AF717891

Voluntary Disruptions

Transformations in Governance

Transformations in Governance is a major new academic book series from Oxford University Press. It is designed to accommodate the impressive growth of research in comparative politics, international relations, public policy, federalism, and environmental and urban studies concerned with the dispersion of authority from central states to supranational institutions, subnational governments, and public–private networks. It brings together work that advances our understanding of the organization, causes, and consequences of multilevel and complex governance. The series is selective, containing annually a small number of books of exceptionally high quality by leading and emerging scholars.

The series is edited by Liesbet Hooghe and Gary Marks of the University of North Carolina, Chapel Hill, and Walter Mattli of the University of Oxford.

Organizational Progeny: Why Governments are Losing Control over the Proliferating Structures of Global Governance
Tana Johnson

Democrats and Autocrats: Pathways of Subnational Undemocratic Regime Continuity within Democratic Countries
Agustina Giraudy

A Postfunctionalist Theory of Governance (5 Volumes)
Liesbet Hooghe and Gary Marks et al.

Constitutional Policy in Multilevel Government: The Art of Keeping the Balance
Arthur Benz

With, Without, or Against the State? How European Regions Play the Brussels Game
Michaël Tatham

Territory and Ideology in Latin America: Policy Conflicts between National and Subnational Governments
Kent Eaton

Rules without Rights: Land, Labor, and Private Authority in the Global Economy
Tim Bartley

Voluntary Disruptions

International Soft Law, Finance, and Power

Abraham L. Newman and Elliot Posner

OXFORD
UNIVERSITY PRESS

OXFORD
UNIVERSITY PRESS

Great Clarendon Street, Oxford, OX2 6DP,
United Kingdom

Oxford University Press is a department of the University of Oxford. It furthers the University's objective of excellence in research, scholarship, and education by publishing worldwide. Oxford is a registered trade mark of Oxford University Press in the UK and in certain other countries

© Abraham L. Newman and Elliot Posner 2018

The moral rights of the authors have been asserted

First Edition published in 2018

Impression: 1

All rights reserved. No part of this publication may be reproduced, stored in a retrieval system, or transmitted, in any form or by any means, without the prior permission in writing of Oxford University Press, or as expressly permitted by law, by licence or under terms agreed with the appropriate reprographics rights organization. Enquiries concerning reproduction outside the scope of the above should be sent to the Rights Department, Oxford University Press, at the address above

You must not circulate this work in any other form and you must impose this same condition on any acquirer

Published in the United States of America by Oxford University Press
198 Madison Avenue, New York, NY 10016, United States of America

British Library Cataloguing in Publication Data
Data available

Library of Congress Control Number: 2017954540

ISBN 978–0–19–881838–0

Printed and bound by
CPI Group (UK) Ltd, Croydon, CR0 4YY

Links to third party websites are provided by Oxford in good faith and for information only. Oxford disclaims any responsibility for the materials contained in any third party website referenced in this work.

To Craig and Gillian

Preface

The Great Recession was a call to arms. People wanted to know how the financial crisis happened and what to do about it. This book began with an invitation from Daniel Drezner and Kathleen McNamara to participate in a working group devoted to these questions. As any scholar of international finance knows, this area of our social world is far from ungoverned space but teems with rules of all sorts: voluntary standards, principles, best practices and guidance, created in transnational forums and labeled international soft law. After the crisis, we wondered how such a collection of rules and its creators might mitigate, exacerbate, or respond to global shocks. We soon found ourselves well beyond the original task of identifying the causes and lessons of economic crisis. Finance had become our window into a fundamental transformation in global politics: the rise, use, and consequences of international soft law.

Three initial observations caught our attention and motivated us to write a book. First, experts were well aware that in one important respect finance looked like the environment, labor, and many other areas: governance by international soft law, as opposed to treaty-based commitments, was rapidly expanding. Yet despite a few exceptions and a growing interest, attention by political scientists, sociologists, and legal scholars had lagged. We believed that a phenomenon so prevalent deserved more thought and scrutiny, especially with respect to its relationship with power and distributive politics, the bread and butter of international political economy, our subfield of international relations.

Second, we kept running across cases that did not make sense. The standard storyline among many scholars and the media is that international soft law reflects best practice designed by technocrats and geared toward solving regulatory problems arising from a globalizing economy. In some cases, this view rings true but in many others does not. A mismatch exists between the abundance of effort and time that goes into creating international standards and the decidedly checkered record of implementing them. These observations led us to explore soft law's possible roles beyond solving problems and to challenge what turned out to be overly myopic conceptualization and theory. Our breakthrough, we believe, was to treat soft law as an institution, which, like other institutions, reflects political contests and bargains and, once created, produces winners and losers and reconfigures power relations. Understanding soft law as an institution with disruptive and distributive sides opened new avenues of thinking and helped us to explain curious patterns and theoretical inconsistencies.

Finally, we noticed the repeated echoes of soft law over time. The earliest soft law agreements of the 1980s deeply conditioned the causes and responses to the 2008 crisis, and not in ways that the originators had planned. So much of the existing research focuses on soft law's creation and immediate effects. Yet early in our collaboration, we came to believe that any compelling analytic framework for understanding the contemporary international financial architecture must incorporate temporal processes: the fits and starts of soft law's creation, its uneven development and gravitational pull, the myriad actors who interpret and use it for their own purposes, and the ever-present result of domestic and international political disruption.

Upon these initial observations, we rejected not only the idea that soft law may safely be ignored but also that the problem-solver depiction comes anywhere close to capturing the complete story. After many years of research, we concluded that existing accounts miss the ways that international soft law contextualizes power and, above all, the way international soft law is political. If we have a lesson for policy-makers, it is that they ask for whom soft law is effective and how it is being used. This book suggests that the answers will go beyond "the public" and "to maximize social welfare," respectively, and will include policy activists in pursuit of political fortunes and agendas.

The book's origins and progression are inextricably linked to the people in our scholarly networks. We would like to thank Jeff Anderson, David Bach, Karen Beckwith, Justin Buchler, Brian Burgoon, Marc Bush, Charlotte Cavaille, Jeffrey Chwieroth, Richard Deeg, Renaud Dehousse, Daniel Drezner, David Edelstein, Henry Farrell, Stavros Gadinis, Matthew Gravelle, Julia Gray, Jessica Green, Emiliano Grossman, Eric Helleiner, Tana Johnson, Miles Kahler, Manolis Kalaitzake, David Kempthorne, Jonathan Kirshner, Peter Knaack, Kathryn Lavelle, Kelly McMann, Kathleen McNamara, Pete Moore, Manuela Moschella, Daniel Mügge, Daniel Nexon, Stefano Pagliari, Cesar Garcia Perez de Leon, Mark Pollack, Tony Porter, Tonya Putnam, Lucia Quaglia, Nora Rachman, Paul Schroeder, Katrin Seig, Susan Sell, Gregory Shaffer, Eleni Tsingou, Geoffrey Underhill, Nicolas Véron, Anna von der Goltz, James Vreeland, Andrew Walter, Steven Weber, Holger Wolf, Cornelia Woll, Alasdair Young, David Zaring, Jonathan Zeitlin, and Nicolas Ziegler. We received outstanding research assistance from Nikhil Kalyanpur, who played an invaluable role in improving and finalizing the manuscript, and excellent editing from Gillian Weiss, who read the entire manuscript before it went to press.

We presented parts of the manuscript at Georgetown University, the London School of Economics, Sciences Po (Paris), the University of

Amsterdam, the University of California at Berkeley, the University of Minnesota (Twin Cities), and the University of Waterloo, and at the annual meetings of the European Union Studies Association (2015), International Studies Association (2016), the American Political Science Association (2017) and the Society for the Advancement of Socio-Economics (2013 and 2015). We were lucky to receive a great deal of constructive criticism at these venues and are grateful to the audiences, participants, and discussants.

We also benefited tremendously from peer review, first in the case of two articles published by the *Review of International Political Economy* (pieces of which comprise parts of Chapters 4 and 5) and then in the case of this manuscript. The many careful and astute comments by expert anonymous reviewers much improved the book. We thank Taylor & Francis for the permission to reprint portions of the articles (Newman and Posner 2016a, 2016b).[1] We also appreciate the roles of our editor Dominic Byatt, the series editors Liesbet Hooghe, Gary Marks, and Walter Mattli, and the larger Oxford group. The professionalism and speed of the review and publication processes were exceptional, and their strong encouragement was a welcome shot in the arm that helped us bring this five-year project to completion.

The book would not have been possible without substantial institutional support. We are grateful to our home universities, Case Western Reserve and Georgetown, which provided necessary time and financial support for a project of this kind. Elliot extends his gratitude to the Fulbright Commission of Belgium and Luxembourg and the Academic Careers in Engineering and Science program at CWRU (ACES+ Initiative) for financial support; the Centre d'études européennes of Sciences Po in Paris and Bruegel in Brussels for hosting him and providing stimulating environments during the initial stages of the research; and Phoenix Coffee on Lee Road for brewing a perfect latte and providing just the right din for writing. Abe expresses his thanks to the faculty and staff at the BMW Center for German and European Studies, the Mortara Center for International Studies, the Government Department, and School of Foreign Service; and to the view of the Hilltop for inspiring another go at the manuscript.

The research behind this book depended on the willingness of policymakers and stakeholders to meet with us and discuss their views. For the kind of qualitative research that we carried out, there is no substitute for candid conversations with the people involved. While withholding names to protect their anonymity, we acknowledge their extraordinary generosity and thank them for it.

A multiyear collaboration with another academic is not without potential perils. Revealing half-baked thoughts is a risky business. Yet in our case it led

[1] The articles are available at <http://www.tandfonline.com>.

to a rewarding and intimate intellectual exchange. As we send this book to press, we realize with a tinge of nostalgia how much the daily check-ins and constant exchanges deepened our friendship. We enjoyed a rare opportunity to build something greater together than we could have as individuals. We are so lucky that we took the time to meet over a beer at APSA's 2004 meeting in Chicago.

Finally, we cannot adequately express our gratitude to our families. We thank Hugo and Oliver who (with only a little help from Minecraft, chess, baseball, soccer, basketball, devoted grandparents, Wyatt, and other diversions) survived a grumpy, book-finishing dad, and we thank Micah and Sadie who would have preferred more time playing Ticket to Ride but still got in plenty of tickle wars between chapter edits. We thank our spouses Gillian and Craig whose emotional and intellectual support showed no limits. We dedicate this book to them. They know why.

Contents

List of Figures and Tables

Figures

Tables

1

Introduction

Consider the most mundane of financial products: a home mortgage in the United States. When our parents purchased houses in the 1970s, financing was locally arranged between the buyer and a domestic bank. Today, global financial conglomerates purchase, bundle, and resell mortgages, uprooting home loans and trading the derived assets on international markets. Like so many other parts of our lives—from medical tourism to the manufacturing of iPhones—home mortgages are part of a dizzying process of internationalization (Henderson et al. 2002; Schwartz 2009; Locke 2013).

The astonishing complexity of international economic exchange may seem ungoverned. Yet this shift in the economy remains bound by rules—tacit understandings and explicit agreements that set, condone, constrain, and enable the terms of international market competition (Fligstein 1996; Vogel 1996; Gereffi et al. 2005; Abdelal 2007). Scholars, policy-makers, and the media tend to concentrate on one component of international economic governance—treaty-based rules like those promulgated by the World Trade Organization or preferential trade agreements signed among states. The effects and politics of this classic form of international law continue to draw academic controversy and debate (Davis 2004; Pelc 2009; Carnegie 2014).

Voluntary Disruptions addresses another component of economic governance: international soft law. Far from the staid world of treaties and state-to-state diplomacy, soft law comprises a different class of international market rules made up of voluntary standards, best practices, and recommended guidance. Its creators are an assortment of obscure and well-known international organizations. Their involvement along with the soft law they generate signals a fundamental transformation in the nature of global governance.

Despite the proliferation and prominence of international soft law, academics have paid relatively little attention to its political consequences. Some see it through a problem-solving lens, as a defining element in robust future governance architectures (Slaughter 2004; Sabel and Zeitlin 2010). Others dismiss it as a guise for the agendas of powerful states and interests (Drezner 2007).

The debate unnecessarily limits analysis to short-term questions of who adopts soft law and to what degree they implement it, and to technical and depoliticized issues surrounding global regulatory challenges.

Voluntary Disruptions sets out to widen the discussion by shifting attention to the full range of international soft law's political and distributional effects. It is no secret that soft law matters in determining globalization's winners and losers. Voluntary rules developed by the Basel Committee on Banking Supervision affect the prices of contemporary home mortgages in the United States and the values of securities derived from them and sold internationally (Thiemann 2014). A similarly arcane body, the International Accounting Standards Board, establishes the financial reporting parameters that contribute to the stock values of publicly listed companies and help to root out corruption (Véron 2007). Voluntary standards developed by the International Labour Organization constrain the actions of international brands from Nike to Ivanka Trump.[1]

This book's theoretical framework examines the political effects of international soft law as it has evolved over time. While certainly assisting in cross-border policy coordination, soft law also leaves a deep political imprint, providing new resources to some groups while not to others and altering the sites of contestation and the actors who participate in them. *Voluntary Disruptions* explains how soft law, typically viewed as limited by its voluntary nature, disrupts and transforms the politics of economic governance.

International Soft Law

Scholars of global governance know soft law when they see it, and these days they see it everywhere: in best practices, policy guidelines, and technical standards (Abbott and Snidal 2000; Trubek and Trubek 2005; Schäfer 2006). All agree that international soft law's incorporation into national law or regulatory and business practices is voluntary, even if a single definition still eludes legal scholars and other experts (Chinkin 1989; Hillgenberg 1999; Guzman and Meyer 2010). In Chapter 2 we discuss the debate and explain why we define soft law as a set of written, advisory prescriptions.

Experts also agree that endless streams of soft law flow from an array of organizations, including established state-led international organizations like the Organisation for Economic Co-operation and Development (OECD) and the International Monetary Fund (IMF) as well as less formal intergovernmental, transgovernmental, and private standard setting bodies such as the G7,

[1] "Better Work," betterwork.org, last accessed July 31, 2017, <https://betterwork.org/dev/>; Matea Gold, Drew Harwell, Maher Sattar, and Simon Denyer, "Ivanka Inc," *Washington Post*, July 14, 2017.

the Basel Committee on Banking Supervision, Forest Stewardship Council, and Fairtrade International (Karlsson-Vinkhuyzen and Vihma 2009; Shaffer and Pollack 2009; Kirton et al. 2010; Brummer 2011; Green 2013; Vabulas and Snidal 2013). Examples of international soft law are as different as the Basel Committee's *Global Regulatory Framework for more Resilient Banks and Banking Systems*[2] and Fairtrade International's *Standard for Hired Labour.*[3]

The gradual but steady accumulation of international soft law long remained the esoteric domain of regulatory authorities, international lawyers, and academics, lying in the shadow of a stylized version of treaty-based rules that emphasized formal enforcement. This is no longer the case, especially since the great financial crisis, when the G20 showcased international soft law as the centerpiece of its program to improve global economic stability and coordinate national regulatory reforms (Shaffer and Pollack 2009; Helleiner 2010; Kirton et al. 2010; Brummer 2011).

Even though policy experts and lobbyists now widely recognize international soft law's importance, public attention has yet to catch up. And scholarly understanding remains stuck within a narrow band of two competing storylines that focus on soft law's ability to smooth out the frictions posed by globalization. The first holds that decision-makers rely on international non-binding rules to help manage challenges requiring cross-border cooperation, from climate change to terrorism. They use soft law to improve national policy-making and coordinate with other jurisdictions, without the heavy-handed enforcement and compliance penalties of treaty-based international "hard" law (Chinkin 1989; Boyle 1999; Zaring 2004; Andonova and Tuta 2014). Some in this camp have gone so far as to conclude that soft law is part and parcel of a new world order of global governance (Slaughter 2004; Cohen and Sabel 2005; Sabel and Zeitlin 2010). Drawing from these findings, proponents of this view encourage further development and use of soft law and predict broad-based compliance, arguing that it offers quick, flexible, technically sound governance solutions to coordination problems in a complex and fast-changing world (Zaring 1998; Slaughter 2004; Brummer 2011).

The second storyline is less sanguine. Rather than see soft law as efficiency enhancing and politically neutral, skeptical scholars maintain that soft law reflects (and is epiphenomenal to) the agendas of powerful jurisdictions and industries, arguing that national compliance with international soft law is intermittent and superficial (Goldsmith and Posner 2006; Drezner 2007; Verdier 2009). From these findings, critics conclude that soft law lacks

[2] "Basel III: A Global Regulatory Framework for more Resilient Banks and Banking Systems—revised version June 2011," bis.org, last accessed July 31, 2017, <http://www.bis.org/publ/bcbs189.htm>.

[3] "Standard for Hired Labour," fairtrade.net, last accessed July 31, 2017, <http://www.fairtrade.net/standards/our-standards/hired-labour-standards.html>. See Seidman (2007).

democratic legitimacy and proves ineffective in situations where actors have an incentive to cheat or renege on pledges to cooperate (Papadopoulos 2007; Steffek 2010). At best, soft law promotes technocratic elitism; at worst, it is nothing more than sham standards.

The attention to likely and actual patterns of compliance is, of course, important. Yet by focusing on the adoption or non-adoption of international advisory prescriptions (Ho 2002; Falkner et al. 2005; Ferran and Alexander 2010; Guzman and Meyer 2010), current analyses miss other—frequently distributional—ways that international soft law contributes to broad, deep, and significant change in national, regional, and transnational policy-making. Using the realm of global financial regulation as its laboratory, *Voluntary Disruptions* redirects research toward these politically transformative consequences as they unfold over time.

Soft Law's Second-Order Effects

Our starting point is that soft law is a political institution that has the potential to govern and regularize social behavior and is thus inherently contentious (Finnemore and Toope 2001). Some existing scholarship already highlights the politics of competing interests in the creation of and compliance with international soft law at any given moment (Kapstein 1992; Oatley and Nabors 1998; Mattli and Woods 2009; Büthe and Mattli 2011). Yet once created, rules also figure prominently in future politics—empowering and favoring some actors more than others, altering preferences and strategies, sparking opportunistic behavior, and simply being hard to change legally and cognitively (Moe 2005; Mahoney and Thelen 2009).

Taking cues from a long line of research in comparative politics, American political development, and international relations that traces the temporal effects of institutions, we argue that the second-order consequences of soft law similarly restructure politics (Thelen and Steinmo 1992; Zysman 1994; Shickler 2001; Sheingate 2003; Posner 2009a, 2010a; Farrell and Newman 2010; Sell 2010; Fioretos 2011). Moving from first-order to second-order questions, we shift from issues of rule development and rule compliance to the ways voluntary prescriptions, once created, are taken up and deployed by political actors. Like domestic institutions, international soft law shapes actors' goals, agendas, strategies, resources, and identities and alters the distribution of political winners and losers.

Such consequences are not limited to the weak. A central theme of the book is that soft law's second-order effects recast policy battles inside the most powerful jurisdictions and change the way influential industries engage in global and domestic politics. In sum, international soft law does much more than provide focal points that help political actors with common goals to coordinate and otherwise smooth out the bumps of globalization at single points in time; it disrupts and transforms political landscapes and their participants.

How does international soft law effect such political change? We focus on two mechanisms: legitimacy claims and arena expansion. First, soft law gives policy entrepreneurs new political resources for intervening in, influencing, and opening up domestic fights. In issue areas where competing regulatory factions struggle to set the policy agenda, opportunistic and skilled political actors take advantage of the various forms of legitimacy (or illegitimacy) associated with soft law and the bodies that create it. These include perceptions of expertise, morality, and neutrality (or of elitism, unaccountability, and partisanship) (Risse-Kappen 1995; Abbott and Snidal 2002; Barnett and Finnemore 2004; Karlsson-Vinkhuyzen and Vihma 2009; Mattli and Woods 2009). Framing soft law as "state-of-the-art" or as politically neutral and non-partisan can be an attractive and powerful resource in domestic political struggles (Porter 2005b); so too can presenting it as unaccountable and elitist. We do not argue that in these circumstances the advisory prescriptions under question reflect best, appropriate, or unaccountable policies. They may or may not. Our point is that policy actors make claims intended to leverage perceptions of (il)legitimacy as they do political battle (Posner 2005; Jabko 2006; Quack 2009, 2010; Halliday et al. 2010). For skillful actors, international soft law offers a resource that helps to disrupt domestic political contests in their favor and, in turn, to reverberate back into transnational processes (Fligstein 2001).

Second, international soft law is politically disruptive because it involves the expansion of contestation to new arenas. In contrast to traditional international law forged through formal negotiations and by heads of state, soft law typically depends for its creation on an additional cast of characters—sub-state officials and private actors including national regulators, international bureaucrats, firms and their associations, professional assemblies, and NGOs (Slaughter 2004; Green 2013; Farrell and Newman 2015, 2016; Kahler 2016). These actors sometimes produce soft law in international organizations dominated by national foreign ministries, but they also do so in transnational and transgovernmental forums (Andonova et al. 2009; Mattli and Woods 2009; Djelic and Quack 2010). The making of soft law thus breaks up the state's monopoly of professional diplomats, allows for transnational alliances of like-minded factions across jurisdictions, and expands policy-making to new arenas.

Like the legitimacy claims mechanism, expanding the arena has temporal effects that bring about political change. Because of resource and organizational constraints, access to and influence over the new arenas is unequal

(Joachim 2003; Djelic and Quack 2010; Lall 2014; Farrell and Newman 2015). Moreover, as the sites of political contestation expand to the transnational level, some participants reorient themselves to the new arena (Tarrow 2001), undergoing internal transformations. Powerful actors like states, regulators from leading markets, and multinational firms and industry associations not only react to and deploy soft law to achieve political ends. They are also shaped by it. Over time, *arena expansion* contributes to shifts in policy priorities and to the reorganization of regulatory authorities and interest groups, ultimately having wide-ranging repercussions for the rules that govern domestic and global markets.

This book, then, explores the political consequences of international soft law over time. It uses the example of market rules and, in particular, financial regulation, a domain in which powerful actors—the European Union, influential financial industry associations, and even the United States—have not escaped the political effects of international soft law as they disrupt domestic regulatory struggles and expand contestation globally.

Soft Law and Financial Regulation

In addition to engaging with the theoretical concerns of social scientists, *Voluntary Disruptions* provides answers to compelling real-world questions about economic governance and, in particular, financial regulation:

(1) How should we describe and account for the international financial regulatory architecture that emerged after the Bretton Woods period?

(2) What explains the alignment of financial regulatory approaches during the 1990s and 2000s between the United States and the European Union, the two rule-making giants—a development that set the stage for the Great Recession?

(3) What explains the direct and prominent role of transnational financial industry associations in making global banking rules during the 2000s? And why were some associations more influential than others?

(4) And what explains post-crisis US financial reforms and their relationship to international markets and foreign jurisdictions? Why did banking and derivatives reforms, in particular, take divergent and seemingly random paths, with different consequences for international finance?

We show that these questions represent important gaps in current understanding of pre- and post-crisis financial governance. We also demonstrate that answers to them lie in the development (or lack thereof) of international soft law and its role in providing political resources to powerful actors and shaping their preferences, strategies, and political channels of influence.

In the rest of this chapter, we first discuss our empirical terrain. As the above questions indicate, the book turns as much on understanding financial governance at the international level as on theoretical concerns. We review the centrality of financial rules in contemporary economic and social life, the merits of international financial regulation as a social scientific area of study, and its relationship to international soft law. We then discuss our methods and offer a few key implications of the book's findings, before giving a chapter-by-chapter overview.

Financial Regulation as a Site of Investigation and Other Methodological Concerns

As the banking, sovereign debt, and economic crises that started in 2008 demonstrate, financial rules matter and have distributive consequences for firms, societies, and governments and economic implications that span political frontiers (Helleiner 1996; Oatley and Nabors 1998; Singer 2007; Mosley and Singer 2009; Grossman and Woll 2013; Calomiris and Haber 2014; Drezner 2014; Mian and Sufi 2014). The location and back-office operations of derivatives trading or the coordination protocol for public officials in the process of resolving insolvent multinational banks may seem overly technical but they influence the stability of national and global financial markets, the fiscal and political prospects of governments, and the most fundamental pocketbook issues of ordinary citizens. Rules about where derivatives are traded affect the safety of retirement savings, and capital requirements set by the Basel Committee determine, at least in part, the cost of a mortgage. Moreover, international soft law in the area of financial regulation, aggregated into the Compendium of Standards[4] and kept under the guardianship of the Financial Stability Board and the IMF and ultimately under the auspices of the G20, has been accumulating for thirty-five years (Eichengreen 1999; Davies and Green 2008; Brummer 2011). Its place within the overall canvas of financial rules—domestic, regional, and international—is manifest and certainly perceived as significant by stakeholders (Lall 2012; Young 2012; Pagliari and Young 2014). In short, we choose to focus on international financial governance because of its intrinsic real-world relevance.

[4] The Compendium of Standards includes the Financial Stability Board's twelve sets of "key standards" as well as other financial regulatory standards created by an array of fifteen standard-setting bodies. "FSB: The Compendium of Standards," fsb.org, accessed July 26, 2017, <http://www.fsb.org/what-we-do/about-the-compendium-of-standards/>.

Theoretically, the considerable and rich literature on the politics of financial regulation has made it possible to identify central research questions (Underhill 1995; Porter 2005a; Singer 2007; Helleiner and Pagliari 2011). The empirical anomalies and analytic puzzles that motivate the substantive chapters grow directly from this literature. For example, the starting point of Chapter 4 is the emergence of the European Union since the late 1990s, from a financial "rule-taker" to a "rule-maker" (Posner 2009a). The European Union's rise seemed to spell the end of US financial hegemony, yet the new configuration of power did not undermine global regulatory cooperation in the pre-crisis period, an unexpected empirical development running contrary to the expectations of prominent theoretical approaches (Drezner 2007; Fioretos 2010). Similarly, the question motivating Chapter 5 has not been resolved by existing studies of financial industry participation in the Basel accords, which cover capital adequacy levels for banks: despite high levels of capital mobility, why have scholars found little direct industry involvement in early periods of transnational coordinating efforts, but significant direct influence in later ones (Goodhart 2011; Lall 2012; Young 2012; Tsingou 2015)?

Financial regulation is also a fertile laboratory for social scientific investigation of the politics of international soft law. An area of international-level economic governance where soft law emerged early, in variant forms and with uneven patterns of development, financial regulation offers an enormous field of observations for cross-temporal and subsectoral comparison. The immense variety of within-domain soft law cases goes a long way to minimize one potential bias: that financial regulatory soft law, because as a whole it is more developed, official, and legitimate than soft law in other domains (such as the environment or online markets), is not representative and therefore not useful in drawing theoretical generalization. There are at least five major and distinct regulatory regimes: banking, securities, accounting, derivatives, and insurance. Each subsector has its own history of subissues and debates ranging from the architecture and processes of oversight to substantive rules, and its own pattern of development (discussed in Chapter 3). These differences make temporal comparison within and across subsectors possible.

As for our methods, all the empirical chapters, in one form or another, rely on structured small-n comparisons to evaluate the relative merits of competing causal claims (Mahoney 2003; George and Bennett 2005). Specifically, to draw inferences, we rely on congruence analysis (which applies a correlational logic to assess whether evidence matches expected relationships between variables) and process tracing (which assesses whether evidence supports the expected causal mechanisms), and use a panoply of sources including original interviews, primary documents, secondary research, the financial press, and archival material. The studies conducted in Chapters 4, 5, and 6 explore the explanatory power of the key mechanisms, legitimacy claims (Chapters 4 and 6), and arena expansion (Chapters 5 and 6). Where relevant in the empirical chapters, we discuss case selection and other methodological decisions and challenges. We also make judicious use of negative cases where soft law was absent, underdeveloped, or illegitimate. These methods and transparency standards enhance the rigor of a largely positivist comparative analysis. We also hope they reveal the judgment and interpretation that not only inform the pre-analysis components such as conceptualization and measurement decisions but also seep into most other aspects of a comparative study of this kind.

Aside from the potential for answering theoretical and empirical questions through a structured comparative method, our selection of cases is significant for another reason. By looking at influential actors in the international system—the European Union, the United States, and the associations of systemically important banks—we chose hard cases that are the least likely to support our hypotheses. Analysts most dismissive of soft law are especially skeptical about its ability to condition the behavior of the powerful as it is said to be epiphenomenal to their interests. If soft law has an impact on such actors, one implication is that it is also likely to have an effect on weaker ones. We thus target powerful actors as a methodological strategy for probing the scope of our claims.

Contributions and Implications

In rethinking international soft law and answering pressing questions about the politics of financial regulation, we strive to make several contributions. The book's approach for understanding international-level economic governance views soft law as more than just a vehicle for solving market frictions or failures, especially through coordination. Akin to other social, political, and economic institutions, soft law is also a driver of distributive politics, where actors win or lose (Knight 1992; Moe 2005; Voeten Forthcoming), and of foundational and constitutive processes (Berger 1983; Zysman 1994; Fligstein 1996, 2001; Blyth 2002; Woll 2008). Here, we hope the book will inject such politics into debates about international economic governance.

Voluntary Disruptions emphasizes temporal analysis. Too much existing research on domestic–international interactions relies on snapshot outcomes and thus misses soft law's potential to disrupt political contests. Work on compliance, for example, has focused on the adoption or non-adoption of soft law rules. This effort (often treating compliance as a binary), however, ignores the ways soft law is embedded or resisted (Halliday and Carruthers

2009; Mosley 2010). In many cases, even when soft law fails to be adopted, it disrupts the balance of political authority between competing regulatory factions. Moreover, such failures can have recursive effects on the transnational process. Politics is an ongoing struggle, where actors stymied at one moment generally live to fight another day. By investigating soft law's temporal effects, this book builds on research from comparative politics and international relations that pays greater attention to endogenous processes and the causal effects of sequences and timing (Büthe 2002; Pierson 2004; Farrell and Newman 2010; Posner 2010a; Fioretos 2011).

Moreover, *Voluntary Disruptions* revisits core debates about institutions, power, and actors in international politics. Standard power-based accounts often emphasize state-to-state interactions as if countries and the European Union behave as single, unified entities led by heads of government (Helleiner 1996; Drezner 2007). As we show in the empirical chapters, an expanding number of actors—regulators, firms, legislators, international organizations—participate in global financial regulation. Chapters 4, 5, and 6 demonstrate that the most significant of these actors are not necessarily coterminous with the heads of government but rather those who leverage political resources made available by soft law. As a result, key political fights often include adversaries from the same jurisdiction as well as from different ones. We make an effort in this book to decouple power from the state and to locate it in the competing political factions struggling within and across countries.

As the preceding points indicate, this book takes power seriously. Yet it rejects perspectives—whether prioritizing the power of states or the structural power of organized business interests—that reduce institutions to the preferences of powerful actors. The empirical chapters instead show how international institutions—soft law—contextualize preferences and behavior, and influence relations. One of our main conclusions is that differences in international soft law (levels of development; presence or absence) over time and across subsectors affect the policy strategies and resources of these actors.

Finally, this book improves our understanding of contemporary developments in the politics of finance. Viewing soft law through its lens helps to make sense of the real-world consequences that seemingly technical standards have for political economies. Rather than only a neutral solution to the problems that arise from globalization, soft law is also a political weapon employed by competing factions and a structuring institution with deeply penetrating effects on powerful actors. The book's approach decodes the politics lurking behind justifications for or against international soft law and identifies the non-economic objectives that potentially skew the effects of policy intervention. As such, we hope to help policy-makers better decipher the motives behind and potential consequences of these competing claims and in turn improve regulatory outcomes.

Plan of the Book

Chapter 2 is a detailed development of our approach that emphasizes soft law's second-order consequences, including the way it disrupts the politics of economic governance. The chapter begins with a definition and the existing literature, which tends to focus on issues surrounding compliance. It then turns to the book's main argument, outlining the logic behind two important mechanisms of political disruption: legitimacy claims and arena expansion. This theoretical chapter thus sets up the key concepts and propositions used in the following empirical chapters.

Chapter 3 describes the international financial regulatory architecture, providing necessary background for the substantive studies that follow. It gives special attention to the architecture's two defining aspects: the soft law character of the rules it produces and the fragmentation of rule-making by subsectors. A matrix of forums develops advisory prescriptions for specific financial policy areas. The chapter traces the architecture's origins and evolution, including how policy-makers and standard-setting organizations dealt over time with the breakdown of traditional boundaries between markets and subsectors. Its main purpose is to provide background on the book's featured causal variable: international soft law. A secondary purpose, however, is to put forth an original explanation for the architecture's key features. We highlight the prominent role of domestic institutional arrangements within the United States and other jurisdictions with important markets for the early development of soft law-creating organizations and establish the role of contingency, sequence, and endogeneity (with reference to post-war international developments and domestic institutions) in the architecture's evolution.

The next three chapters explore international soft law's effects over time by evaluating the evidential support for our arguments about legitimacy claims and arena expansion. Chapter 4 focuses on soft law's second-order consequences for rising regulatory powers. One of the key puzzles in the international regulation of finance is the persistence of cooperation even as the number of economic great powers increases. The emergence of the European Union as a financial rule-maker in the late 1990s and early 2000s, roughly on par with the United States, resulted in a transatlantic alignment of regulatory approaches, not conflict over the fundamentals. This chapter demonstrates how soft law was used by reform-minded factions in Europe to legitimize their claims and tip in their favor political contests over the modernization of internal regulation. International soft law served as a mechanism of endogenous change, helping to foster a great power preference alignment along market-friendly paths and setting the stage for the financial crisis.

In Chapter 5, we shift focus from soft law's effects on great powers to its impact on influential business groups. We argue that by expanding arenas of contestation to the transnational level, soft law transforms business representation as well as individual industry associations. The chapter's empirical focus is on banking regulation from the 1980s to the 2000s. Much of the literature on transnational banking standards centers on the role of industry associations and, in particular, on the Institute of International Finance (IIF). In this chapter, we explain the rise of direct industry participation in and influence over Basel-based standard setting. We show that the orientation and priorities of the IIF as well as its membership and internal structure were deeply conditioned by 1980s international soft law. The IIF's transformation subsequently set off a series of changes to the ecology of financial industry associations and the politics of financial regulation.

The final empirical chapter, Chapter 6, examines the long-term recursive effects of international soft law on policy in the United States since 2008. The extent and type of post-crisis US cooperation with foreign jurisdictions has varied considerably with far-reaching ramifications for international financial markets. Focusing on the international interaction of reforms in banking and derivatives, we use our approach to understand the domestic politics of US regulation in the wake of the Great Recession. We attribute seemingly random variation in the US relationship to foreign regulation and markets to differences in pre-crisis international soft law. Here, the existence (or absence) of robust soft law and standard-creating institutions determines the resources available to policy entrepreneurs as well as their orientation and attitudes toward international cooperation. Soft law plays a central role in the evolution of US regulatory reform and its interface with the rest of the world.

In the Conclusion, we elaborate on the book's substantive and theoretical implications and probe the limits of its argument by considering other empirical domains outside of finance. We draw lessons about international soft law in a climate of rising anti-expertise disdain and offer recommendations for improving representation in the transnational arenas where financial soft law is made. The chapter calls on scholars of international relations, comparative politics, and international law to rethink the interaction of institutions, actors, and power.

To some soft law is malleable and thus well suited to our increasingly complex world. To others this flexibility suggests inconsequentiality. For us, soft law is not just about fixing market problems. Like any other political institution, it becomes consequential in real political struggles as powerful actors use it and are transformed by it.

2

International Soft Law and Mechanisms of Political Disruption

International soft law is an enormous and growing component of economic governance (Shaffer and Pollack 2009; Brummer 2011; Pauwelyn et al. 2012; Green 2013). Organizations as diverse as the OECD, the Forest Stewardship Council, and the Basel Committee on Banking Supervision generate a slew of voluntary best practices, prescriptive standards, and advisory guidance. The targets are national and regional legislators, rule-making regulatory authorities, and ultimately market actors across a wide range of sectors and industries including capital markets, foreign investment, Internet governance, energy production, sustainable practices, and food safety to name a few.

Despite the proliferation of international soft law, relatively little scholarly work has been devoted to understanding its use and consequences. This chapter proffers answers to two questions: what is international soft law, and what are its effects on regulatory politics and, more broadly, the politics of economic governance? We start with a definition, which emphasizes soft law's written yet advisory nature and articulates more precise boundaries of the concept than existing definitions. In addition to serving as a brush-clearing exercise, we believe that our definition helps to dispel exaggerated claims about soft law as either panacea or epiphenomenon in global economic governance.

We then turn to the central question of international soft law: how can advisory rules matter? Put another way, soft law's increasing centrality in economic governance is occurring without the defining characteristic of traditional formal institutions: legally binding rules, often based on clear penalty mechanisms, designed to increase confidence that others will adhere to the agreed terms and thus to overcome commitment problems (Abbott and Snidal 2000; Koremenos et al. 2001). The question is: what are the possible channels through which soft law, without these attributes, might still have effects on governments, regulatory authorities, industries, and civil society groups.

The leading answer, much discussed in political economy research, captures soft law's function in solving global governance challenges by providing a focal point, facilitating coordination of different national regulation at a given moment, and, like traditional "binding" rules, helping to overcome cooperation problems (Garrett and Weingast 1993; Abbott and Snidal 2000; Mattli and Büthe 2003; Verdier 2009). We do not dispute that soft law provides a coordinating function. Yet by restricting itself to a relatively narrow view of institutions, this research misses soft law's broader and equally fundamental political and distributional consequences that tend to unfold over time.

Building on insights from the fields of comparative politics, American political development, and, more recently, international relations, we advance an answer to the conundrum that addresses these core political concerns. Our approach treats soft law as an institution with the potential to restructure and disrupt domestic and transnational politics, to provide resources to some (and not others), to affect economic governance agendas, and ultimately to alter the organization and preferences of powerful political actors. The argument highlights two mechanisms: legitimacy claims and arena expansion. Through the first, soft law, under specified conditions, serves as a political resource for regulatory factions hoping to unsettle a policy status quo, often within their home jurisdiction. Through the second, it serves to reorient political actors, by expanding sites of contestation beyond strictly domestic arenas, by altering policy agendas, and by shaping organizational missions and goals. In short, this chapter argues that international soft law does more than coordinate actors or solve problems; and despite its doctrinal advisory nature, it upsets existing political dynamics within and across political frontiers.

The chapter puts forth the book's main theoretical proposition. Written, yet voluntary rules, once generated within an eclectic field of transnational standard-setting bodies, over time alter the balance of authority among competing regulatory factions, and restructure the interest group landscape across and within territorial frontiers as well as the regulatory politics of economic great powers. International soft law does not exist in a vacuum but is deeply tied to and embedded in domestic political struggles among groups hoping to influence market rules. As a result, soft law may transform both domestic and international regulatory politics. In addition to addressing important, enduring real-world questions about financial regulation, the empirical studies discussed in Chapters 4, 5, and 6 evaluate specific expectations drawn from this chapter's two proposed mechanisms.

What is International Soft Law?

A long tradition across academic disciplines (economic sociology, political economy, and legal realism) understands markets to be social and political institutions made up of rules: implicit and explicit, written and unwritten, enforced by coercion and obeyed because of material incentives and logics of appropriateness, habit, and practice (Polanyi 1944; Hall 1986; Fligstein 1996; Vogel 1996; McNamara 1998; Sunstein 1998; Finnemore and Toope 2001). Market rules determine who is allowed to buy and sell, what they may exchange, and on what terms. Market rules also set the degree to which foreign companies may access local markets (Zysman 1994).

Governments have long used treaties to smooth out the inevitable differences in national market rules that obstruct cross-border commerce and the transnational interoperability of companies. In recent decades, the proliferation of written, advisory rules originating inside and outside treaty-based organizations has gained policy prominence. Often labeled "soft law," these rules are created in a complex web of organizations (public, private, and hybrid) staffed by a wide array of actors including regulators and industry experts. These organizations release guidance for market participants and government authorities on topics as far-ranging as the level of capital that banks should hold, the appropriate conduct of multinational corporations, and the procedures for cooperation among supervising authorities.[1]

Despite its recent proliferation, soft law is understudied, and the existing scholarship lacks consensus on core issues, including a definition (Chinkin 1989; Boyle 1999; Abbott and Snidal 2000; Shaffer and Pollack 2009; Guzman and Meyer 2010; Brummer 2011). We define international soft law as a set of written, advisory prescriptions. This minimalist definition distinguishes soft law from other types of international rules. First, soft law consists of written prescriptions, which detail specific actions intended to shape behavior. It differs from unwritten norms or beliefs that may guide practice but have not been explicitly articulated or codified (Zaring 2015b). Norms of democracy and transparency, for example, have been associated with the behavior of multinational firms investing in foreign countries (Li and Resnick 2003; Büthe and Milner 2008; Nelson 2014). Such norms, though, are distinct from soft law, like the *Guidelines for Multinational Enterprises*, agreed by OECD members to shape the behavior of companies that engage in foreign direct investment.[2] In the same vein, we distinguish soft law from political rhetoric. Political

[1] Some scholars use a narrower definition that only includes "agreements between regulators in two or more countries" as opposed to ours which also includes agreements made in private transnational organizations (Zaring 2015a: 1257–8).

[2] "2011 Update of the OECD Guidelines for Multinational Corporations," oecd.org, last accessed July 27, 2017, <http://www.oecd.org/daf/inv/mne/oecdguidelinesformultinationalenterprises.htm>.

leaders frequently trumpet vague goals of cooperation but do not specify written recommendations or guidance (Guzman and Meyer 2010).

Second, while soft law agreements prescribe appropriate market behavior and national regulation, they do not include formal adherence obligations, mutually agreed by the objects of regulation, whether sovereign states, their representatives, international organizations, or private actors. In contrast to some provisions of treaties and other types of international "hard" law, soft law does not constitute a legal contract among sovereign states in the traditional sense. In doctrinal terms, states have not given their consent to be bound by the standards or principles (Guzman and Meyer 2010). Rather than expressions of collective agreement by those governed to enforce and implement, soft law texts give advice, guidance, recommendations, and best practices.

This difference distinguishes international soft from hard law and should be clear in any definition—though not for reasons often put forward. Here, we depart from legal scholars who make a stark distinction between binding, treaty-based and non-binding, non-treaty-based international law, with soft law falling into the latter category (Klabbers 1998; Shelton 2003). It is true that the texts of treaties often establish commitments, monitoring and dispute-settlement mechanisms, and penalties and sanctions for non-compliance; and that parties signing soft law agreements acknowledge that implementation of the strictly advisory prescriptions depends on voluntary efforts (Hillgenberg 1999). Nevertheless, the dichotomy is problematic, with its chief flaw being that it ignores the practical significance of hard and soft law's lived experience.

In the first place, there are conceptual limitations to "binding" international law. A long line of legal scholars and political scientists have argued that even treaties—perhaps the most "binding" of international legal contracts—are only binding under certain conditions and cannot easily be equated with contracts agreed under national laws (Simmons 2000; Goldsmith and Posner 2006; Hafner-Burton and Tsutsui 2007; Pelc 2009). Moreover, many treaty texts include advisory prescriptions that do not fall under the traditional definition of hard law but more resemble soft law (Guzman and Meyer 2010).

Our skepticism about the practical significance of the binding/non-binding and treaty/non-treaty dichotomies, moreover, lies not only in conceptual limitations and ambiguities but also in soft law's influence on actor behavior. Soft law routinely has legal and practical bite. The proviso is that the source of legal boundedness lies outside the text itself. Soft law is used by international and domestic courts to inform opinions and is incorporated into domestic legislation and the bylaws of international bodies; important actors such as the International Monetary Fund, the World Bank, credit rating agencies, international lenders, the Financial Stability Board, and regulators of the largest markets employ it to evaluate the behavior of others in the international system, and multinational corporations adopt it into their business practices (Cashore 2002; Ho 2002; Brummer 2011; Zaring 2011; Galbraith and Zaring 2013; Newman and Bach 2014).

Our reservations about the binding/non-binding and treaty/non-treaty distinctions notwithstanding, the absence in soft law of mutually agreed obligations by its objects is still an important distinguishing characteristic for other—political—reasons. Two stand out. The first, a theme in the compliance debates discussed later in this chapter, is that soft law frequently emerges through different processes than international treaties. Compared to intergovernmental organizations that create hard law, soft law's generators come in a variety of organizational types, many of which are without legal personality or other formal organizational features. The wide array includes international organizations, transnational private business associations, transgovernmental networks, and NGOs. Even when originally created to achieve differing tasks with varying degrees of delegated responsibility, treaty-based as well as non-treaty-based organizations produce soft law. Thus, the list of soft law generators includes both the International Accounting Standards Board (a private body, albeit with some public oversight since 2009, composed of industry experts) delegated by the European Union in the Regulation on the Application of International Financial Reporting Standards[3] to produce reporting standards for publicly traded companies (Trubek and Trubek 2005) and the Basel Committee (a more traditional transgovernmental network) used by US banking authorities to help carry out the US Dodd-Frank Act's[4] provisions for bank capital adequacy requirements.

The point, as the political science literature (Abbott and Snidal 2000) has emphasized, is that soft law avoids important barriers to its creation. Unlike hard law, it does not require the same types of national ratification processes as treaties; therefore, even when the negotiating parties are governments or their officials and agencies, fewer hurdles stand in the way of finding common ground. This does not mean that soft law eliminates domestic politics. For example, it is often implemented through national legislation or rule-making procedures, which activate veto players and points (Posner 2010b; Newman and Bach 2014). But here the rules of intergovernmental diplomacy are replaced by administrative procedures or domestic legal rules. Negotiators, moreover, are often double hatted as they participate in transnational standard setting and simultaneously carry out domestic oversight authorities. This blurs the traditional domestic–international distinction and has the potential

[3] "Company Reporting and Auditing," ec.europe.eu, last accessed July 27, 2017, <http://ec.europa.eu/finance/company-reporting/ias-regulation/index_en.htm>.

[4] "H.R. 4173 (111th): Dodd-Frank Wall Street Reform and Consumer Protection Act," govtrack.us, last accessed July 27, 2017, <https://www.govtrack.us/congress/bills/111/hr4173/text>.

to ease implementation as negotiators serve also as on-the-ground enforcers (Newman 2010).

The second political reason that the absence of mutually agreed obligations is important is that scholars and practitioners often claim that soft law reflects state-of-the-art knowledge devised through politically neutral and technocratic processes, rather than a diplomatic bargain negotiated by representatives of the state executive. We elaborate on soft law's perceived aura of legitimacy (or illegitimacy) and the political implications later in this chapter.

Despite a great deal of overlap, our definition of soft law differs in a few respects from the most common one used in political science. Like our definition, Abbott and Snidal (2000) consider the relative lack of mutually agreed obligations as an essential characteristic of soft law, separating it from hard law. Soft law prescriptions do not create explicit enforceable penalties for non-compliance in the text; nor do they mandate use of dispute settlement mechanisms that could coercively sanction. We agree that categorizing an agreement as soft or hard law may not always be a matter of black or white but as lying somewhere on a continuum. Still, we do not include Abbot and Snidal's other two dimensions—levels of precision and delegation.

Soft law is not necessarily less precise than hard law. There are plenty of examples of well-defined and articulated prescriptions that would not qualify under anyone's definition of hard law. For an example featured in later chapters, the Basel Committee on Banking Supervision's standards have steadily become more precise over time but remain advisory and without mutually agreed obligations. Instances of the converse—of imprecise principles constituting treaty-based, hard law—also abound. We therefore emphasize the written and prescriptive nature of soft law, which distinguishes it from vague statements made as political rhetoric or unspoken norms and customs and contributes to its frequently invoked aura of legitimacy.

Similarly, we leave out the level of third-party delegation "to interpret, implement and apply the rules; to resolve disputes; and (possibly) to make further rules" (Abbott and Snidal 2000: 401). Without mutually agreed obligations, soft law texts tend to grant either no or only modest delegations of implementation, monitoring, adjudication, and enforcement authority. Even so, just as some soft law agreements delegate these functions, hard law texts frequently provide little or no delegation of authority (Abbott and Snidal 2000: 406). For example, since the 2008 financial crisis, generators of financial regulatory soft law, like the Basel Committee and the Financial Stability Board, have assigned themselves or their constituent members (usually in adjacent agreements separate from the texts containing the prescribed standards) the tasks of monitoring and assessing implementation of standards.

In sum, this book's parsimonious definition, highlighting soft law's written and advisory nature and its origins in a patchwork of transnational private, intergovernmental, and transgovernmental organizations, distinguishes soft law from other types of international rules and turns attention to politics. In the next section, we review some key findings of existing research on the impact of soft law, which focuses on atemporal questions of coordination, before laying out our argument about the distributional politics of international soft law over time.

Does Soft Law Matter? Soft Law as Coordination Mechanism and the Compliance Debate

The meteoric increase of non-traditional (that is, non-state) actors in international affairs at the end of the century has widespread implications for international relations theory, built largely on statist foundations (Slaughter 2004; Della Porta and Tarrow 2005; Djelic and Quack 2010; Kaldor 2013). It prompted research on intergovernmental, transgovernmental, private (that is, professional, industry and advocacy), and hybrid networks, forums, "authorities," and architectures (Rosenau 1990; Sinclair 2005; Cerny 2010; Sabel and Zeitlin 2010). Many studies center on market rules produced through these various sources and, in particular, on international soft law (Zaring 1998; Slaughter 2004; Green 2013; McKeen-Edwards and Porter 2013). Given the advisory nature of soft law, proponents and skeptics naturally want to know to what degree, why and by what mechanisms states, firms, or NGOs adopt it. The underlying objective is to analyze whether soft law could effectively solve important global governance challenges.

One set of arguments sees soft law as a flexible and quick means to promote cooperation based on mutual interests and as a suitable solution to clashes between national regulatory systems, which have overtaken traditional obstacles to cross-border exchange. In settings where multiple, conflicting national market rules exist, soft law offers a useful coordination device for helping parties cooperate and improving their self-perceived welfare (Abbott and Snidal 2000; Slaughter 2004). As soft law is void of mutually agreed compliance obligations and typically lacks legislative approval requirements, it is often easier for parties to agree on the details of the prescriptions (Raustiala 2002). Moreover, soft law offers a path to better regulation as it is formulated in a technocratic environment that prioritizes regulatory effectiveness over political and material advantage (Porter 2003). Some soft law optimists contend that compared to intergovernmental agreements or rules imposed by the United States and other powerful polities, soft law is also more likely to promote democratic norms at the global level, as it is produced through deliberative processes involving dynamic feedback, learning, and revision of key standards (Cohen and Sabel 2005; Trubek and Trubek 2005; Sabel and

Zeitlin 2010). Overall, this more optimistic strand of work has emphasized soft law as a potential tool to mitigate the frictions associated with globalization.

Critics, by contrast, cast doubt on soft law's efficacy. They see soft law as epiphenomenal to observed patterns of national regulation and firm behavior, arguing that legal rules have little independent binding effect. Powerful actors, they contend, use soft law as long as it is already in line with their interests but are unlikely to be constrained by such prescriptions (Goldsmith and Posner 2006; Drezner 2007), and several studies document patterns of "mock" compliance and high-profile instances, such as the second Basel Committee accords in the United States, which illustrate poor, delayed, or no implementation (Walter 2008; Halliday and Carruthers 2009; Mosley 2010; Lavelle 2013). In other words, soft law reflects distributional issues but has little independent effect.

An additional critique, derived from the rational institutionalist perspective, argues that soft law's usefulness is limited to a small class of global problems (Whytock 2005; Verdier 2009). In relatively rare cases, all parties want to coordinate around a common standard and are largely indifferent to which standard is used. In these "simple coordination games," soft law may serve to promote cooperation. Yet most cases of global governance display significant enforcement problems. Some parties may find it in their interest to shirk or not implement the standards. Because compliance often entails some costs, a state might find it in its interest to defect from the standard, leaving other states to bear the burden of compliance (Abbott and Snidal 2000). Soft law standards are criticized as ill-suited to address such enforcement problems as they lack a commitment mechanism such as a formal dispute settlement system to induce cooperation (Klabbers 1998).

Addressing these doubts and evidence that reveals greater variance in implementation than earlier studies suggested, scholars seek to identify channels—separate from provisions in the agreements and beyond simple coordination logics—to explain the circumstances for compliance. In some cases, soft law creates a reputational dynamic (Ho 2002; Brummer 2011). Third parties such as credit rating agencies, retailers concerned about consumer values, or other states evaluate actor behavior based on whether or not they follow soft law prescriptions. Incentives for behavioral change stem not from the prescriptions themselves, but the decisions taken by third parties (lowering credit ratings, threatening to cut off product suppliers, limiting access to preferential loans) based on compliance with such standards (Sinclair 2005; Abdelal 2007; Gray 2009). Taking the logic further, some scholars explain the adoption of mutually agreed and flexible soft law as part of the widespread emergence of experimentalist architectures that respond to the failure of more traditional command and control regulation. Such architectures include not only reputational mechanisms such as joint monitoring and peer reviews, but also structured deliberation by relatively autonomous implementers of shared goals.

Regulators and market actors engage in an ongoing dialogue with one another, producing flexible yet refined regulatory practices and implementation buy-in, which is alleged to ultimately improve overall governance outputs (Dorf and Sabel 1998; Sabel and Zeitlin 2010; Zeitlin 2015).

Research also uncovers coercion as a mechanism leading to compliance. Polities with large internationalized markets such as the United States and the European Union use conformity with soft law as a condition of market access. Foreign firms (or their respective governments) then follow soft law or face exclusion from these important markets (Kapstein 1992; Singer 2007; Posner 2009a).

Finally, a stream of research shows the role of network effects in bringing about compliance with soft law. When firms or countries seek a common standard, even in the face of distributional conflict, soft law may serve as a focal point (Abbott and Snidal 2000; Büthe and Mattli 2011). Compliance occurs when an organization is the first to produce a standard or a large jurisdiction incorporates it into national laws (Simmons 2004; Newman and Bach 2014), creating network effects whereby the more actors that adopt them, the more beneficial they become (David 1985). Over time, it is costly to deviate from the standard because so many others already follow it.

This robust debate on compliance generates important contributions concerning the role of international soft law in global governance. Often attentive to politics and power, the research challenges scholars to uncover mechanisms that might promote adoption and that might account for variance in patterns of compliance. This book's arguments about the politics of soft law over time benefit from these ideas and the scholarship behind them. At the same time, however, the empirical chapters demonstrate that much more is going on than the simple adoption or non-adoption of regulatory standards implied by the compliance literature and its emphasis on soft law as a solution to global governance challenges.

At the end of the day, there remains a serious mismatch between the decidedly mixed record of direct compliance and the vast resources and time expended by governments, industry associations, and other stakeholders to influence the content of international soft law. The Basel Committee, for example, was the site of considerable lobbying by global firms (Lall 2012; Pagliari and Young 2014). Similarly, the European Union recently engaged in a high-level dispute with the International Federation of Organic Agriculture Movements, the leading transnational standard setter for organic food labeling (Mutersbaugh 2005; Padel et al. 2009).[5] If skeptics are right and national implementation of international soft law is so limited, why would

[5] "History," ifoam.bio, last accessed July 27, 2017, <https://www.ifoam.bio/en/about-us/history>.

stakeholders or governments devote so much to achieve so little? The possible benefits would appear incommensurate with the costs.

The answer, borne out in the empirical studies discussed in the following chapters, is that existing arguments deeply underestimate soft law's impact. Theory needs to go well beyond the narrow band of questions concerning soft law and compliance and the underlying assumption that institutions reflect equilibria in which actors assess the costs and benefits of adopting proposed standards. We do not dispute that soft law may have such coordination properties. Yet following Moe (2005) and Knight (1992), we suggest that too much thinking underestimates international soft law's indirect, yet systematic, second-order political and distributional effects.

International Soft Law's Second-Order Effects

This book's central argument emphasizes how soft law, like other institutions, has important effects that evolve over time. In developing this argument, we shift attention away from issues of compliance, coordination, and problem solving and join the small but growing band of scholars who have explored the distributive politics associated with soft law (Kapstein 1992; Oatley and Nabors 1998; Simmons 2001). In contrast to much of this work, we do not focus on soft law's first-order issues such as the decision to cooperate or its immediate market effects. In other words, most existing distributional accounts have a relatively thin account of institutions.

We take as given that soft law is generated through a political process with distributive dimensions and instead highlight soft law's second-order consequences for political arenas and ecosystems. Most important, we take seriously the ways that soft law as an institution generates political winners and losers. In particular, we explore soft law's potential to become a political resource at the disposal of policy entrepreneurs and a new and disruptive social fact that repositions, reorients, and constitutes political actors (March and Olsen 1983; Thelen and Steinmo 1992; Campbell 2004; Helmke and Levitsky 2004). By definition soft law is voluntary, lacks mutually agreed upon obligations, and needs to be adopted, transposed, and implemented by national and regional rule-making authorities. Even so, it may also be politically disruptive (Finnemore and Toope 2001). Whereas first-order consequences, the focus of the existing literature, revolve narrowly around soft law's functional and intended aspects, we turn to the downstream mechanisms through which over time it shapes political actors who take up, respond to, bend and manipulate its prescriptions and by doing so shift the balance of authority among competing regulatory factions.

Voluntary Disruptions builds on a large literature in comparative politics, American political development, and international relations that shares an interest in second-order institutional effects (Thelen and Steinmo 1992; Carpenter 2001; Shickler 2001; Sheingate 2003; Thelen 2004; Mahoney and Thelen 2009). Take the case of interest group representation in the context of the welfare state. Research has demonstrated that elderly citizens were relatively unorganized prior to the creation of formal state pension systems. With the passage of Social Security in the United States and similar policies in other countries, elderly citizens formed formal interest groups that fought to maintain and expand such programs (Pierson 1993; Campbell 2003). Levy (1999) demonstrates the reverse process, in which French centralization policies undermined the strength of regional and local governance structures during much of the post-war period. As the French state attempted to devolve economic governance to the regions as part of a liberalization strategy in the 1990s, it found few credible partners available. Such policy feedback, both positive and negative, is just one way by which institutions become endogenous sources of change.

International relations scholarship has also shown that institutions shape actor preferences, organization, and power resources (Finnemore 1996; Jabko 2006; Woll 2008; Sell 2010). Research on the European Union, for example, is replete with cases of endogenous institutional change that alters political dynamics over time (Pierson 1996). In many policy domains, the European Commission fostered the development of transnational interest groups to achieve a specific policy goal. Subsequently, these groups evolve into independent political actors with autonomous preferences, agendas, and resources, have been issue entrepreneurs, and have given the Commission important allies from industry and civil society in domains unrelated to the original policy (Sandholtz and Zysman 1989; Stone Sweet et al. 2001; Posner 2005, 2009b). Likewise, EU agencies, authorities, and committees, initially designed to coordinate the national implementation of EU legislation, later become independent political actors (Newman 2008b; Posner 2010b). At the international level, treaty-based law has also been shown to have similar consequences. The Agreement on Trade-Related Aspects of Intellectual Property Rights generated significant domestic regulatory reforms, including the creation of bureaucratic structures across developing countries. Subsequently, the new agencies began to assert themselves in the politics of the international regime's evolution (Helfer et al. 2009; Sell 2010). Research on the World Trade Organization has also found important examples of how the regime generated institutional change in the participating states that, in future periods, put new pressures on the trade regime (Goldstein 1996; Shaffer 2012). Across these examples, powerful actors are bound up in the new institutional context.

In accordance with similar logics, soft law is part-and-parcel of dynamic, temporal processes that alter the preferences, resources, and political landscapes of powerful actors. Put differently, soft law spawns endogenous change and thereby does not merely reflect existing and exogenously determined interests and resources. As the examples from the domestic and international contexts suggest, soft law's temporal consequences may at times result from the intentional actions of political entrepreneurs. But they may also emerge from unanticipated experimentation with institutions as the larger political setting evolves. Given that transnational politics is as complex and contingent as other domains, we assume bounded rationality: decision-makers cannot fully appreciate the future direction, complexity, and meaning of institutional change—even though they may recognize that institutions have temporal consequences (Jupille et al. 2013; Poulsen and Aisbett 2013). We do not suggest that such consequences are more important in soft law's case than, say, in hard law's. Rather, we emphasize a largely unappreciated phenomenon: that soft law has similar second-order effects even in the absence of legal commitment mechanisms typical of hard law.

International soft law restructures politics in at least two prominent ways. First, it involves claims based on soft law's perceived legitimacy (or illegitimacy) and, second, it expands the political arenas where contestation over market rules occurs. In both cases, we highlight channels through which soft law may be used by a regulatory faction to promote its position over that of other factions. The "may" in the previous sentence is important because we view causality as probabilistic and contingent. Thus, the channels we describe are not meant to be determinative of outcomes. They are hypotheses that soft law will have the ascribed effect with a high degree of likelihood.

Legitimacy claims

The politics of economic governance typically involves pro- and anti-status quo camps or regulatory factions that compete to set the political agenda (Mahoney and Thelen 2009). Domestic and international conflicts of this kind feature prominently in the comparative and international political economy (IPE) literatures, respectively, but the two spheres are typically treated as discrete and separate (Callaghan 2010; Oatley 2011; Farrell and Newman 2015). Comparativist analysis, modeling international variables as exogenous forces, exaggerates the extent to which domestic political arenas are closed off from transnational developments. IPE theorists either assume away internal domestic conflicts under unitary national positions or depict "national positions" as the outcome of government efforts to filter settled and separate domestic contests at a previous moment in time.

Our first mechanism—legitimacy claims—suggests a more complex, fluid, and integrated relationship between domestic and international politics. It highlights how international soft law interacts with internal political struggles so as to reshape national debates and policy outcomes and then to have knock-on consequences for economic governance over time. We ask, what likely happens when internationally produced soft law is inserted into the "domestic" analytical scenario of a regulatory battle with pro- and anti-status quo camps? We suggest that soft law unsettles the contest by providing new political resources to some regulatory factions as they advocate for and advance their positions or attack and erode the positions of others (Joachim 2003; Della Porta and Tarrow 2005; Jabko 2006).

Similar to the way that ideas developed by transnational advocacy organizations help national-level reformists advance their causes (Risse-Kappen 1994; Keck and Sikkink 1998), international soft law offers policy entrepreneurs additional political resources. In particular, we argue that these political actors introduce soft law in the form of claims about its legitimacy or illegitimacy and then use them to support or oppose reform. The potential for and character of policy change is not only defined by the available range of ideas but also by the extent to which those ideas are perceived to have the legitimacy necessary to navigate through political conflict. Following Hurd (1999: 381), legitimacy is the "belief by an actor that a rule or institution ought to be obeyed." Legitimacy is thus a relational concept between actors and institutions. By associating preferred policy alternatives with international soft law and the bodies that generate it, a policy entrepreneur extends the perceived legitimacy or illegitimacy of the latter to shape conflict and opposition to such proposals at home.

In making claims about soft law's legitimacy, policy entrepreneurs draw from several sources (Barnett and Finnemore 2004; Bernstein and Cashore 2007). First, global standards often enjoy an aura of political neutrality that policy entrepreneurs use to boost the legitimacy of a preferred policy (Zaring 1998; Porter 2003; Slaughter 2004). In the context of internal political struggles, policy alternatives easily become tainted or lose traction by their association with perceived partisanship or, in the context of the European Union, national agendas. International soft law, by contrast, appears deracinated from the national context and any one political group, muting claims of bias (McNamara 2015). It may also appear as internationalist and cooperative, enjoying the support of a broad range of national perspectives. Implicitly, soft law often embodies the claim that it has passed the muster of a large number of national representatives with a broad range of potential objections. In terms of types of legitimacy, soft law, here, embodies the processes of "throughput" legitimacy, in which the prescriptions and rules are perceived as being generated through impartial or unbiased procedures (Risse and Kleine 2007; Quack 2010; Schmidt 2013).

Second, international soft law is frequently produced in highly specialized bodies that are viewed by policy-makers as enjoying a certain degree of expert authority. A large literature demonstrates the informational limits of policy-makers as well as citizens who are unable to know the exact effects of particular policy proposals (Haas 1992; Zito 2001; Hawkins et al. 2006). These groups, in turn, rely on specialized organizations such as credit rating agencies or scientific panels to fill these gaps in information and causal relationships. Research suggests that specialized organizations composed of professionals from a distinct policy domain often receive considerable deference from policy-makers seeking reassurance about the potential output legitimacy associated with their actions (Porter 2003; Barnett and Finnemore 2004; Cutler 2010). Policy alternatives generated by such bodies, when wrapped in a "cloak of scientific respectability" (Majone 1984: 15), become viewed as best practice, beating out alternative policy proposals even though the soft law producing bodies themselves may be unsure as to the ultimate effects of their policy prescriptions (Cutler et al. 1999; Gray 2009; Conti 2010; Brooks et al. 2015). In the absence of an experimental setting to test the effectiveness of soft law, expertise connotes a degree of "output" legitimacy on such prescriptions (Quack 2010; Schmidt 2013).

Finally, regulatory factions use international soft law to argue that the domestic status quo is unstable (Sikkink 2005; Andonova et al. 2009; Bartley 2011; Farrell and Newman 2015). In the absence of soft law, market actors follow domestic policy as their regulatory reversion point, that is, the regulatory status quo absent policy action (Richards 1999). But in a world of global economic exchange, market actors confront a series of potentially conflicting domestic rules that may undermine the reversion point. Soft law offers a concrete path to resolve such uncertainty. As market participants gravitate toward soft law, political actors point to these defections and argue that the regulatory reversion point is no longer best practice. Motivated political actors then insist that domestic policy confront (and be brought into line with) international soft law to avoid regulatory arbitrage. Because soft law offers a clear policy alternative to the domestic status quo, those seeking to maintain existing rules and institutions may no longer simply argue that there is no alternative. Instead, they face a new political situation in which they must defend the status quo against a written set of advisory prescriptions.

The legitimacy claims associated with soft law are thus derived from a range of sources—including perceived neutrality and expertise (Barnett and Finnemore 2004); and in domestic struggles, they serve to break internal policy paralysis by offering an external alternative. In sum, political groups leverage the legitimacy surrounding soft law as they wage their political battles.

Legitimacy claims associated with soft law need not be cast in a positive light. There are plenty of instances when soft law or the bodies that produce it are framed as suffering from bias or lacking the technical expertise that others claim or the accountability expected in a democracy. During the early 2000s, to give an example discussed in Chapter 5, the Basel Committee became increasingly subjected to criticisms that it had been captured by the transnational financial industry and thus lacked proper "input" legitimacy—a development that prompted reforms, including the introduction of new procedures similar to the notice and comment systems of domestic US agencies (Barr and Miller 2006). In the aftermath of the 2008 financial crisis, moreover, widespread accusations of technocratic standard-setting bodies being disembedded from domestic politics and prone to dogmatic forms of regulatory liberalism opened the door to policy entrepreneurs who pushed against reliance on international standards (Mügge 2011b).

As this discussion suggests, whether claims of legitimacy or illegitimacy are made and when they resonate is likely to vary by context and by the needs and skills of the policy entrepreneurs. The composition and characteristics of the soft law generator—that is, whether it is an international organization (IO), NGO, or transgovernmental network—are certainly important factors behind perceptions of credibility. For example, lobbying activities by private standard setters might diminish their political value when claims about neutrality and impartiality ring hollow. As we show in Chapters 5 and 6, the International Swaps and Derivatives Association experienced this at several junctures. Indeed, the case shows that opposing regulatory factions use such perceptions of bias to delegitimize soft law and promote their own agenda (Morgan 2010). That said, our evidence suggests that the organizational actor-type matters less than the quality and characteristics of the specific body responsible for generating the particular piece of soft law (Fourcade 2009). More to the point, our focus on legitimacy claims shifts attention to how policy entrepreneurs turn the reputations and perceptions of soft law and its generators—regardless of actor-type—into political resources for waging battles against competing regulatory factions.

In this way, the contests between regulatory factions that we describe produce outcomes that are far more than the adoption of or compliance with international standards and include the rebalancing of political power. As domestic struggles evolve, national positions may shift as well, altering subsequent possibilities for global cooperation.

Arena expansion

International soft law also transforms the politics of economic governance by expanding the sites of contestation. Like legitimacy claims, arena expansion is a temporal process by which international advisory rules and the transnational bodies that produce them are politically disruptive. Arena expansion alters the regulatory factions that have access (and those that do not) to agenda setting and decision-making, changes the number and types of actors involved, facilitates the creation of transnational coalitions and alliances, and shifts actor priorities toward the transnational level.

Traditional forms of diplomacy privilege the national executive by, among other things, giving foreign ministries control of treaty negotiation processes. Input from regulators, industries, NGOs, and other actors is typically filtered through their respective national executives in line with the metaphor of the two-level game (Evans et al. 1993; Milner 1997). In this classic image of international politics, interest groups and other actors must mobilize domestically and find their political goals filtered, aggregated, and molded by the national executive.

International soft law, by contrast, generally falls outside the direct control of national executives (Zaring 2004; Brummer 2011). A wide variety of bodies produce it, including organizations housing informal networks of national regulators and collections of private actors. One result is the emergence of a transnational level of political contestation, as actors of all kinds recognize soft law's potential importance to their industries, domains, or values (Sikkink 2005; Shaffer 2012; Farrell and Newman 2015; Halliday and Shaffer 2015). In transnational arenas, potential stakeholders coordinate and collaborate with like-minded counterparts from other jurisdictions (Burley and Mattli 1993; Alter 1998; Hale 2015). Arena expansion is particularly likely to facilitate the creation of transnational organizations when actors find their policy agenda blocked domestically (Farrell and Newman 2015). By organizing transnationally, political actors press their interests directly at the transnational level and, while not necessarily bypassing traditional two-level politics, are likely to disrupt it.

This shift has important consequences for the agendas that are developed at the transnational level as the new factions are composed of unique and often divergent preferences from those of traditional diplomats (Farrell and Newman 2014). In addition, transnational soft law arenas may shift the relative influence of competing factions, away from the ones previously prominent in policy development and agenda setting at the domestic level. Some organizations—regulators, NGOs, or firms, for example—will be better able to organize and insert themselves into transnational policy-making while others will lack the resources and expertise to span national and global conversations (Barr and Miller 2006; Overdevest 2010; Quack 2010; Büthe and Mattli 2011). Although transnational contestation and participation promise to alter the mix of actors involved, they do not necessarily promise greater transparency or inclusion than traditional two-level politics.

Like legitimacy claims, the expansion of arenas undermines contentions of no policy alternatives and therefore has the potential to reopen previously settled debates. Soft law proposals, by providing new policy ideas, force the engagement of competing regulatory factions (Fox and Stephenson 2015). In this way, transnational policy proposals become political facts that undermine a blocking faction's defense of the status quo and pressure them into the more challenging role of accepting or rejecting the new transnational agenda. As a result, arena expansion has the potential to alter the balance of authority and political resources among regulatory factions. Those groups that had been frustrated in purely domestic channels now have opportunities to re-litigate and find support for their position in a new transnational setting. Moreover, actors may exploit their access within transnational arenas to enhance their clout in the domestic arena and circumvent opposition from those factions that do not have access to the transnational level.

The emergence of international soft law arenas also has a deep imprint on participating stakeholders—on their internal goals, identities, and organization as well as the ecology within which they operate. Here, our argument draws from historical institutionalist scholarship about the impact of institutional context on interest groups (Berger 1983; Pierson 1993; Campbell 2003; Falleti and Lynch 2009). These studies show that public institutions (policies, in this instance) "frame the choices of political actors both by creating resources and incentives and by influencing the efforts of individuals to interpret the social world" (Pierson 1993: 628). An important strain of this literature examines how such policies affect the organization of business and industry–government relations. For example, David Vogel's early research on the role of business in US regulatory politics reveals the critical role that new policies like the endorsement of class action lawsuits and transparency requirements played in making "business executives much more conscious of their common class interests, which in turn led to both the formation and revival of political organizations" (Vogel 1989: 14).

We extend this general logic, positing that soft law may have a strong restructuring effect on competing regulatory factions and interest groups. Within any policy domain, there is an ecology of organizations that seek to survive and maintain their authority (Abbott et al. 2016). To do this, they need to attract members and financial resources and foster political legitimacy, which means finding ways to be perceived as useful and valuable. The expansion of the political arena changes what it means to be relevant. New transnational institutions shift the locus of political attention, encourage the organization of interests at the transnational level, and, we argue, reshape the priorities and missions of individual organizations. Transnational arenas narrow the issues and topics that become salient politically, refocusing the attention and agenda of regulatory factions (Porter 2003). In this way, international soft law transforms the nature of interest group representation, the priorities and fate of particular organizations, and who has a say in the creation of market rules.

Conclusion

Over the course of the book, we demonstrate that soft law is more than simply a coordination mechanism deployed to solve global governance challenges and that its political and distributional consequences extend well beyond the first-order effects discussed in existing accounts (Knight 1992; Kapstein 1994; Oatley and Nabors 1998; Simmons 2001; Moe 2005; Voeten Forthcoming). Drawing on diverse literatures from American political development, comparative politics, international relations, and sociology, our argument stresses how soft law, like other institutions, has independent distributional effects capable of transforming politics over time. We do not suggest that soft law is exceptional in this way. Like hard law, soft law generates second-order political consequences. Yet it does so even though it does not come with the legal commitments and obligations typical of hard law. We emphasize two processes—legitimacy claims and arena expansion—by which soft law shapes the behavior of powerful actors including leading "rule-making" polities and influential interest groups. Thus, rather than asking whether soft law is adopted or not, we look at how it is wielded by political actors and regulatory factions and how it changes political organization, orientation, and representation over time.

An additional aim of this book is to shed light on a host of real-world questions surrounding pre- and post-crisis financial governance—questions about the policy consensus between the United States and the European Union that helped enable the 2008 financial crisis; about the influence of transnational financial firms over agenda setting for global banking rules during the 2000s; and about the uneven pattern of US cooperation with other jurisdictions in reforming financial regulation in the post-crisis era. Each of these financial regulatory outcomes discussed in Chapters 4, 5, and 6, respectively, was contingent on a wide range of contributing factors. Yet we show that satisfying explanations across all of them depend on shifting the theoretical lens away from soft law as a coordination device toward its role in transforming politics. Before turning to these questions and our explanations, Chapter 3 gives necessary background on international financial regulation and, in particular, on the origins of major soft law initiatives.

3

International Financial Regulation

The book's central proposition is that international soft law has disruptive consequences for the future politics of powerful jurisdictions and interest groups. This chapter provides an overview of soft law's evolution in the area of finance and other necessary background for the rest of the book. In particular, it describes two key properties of international financial regulation[1] that resurface as "causes" in later chapters: the prominence of soft law; and the fragmentation and consequentially uneven development by subsector of rules and rule-making.

The second half of the chapter makes an argument about the origins of these properties as well as of soft law's initial substance: they largely reflect the deep imprint of internal political institutions and dynamics of polities with major financial markets. While other authors note the importance of domestic politics in the creation of international soft law (Kapstein 1989; Singer 2007), they typically emphasize its coordinating function. In this chapter, by contrast, we highlight its origins in domestic distributive politics. In the absence of a treaty-based organization for financial regulation like the World Trade Organization, regulators of leading financial centers, embroiled in factional battles and struggles to preserve autonomy and power at home, created the emergent soft law system to promote their agendas and ambitions. When successful, they left a lasting mark on it, often mirroring internal institutions, priorities, and models.

We underscore that US financial authorities deliberately expanded the regulatory arena and created international soft law as a means to achieving domestic ends. Our argument helps to identify not only the motivations to cooperate in some sectors as opposed to others but also the substance of the soft law resulting from that cooperation. At times, the motivation stemmed

[1] By international financial regulation, we refer to financial regulation created in intergovernmental, transgovernmental, and transnational organizations.

from factional infighting among agencies, rooted in historical US regulatory fragmentation. At other times, regulators used international cooperation to push back against threats—from industry and politicians—to their autonomy and powers. Still, other instances exhibit early examples of soft law's second-order effects, as regulators used the legitimacy of early international standards to win battles at home. Far from simply promoting market stability, soft law shows its roots in distributional conflicts among regulators, industry, and politicians. These clashes and their international implications anticipate central themes running through Chapters 4, 5, and 6: domestic and international regulatory politics are deeply entangled; and rather than treating large polities as cohesive units (e.g. the United States or the European Union) that win or lose in global conflicts, contestation within these polities often has an impact on international developments and vice versa.

As defined in Chapter 2, soft law is a set of written, advisory prescriptions. This type of law abounds in the area of international financial regulation. Few of the major transnational rule-making bodies in this domain are founded on formal treaty-based international law. They instead make up a field of organizations, each with its own operating procedures, governing bodies, and memberships composed of informal networks of collaborating public and private regulators. For the most part, these bodies create voluntary standards that leave implementation and enforcement largely in the hands of national and regional legislators and authorities (Porter 2005a; Alexander et al. 2006; Davies and Green 2008; Brummer 2011; Helleiner and Pagliari 2011; Newman and Bach 2014). In short, global financial regulation consists of rules at multiple levels—domestic, regional, and international—with the international level consisting primarily of *advisory* prescriptions.

The fragmented organization of the rule-making bodies refers to the tendency toward specialization by the subsectors of banking, securities markets, insurance or financial reporting, to list the best-known ones. As market boundaries have blurred with companies offering products and engaging in business that span these divisions, leading governments cooperating in the G7, G10, and G20 have sought cross-subsector coordination. Yet the original fragmentation into separate standard setters remains largely intact and pertinent as subsector regulatory silos have continued to shape most aspects of the pre- and post-crisis international financial architecture (Porter 2005a; Pauly 2009; Baker 2010; Helleiner 2010) and produce uneven cooperation, rule-making, and rules with differentiated political effects (Posner 2015).

Why do we highlight these, as opposed to other features of the international financial architecture? The main reason, as developed in later chapters, is that these constant and common properties generate endogenous processes that have disruptive effects on the politics of financial regulation. International law, like other institutions, we argue, transforms long-existing struggles among powerful actors domestically and internationally. Vital questions about the politics of financial regulation, like the ones we address in the following chapters, cannot be answered without reference to the expansive use of soft law and the fragmented organization of rule-making: Why did the European Union, the rising second mover at the turn of the millennium, align its regulatory approaches with the United States in the pre-crisis decade? Why did the leading transnational lobby for the financial services sector, the Institute of International Finance, become influential in the Basel II negotiations having had an inconsequential impact on Basel I? And why did post-crisis US regulatory reforms contribute to smoother transatlantic cooperation in the area of banking than in others like derivatives? Our answers to these questions in Chapters 4, 5, and 6 highlight the temporal effects of the voluntary and fragmented organization of international financial regulation.

This chapter also provides the methodological basis for organizing and interpreting evidence and for answering the questions posed in subsequent chapters. As a result of the initial fragmented rule-making by subsector, the narrowly oriented networks and standard-setting bodies developed differently and unevenly—a fortuitous (and easily exploitable) pattern from the standpoint of the social scientific study of soft laws' effects. In addition to its having an impact on important real-world outcomes, the differentiation across subsectors highlighted in this chapter is useful in later ones for drawing inferences and answering the concrete questions under investigation; the natural variance allows us to observe what happens with and without soft law's prior existence and under different states of its development.

We note one final justification for our attention to the featured properties, rather than others. The advisory character of the rules and fragmented organization of the financial architecture are of general, real-world importance beyond the specific questions addressed in Chapters 4, 5, and 6. The two properties were central factors behind the architecture's underperformance before and after the 2008 financial crisis (Lall 2012; Helleiner 2014b; Goldbach 2015a). Critics portray the absence of binding burden-sharing mechanisms as the Achilles heel of transnational financial governance, hindering preemptive regulatory responses, leaving bailouts and the lender of last resort functions to leading central banks and uncoordinated national treasuries (Pauly 2009; Drezner 2014; Helleiner 2014b). Likewise, analysts tie the fragmented organization of the architecture to an overemphasis on micro-prudential concerns, such as the standard-setting bodies that monitor and enforce particular subsector behavior in banking or insurance, rather than on the systemic vulnerabilities created by interlinkages across sectors and economies (Haldane and May 2011; Baker 2013; Kalyanpur and Newman 2017).

The International Regulation of Finance: Fragmented Soft Law

What does the international dimension of financial governance look like and how has it evolved? The rule-making bodies feature considerable diversity of participants and members.[2] Some of the organizations are comprised primarily of public sector officials (mostly sub-state-level authorities such as independent regulatory agencies but occasionally ministry-level representatives), others rely on industry representatives, and still others contain a mix of both. And the composition of several standard-setting bodies has evolved over time. In the case of the International Accounting Standards Board (formerly, the International Accounting Standards Committee), for example, a monitoring board including the US Security and Exchange Commission (SEC), the European Commission, other national authorities and international organizations, was imposed in 2009 on an until-then entirely private organization (Posner 2010b). Even among purely private organizations, the membership ranges from individual professionals and experts, to financial industry associations, national standard setters, and firms (McKeen-Edwards and Porter 2013). It is typical for a financial rule-making body to be composed of domestic regulators—public and private—with expertise and often national legal authority in the respective subsector (Raustiala 2002; Porter 2005a; Brummer 2011).

Another uncontroversial observation is that participants typically mirror domestic distributions of regulatory authority. The United States, for example, is represented on the Basel Committee by the Federal Reserve and other banking supervisors,[3] while the US SEC participates in meetings of the International Organization of Securities Commissions (IOSCO). National representatives may differ across the organizations and usually do not include finance ministers or political representatives of the executive. For unified financial regulators, by contrast, one regulator represents countries across subsector organizations, as was the case in the United Kingdom for much of the 2000s. As noted, domestic regulatory structures change over time in response to both international, regional, and domestic political developments that may not be directly related to the work of these bodies, causing national representation to fluctuate as a result (Lütz 1998). Since the late 1990s, the deepening of EU legal, regulatory, and supervisory integration complicates European representation in standard-setting bodies (Posner 2007; Posner and Véron 2016).

[2] For an overview of these and other features of the international financial regulatory architecture, see Brummer (2011: 60–114).

[3] Currently, the United States is represented by the Federal Reserve Bank of New York, the Office of the Comptroller of the Currency, and the Federal Deposit Insurance Corporation.

These areas of agreement notwithstanding, scholarly descriptions of international financial regulation do not always highlight the same properties. Slaughter (2004) and others depict the phenomenon as a network of networks, an apt metaphor in some respects (since clearly networks abound).[4] While still others focus on the nature of the participants, which may be alternatively *transnational* (i.e. industry and non-profit private), *transgovernmental* (sub-national public), or intergovernmental (executive branch public) officials (Zaring 1998; Slaughter 2004; Baker 2006; Büthe and Mattli 2011; Green 2013) and how these groups are associated with the spreading of ideologically driven content under the guise of technocratic neutrality (Perry and Nölke 2006; Underhill et al. 2010). While we pay attention to both the networks behind soft law's production and the actors involved, who participates and how they are organized are not the only factors that influence the political economy of international finance.

Instead, we highlight two properties of the international financial architecture—the heavy reliance on soft law and the fragmented organization of rule generation by subsector. This section describes them, while the next one charts their evolution by stressing the uneven development across subsectors and the domestic institutional and political origins of the substantive content.

Written advisory prescriptions

Unlike the regimes for trade or monetary policy, the international rule-making organizations that govern finance (e.g. those contributing to the Compendium of Standards[5]) rarely use treaty-based international law (Zaring 2004; Brummer 2011; Galbraith and Zaring 2013).[6] While a few treaty-based international organizations (the IMF, World Bank, and OECD) today play a collaborative role, the main standard-setting bodies are collections of regulators and financial industry professionals who initially created their own transnational organizations and meet on an ongoing basis. The best known of these organizations are the Basel Committee on Banking Supervision (Basel Committee),

[4] The term network has a variety of meanings across disciplines. It has been used to describe a form of coordination that contrasts to markets or hierarchies. Alternatively, social network analysis explores the structure of relations between units. Finally, research on policy networks suggests the interactions of experts with similar training and outlooks. The literature on global finance frequently moves between these concepts.

[5] The Compendium of Standards includes standards related to the stability and soundness of financial systems, which is maintained by the Financial Stability Board and is a key pillar of the global governance of finance. "FSB: The Compendium of Standards," fsb.org, last accessed July 26, 2017, <http://www.fsb.org/what-we-do/about-the-compendium-of-standards/>.

[6] The WTO's weak (compared to other areas of the trading regime) Annex on "Financial Services" is an exception. "WTO Financial Services," wto.org, last accessed July 26, 2017, <https://www.wto.org/english/tratop_e/serv_e/finance_e/finance_e.htm>.

the International Organization of Securities Commissions (IOSCO), the International Association of Insurance Supervisors (IAIS), the International Swaps and Derivatives Association (ISDA), the Financial Stability Board, and the International Accounting Standards Board (IASB). With small secretariats responsible for organizing correspondence, committee meetings, and publications, most of the work is conducted by teams of seconded staff from member agencies or participating firms, professionals and experts who collaborate virtually or on the sidelines of economic summits or meetings.

The production of soft law is what binds these organizations together.[7] Among the voluntary prescriptions they embrace are standards for industry-wide contracts or back-office operations, recommendations on the institutional configuration of supervisory authorities, and procedures for enforcement cooperation. For example, the International Swaps and Derivatives Association's *Master Agreement* (a common template for derivatives contracts) (McKeen-Edwards and Porter 2013: 43) bolsters legal certainty, contract standardization, and net-reductions of collateral for counter parties of over-the-counter derivatives transactions McKeen-Edwards and Porter 2013: 43–6). IOSCO, for its part, produces the *Objectives and Principles of Securities Regulation*.[8] Intended for national and regional authorities, it provides a set of thirty-eight principles and is accompanied by an assessment methodology to evaluate national performance. Such regulatory forums have gone so far as to develop specific policy proposals: the Basel Committee's Capital Adequacy Accord,[9] which recommends statutory demands that banks hold a certain amount of capital in reserve to be used during financial stress, and the ISDA's recommendations for national legislators concerning netting of assets and liabilities (Newman and Bach 2014). Table 3.1 gives an overview of many of the most prominent bodies involved in international financial regulation.

As discussed in Chapter 2, governments and the European Union have many reasons—from reputational benefits to coercion—for complying with soft law (Ho 2002; Brummer 2011). Indeed, soft law often finds its way into domestic law, as jurisdictions rely on such prescriptions as they reform their national rules (Bach and Newman 2010; Zaring 2015a). In addition, most standard-setting organizations have stepped up monitoring capacities (notably through more rigorous peer review procedures) since 2008 (Posner 2015).

[7] Transgovernmental bodies (made up of public officials) also focus on information sharing and, since the crisis, monitoring. Transnational associations (composed of industry representatives) sometimes provide advocacy functions and serve technical functions (McKeen-Edwards and Porter 2013).

[8] "OICV-IOSCO," iosco.org, last accessed July 26, 2017, <https://www.iosco.org/about/?subsection=display_committee&cmtid=19&subSection1=principles>.

[9] "Basel III: international regulatory framework for banks," bis.org, last accessed July 26, 2017, <http://www.bis.org/bcbs/basel3.htm?m=3%7C14%7C572>.

Table 3.1. International and transnational bodies that create financial regulatory soft law

Regulatory body	Area	Location	Founding	Membership	Webpage
Basel Committee on Banking Supervision (Basel Committee)[a]	Banking	Basel	1974	28	http://www.bis.org/bcbs
Committee on Payment and Market Infrastructure[b] (CPMI)	Financial market infrastructure	Basel	1990	25	https://www.bis.org/cpmi
Financial Action Task Force (FATF)	Money laundering/ financing of terrorism	Paris	1989	37	http://www.fatf-gafi.org
Financial Stability Board[c]	Derivatives; G-SIFIs; banking resolution	Basel	1999	24	http://www.fsb.org
International Accounting Standards Board (IASB)[d]	Accounting	London	1973	13	http://www.iasb.org
International Association of Deposit Insurers (IADI)	Deposit insurance	Basel	2002	83	http://www.iadi.org
International Association of Insurance Supervisors (IAIS)	Insurance	Basel	1994	200+	http://www.iaisweb.org
International Auditing and Assurance Standards Board (IAASB)[e]	Auditing	New York	1978	18	http://www.ifac.org
International Capital Markets Association (ICMA)[f]	Debt	Zurich	1969	60+	http://www.icmagroup.org
International Monetary Fund (IMF)[g]	Policy transparency	Washington, DC	1944	189	http://www.imf.org
International Organization of Securities Commissions (IOSCO)[h]	Securities	Madrid	1983	115+	http://www.iosco.org
International Swaps and Derivatives Association (ISDA)	Derivatives	New York	1985	68	http://www2.isda.org
Joint Forum	Cross-sectional issues; conglomerates	Basel	1996	18	http://www.bis.org/bcbs/jointforum.htm
Organisation for Economic Co-operation and Development[i]	Corporate governance	Paris	1948	35	http://www.oecd.org
WB/UNCITRAL[j]	Insolvency/creditor rights	Washington, DC	1945	189	http://www.worldbank.org

Notes:

[a] The body was formed as the Committee of Banking Regulations and Supervisory Practices. It changed its name to the Basel Committee on Banking Supervision in 1989.

[b] The organization was first formed as the Committee on Payment and Settlement Systems (CPSS). It was renamed in 2014 as the CPMI. It followed up the work started by the Committee on Interbank Netting Schemes at the Bank for International Settlements.

[c] The FSB was originally created as the Financial Stability Forum. It was renamed the Financial Stability Board in 2009.

[d] Originally named the International Accounting Standards Committee. The name changed in 2001.

[e] Originally named the International Auditing Practices Committee. The name changed in 2002.

[f] Originally named the Association of International Bond Dealers. Its name first changed to the International Securities Markets Association in 1992, and, following its merger with the International Primary Markets Association, the ICMA was formed in 2005.

[g] The IMF devised the Code of Good Practices on Transparency in Monetary and Financial Policies in 1999.

[h] IOSCO started as a regional organization in the Americas known as the Inter-American Conference of Securities Commissions. It was renamed IOSCO in 1983.

[i] Originally known as the Organisation for European Economic Co-operation, the organization was renamed as the OECD in 1961. The first OECD Principles of Corporate Governance were published in 1999.

[j] The World Bank and United Nations Commission on International Trade Law worked together to publish the Insolvency and Creditor Rights Standard in 2001.

None, however, possess a formal dispute settlement mechanism or rule-enforcement capacity that is legally binding among the members.

Subsector fragmentation

A second fundamental feature of the global governance of finance is its primary organizational principle: specialized rule-making by subsector. As described earlier and illustrated in Table 3.1, the generation of international soft law in the area of financial regulation has mostly occurred in forums like the Basel Committee on Banking Supervision (BCBS), IOSCO, IAIS, or IASB, responsible for governance of banking, securities, insurance, and financial reporting, respectively.[10] Other examples include highly specialized bodies like the International Auditing and Assurance Standards Board (IAASB) and the International Swaps and Derivatives Association (Porter 2005b; Alexander et al. 2006; Davies and Green 2008). From the 1970s through the early 1990s, these organizations developed in relative independence from one another with little formal coordination among them.

By the mid-1990s, however, leaders of the major industrial economies realized that the continued subsector organization of the core transnational regulatory bodies was poorly suited to a world of internationalizing financial markets wherein firms increasingly competed across traditional subsector boundaries (Haldane and May 2011; Baker 2013). Prompted into action by the financial crises in Mexico (1994) and Asia (1997), policy-makers under the auspices of the G7[11] and later the G20 attempted to fix the market-regulatory mismatch through the creation of a layer of coordinating forums. The new framework became known as the international financial architecture (Eichengreen 1999; Noble and Ravenhill 2000; Soederberg 2004; Reisenbichler 2015). The first new organization was the Joint Forum, founded in 1996, which brought together the subsector regulators for banking, securities, and insurance to develop common soft law guidelines for issues that touched on all three sectors. In 1999, the Joint Forum was joined by the Financial Stability Forum (FSF), which became the Financial Stability Board (FSB) in 2009 when the G20

[10] For the IMF's list, see: "Standard Setting Agencies," imf.org, last accessed July 26, 2017, <https://www.imf.org/external/standards/agency.htm>. For the FSB's list, see: "FSB: The Compendium of Standards," fsb.org, accessed July 26, 2017, <http://www.fsb.org/what-we-do/about-the-compendium-of-standards/>.

[11] Created in 1974 in response to financial instability associated with the unwinding of the Bretton Woods exchange rate system and the oil shocks, the G7 brings together finance ministers and central bankers from the advanced economies. It includes representatives from Canada, France, Germany, Italy, Japan, the United Kingdom, and the United States (and Russia under the G8), who meet between one and four times a year to discuss and coordinate macroeconomic policy. The G7 is an informal body, which relies on summit agreements to shape policy, rather than an organization founded on a formal treaty.

response to financial crisis deepened the new layer of coordination in the name of mitigating macro-prudential systemic risks (Pauly 2009; Helleiner 2010; Gadinis 2013; Moschella 2013; Posner 2015; Reisenbichler 2015).[12]

As part of the recent effort to give the international financial architecture a more articulated and hierarchical structure, the FSB brings together representatives from national and international regulatory bodies as well as political representatives from the member state finance ministries and treasuries. Originally, the FSF included representatives from the G7 countries and a few others with international financial centers. In 2009, with the FSF's transformation into the FSB, the membership was expanded to reflect the G20's. Each country is allowed up to three representatives, which typically come from the finance ministry, the central bank, and the securities regulator. In addition, the subsector standard setters (e.g. IOSCO, IAIS, and BCBS) and international organizations (the IMF, the World Bank, the OECD, the European Commission, and the European Central Bank) are members.

The FSB is a guardian of the Compendium of Standards, which is the compilation of most international financial and economic standards generated primarily by the subsector bodies, but also by the FSB itself in areas that do not fall neatly under the auspices of the incumbent specialized standard setters.[13] In a delicate division of labor among the IMF, World Bank, and subsector standard setters, the FSB oversees the much-enhanced post-crisis monitoring regime that evaluates the soundness of national financial arrangements and international systemic stability in large part by assessing adherence to the Compendium of Standards—representing the benchmark for international best practices.[14] Figure 3.1 visually displays the development of the international financial architecture since the 1970s.

Despite the first gradual, then more rapid deepening of these coordination efforts, the persistence of soft law-producing bodies fragmented by subsector remains a defining feature of the architecture and permeates most parts of its functioning in at least three ways (Brummer 2011; Helleiner 2014b; Moschella and Tsingou 2014). First, it contributes significantly to the mixed results of G7 and G20 efforts to impose a hierarchical structure over the field of specialized standard setters. The FSB offers a degree of centralized information sharing, rule development, and monitoring. Yet it is weakly institutionalized and grounded in the G20, which is itself an informal institution of cooperating heads of states. The G20 has a relatively small administration that works

[12] "About the FSB," fsb.org, last accessed July 26, 2017, <http://www.financialstabilityboard.org/about/>.

[13] The Compendium of Standards includes standards related to the stability and soundness of financial systems but excludes standards developed by transnational industry organizations such as the ISDA. The IMF's "Standards and Codes" contains most of the same subsector standards.

[14] For variation in their implementation see Mosley (2010).

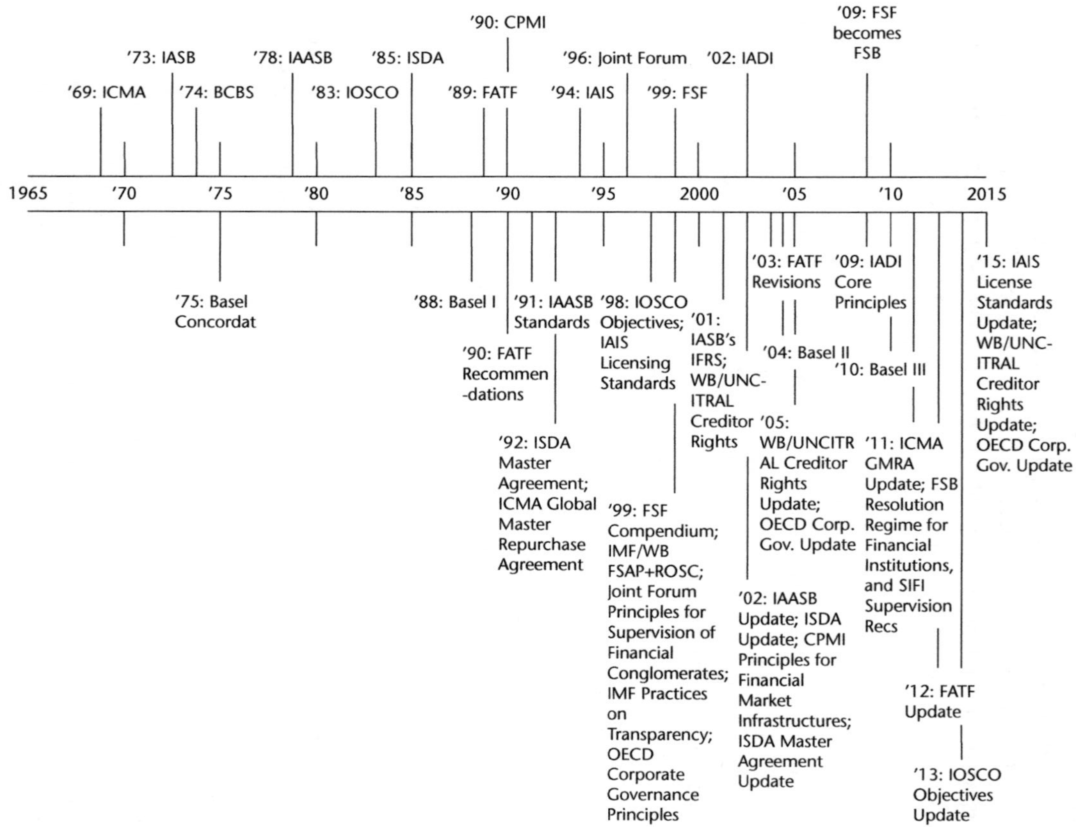

Figure 3.1. Development of international soft law in finance

Source: Authors.

within a voluntary regime with few mutually agreed-upon formal penalties or adjudication options (Ho 2002; Verdier 2009). Among other consequences, this setup makes the FSB dependent on the participation of member representatives, whose resources and fatigued staffs have not generally expanded to meet the post-crisis increase in workload (Moschella 2013; Helleiner 2014b).[15]

More to the point, rather than replacing the subsector standard-setting bodies, the FSB relies heavily on their work for most areas of financial regulation included in the Compendium. Among other problems, the dispersion of authority gives rise to bureaucratic politics, rivalries, and turf wars—at the domestic as well as international level—that undermine the G20's purported goals.[16] The subsectoral divisions and informality generate a backdrop that persistently shapes the regulation of global finance. The divisions, for example, create a tension between those regulators that want to protect their autonomy over a particular regulatory domain and political principals and competing regulators that periodically push for more centralized oversight (Singer 2007).

Mandates from the G7 and G20 add a degree of political oversight, and some argue that the FSB itself, to which the subsector bodies are also supposed to report in the post-crisis arrangements, is an attempt to reassert political control over them (Verdier 2009). Finance ministries are members of the FSB and can inject executive preferences into the standards debates. Sometimes this executive influence can be subtle such as the drawing of red lines (behind closed doors in "staffless" discussions) that prevents the FSB from including items in peer reviews of member countries.[17] Yet most of the networks associated with the subsector organizations are made up of arm's-length independent regulators or private bodies who are variously accountable to respective home governments. The net outcome is that the multiple and complex "chains of command" involving the FSB and the standard setters contribute to the mixed successes of the G7 and G20 efforts to centralize decision-making (Newman 2010).

Continued subsector fragmentation also complicates the IMF's and World Bank's responsibilities to address macro-prudential systemic risks. In 1999, the IMF (and World Bank, in the case of developing countries) launched the Financial Sector Assessment Program (FSAP) and began to issue Reports on the Observance of Standards and Codes (ROSCs). These monitoring exercises are, respectively, assessments of the soundness of a country's financial system and its adherence to the Compendium of Standards. Carried out and made public on voluntary bases, the pre-crisis programs were notoriously weak (in part because China and the United States opted out entirely but also because

[15] Author interview with two FSB officials, Basel, June 24, 2015.

[16] Author interview with former FSB official, Basel, June 28, 2012.

[17] Author interview with US Treasury official, Washington, DC, December 20, 2011.

governments were able to get away with superficial implementation) (Walter 2008; Foot and Walter 2010). Even so, the FSAPs and ROSCs forced the IMF and the subsector standard setters into a new uneasy relationship.

The IMF repeatedly criticized the standard setters for their narrow subsector lenses that failed to deliver on the primary policy goal of limiting macro-prudential systemic risk (IMF 2001, 2002a, 2002b).[18] The tendency was instead for the standard setters to emphasize micro-prudential issues such as regulatory quality (Baker 2010). The clash continues with post-crisis forensics, which repeatedly points to the lack of macro-prudential concern in the regulatory architecture (Haldane and May 2011). Improvements in the post-crisis period, including the participation of the United States and China, and heightened public salience puts political pressure on the standard setters to make reforms in the direction of the IMF's concerns. Yet these reforms do not resolve the underlying tension, a product of subsectoral specialization. Given these realities, it is difficult to make the case that international soft law is driven solely by regulators seeking to resolve cooperation problems or produce market stability (Kalyanpur and Newman 2017).

Lastly and perhaps most important for understanding soft law's disruptive political and temporal effects discussed in later chapters, subsector fragmentation gives rise to a field of highly differentiated organizational setups and uneven levels of soft law development (see Figure 3.1 and Posner 2018). Each network (with its distinctive culture and priorities) creates its own rule-making organization (with unique voting and membership rules) and faces different constraints and opportunities. At any given moment in time, soft law's development (and effects on politics) looks very different across subsectors. We now turn to the origins of this variation in soft law development.

The Evolution of Fragmented Soft Law Governance: Bretton Woods, Domestic Institutional Legacies, and Uneven Development

In this section, we focus on the evolution of international soft law before the crisis of 2008. We argue that decisions made during the post-war Bretton Woods negotiations combined with the peculiarities of domestic regulation and politics in core countries, especially the United States, shaped the development of international financial regulation (Burley 1993; Bach 2010).

[18] An important exception is FATF blacklists, which have a much more coercive feel than most of the more advisory guidelines generated by the other bodies. Even FATF, however, relies on state implementation of its blacklists.

Regulators within these polities, sometimes representing one of several dueling factions, created transnational political arenas and developed international soft law (mostly in their own image) in pursuit of domestic policy agendas. Such an account of soft law as domestic politics by other means contrasts with conventional explanations that emphasize more functionalist drivers such as the nature of the problem or the role of technical expertise (Koremenos et al. 2001; Verdier 2009). Similarly, we depart from domestic political perspectives, which ask whether regulatory cooperation is more or less likely and which emphasize how coordination resolves regulators' dilemmas about market risk and legislative oversight (Singer 2007; Verdier 2009). Taking into consideration a wider set of distributional issues, we argue that such cooperation also serves a range of alternative political goals such as winning bureaucratic turf wars, expanding and defending administrative missions, and pushing back against waves of anti-regulatory sentiments. Once the fragmented system existed, it had two important knock-on consequences that resurface in the narratives of subsequent chapters: first, the uneven development of soft law across the subsectors; and, second, the imprint on soft law's content of a few powerful regulators, sometimes with factional policy agendas.

Bretton Woods and governance gaps

The legacy of the Bretton Woods Agreement, more than any other factor, prompted the subsequent rise of soft law instead of the creation of new treaty-based institutions. A central provision of the post-war monetary regime was the acceptance of national capital controls and other policy tools, which led to the belief that banking systems and financial institutions were cordoned off and therefore unlikely to contribute to global economic instability (Kapstein 1994; Helleiner 1996, 2016). Policy-makers viewed banks and stock markets as domestic institutions that played an important role in the embedded liberalism compromise, i.e. societies could regulate and channel finance in different ways so as to achieve post-war national goals (Ruggie 1982; Zysman 1983). In short, governments did not see the macro- and micro-level health of the financial services sector as an international affair.

The Bretton Woods institutions that the United States and its allies created—the International Monetary Fund and the World Bank—did not possess delegated authority over prudential financial regulation. While the British proposal for a strong international liquidity institution, known as the International Clearing Union, might have encroached into national monetary policy, it was rejected at the summit. Instead, with the exception of IMF responsibilities over capital controls, the new multilateral institutions did not receive expansive authority over what has become known as macro-prudential stability

(Helleiner 2015). By bracketing the issue as a largely domestic concern, the post-war settlement set the stage for a governance gap in the event of a future return of international finance. Despite a string of proposals dating as early as the 1980s (and as recently as 2008[19]) to create a formal treaty-based organization tasked with monitoring and maintaining global financial health, none found much political traction (Rogoff 1999). Among other reasons, domestic regulators, who had grown accustomed to the absence of international institutions and wary of relinquishing their authority, sometimes worked to block such efforts.

Market and political realities quickly challenged the central assumptions of the Bretton Woods system. Starting with the eurodollar markets in the 1960s, the clean separation between national banking systems dissolved (Kapstein 1994; Helleiner 1996). Moreover, the potential for systemic risk inherent in banking crises became clear as bank failure in one country had consequences for banking systems in other countries (Goodhart 2011). Finally, with the end of the dollar–gold standard and the easing of capital controls, the internationalization of currency and capital markets accelerated. The New York and London financial markets saw a dramatic rise in foreign investors, traders, and companies seeking capital. This was particularly true as asset managers and banks, flush with petro-dollars from states that benefited from the 1970s oil crisis, looked for new investment opportunities (Abdelal 2007). It quickly became apparent that the behavior of foreign firms and investors could have consequences for the stability of these markets. Yet no international institution had clear responsibility for them (Porter 2005a; Wood 2005).

Domestic institutions and subsector fragmentation

Because of the absence of treaty-based international regulatory institutions, national officials overseeing the US and other large markets as well as industry associations had to grapple with the governance challenges of financial internationalization without an overarching framework, let alone a central authority. Distinctive domestic regulatory configurations and politics—divisions of authority along subsectors, federalism, the balance between public and industry self-regulation, bureaucratic autonomy from politicians, other agencies and industry, and bureaucratic cultures and priorities (Coleman 1996; Deeg 1999; Konings 2011)—played key roles in producing an international architecture deeply fragmented along subsectors (Hemel 2011). Foreshadowing the two mechanisms (discussed in Chapter 2) through which soft law has second-order effects (i.e. legitimacy claims and arena expansion), political entrepreneurs

[19] Author interview with French Treasury official, Paris, August 17, 2011.

extended regulatory battles to the transnational level and created soft law to bolster their home authorities, agendas, and positions vis-à-vis political opponents. After giving an overview of these domestic spillovers, we turn to the specific origins of the Basel Committee, IOSCO, and IAIS. We use these illustrations to demonstrate both the uneven development across subsectors as well as the importance of specific regulatory agencies, mostly from the United States, in shaping the content of rules in several subsectors.

Compared to some financial systems of Europe, US domestic regulation, particularly after the Great Depression, was highly fragmented by subsector (Government Accountability Office 2004, 2016; Konings 2011; Lavelle 2013). Layered atop state (as in California and Illinois) governance, federal independent statutory regulators like the Federal Reserve (the Fed), the Office of the Comptroller of the Currency (OCC), the Federal Deposit Insurance Corporation (FDIC), and the Securities and Exchange Commission were charged with supervising the domestic commercial and investment banking sectors. But in other areas, regulatory oversight was left largely to the states (e.g. insurance) or primarily to private sector bodies (e.g. accounting standards) (Singer 2007; Büthe and Mattli 2011; Quaglia 2013). Moreover, in response to the Great Depression and as part of the New Deal, the subsectors of banking, securities, and insurance were legally segmented under the 1933 Glass-Steagall Act. The US setup created a particular type of politics that emphasized regulatory silos for each subsector and competition between regulators who sought to maintain bureaucratic jurisdiction and to govern in accordance with their respective regulatory mission, approach, and organizational culture (Coleman 1996; Konings 2011). The legacy of these US regulatory characteristics—arm's-length oversight, sectoral fragmentation, bureaucratic politics, and clashing regulatory approaches—shaped the birth of international soft law (Burley 1993; Bach 2010).

In many, though not all cases, the depth and quality of soft law reflected the capacity and goals of domestic regulators in the United States (Hopkins 1976; Burley 1993; Lavelle 2013). Relatively autonomous sub-state actors such as the SEC and the Fed developed foreign policy agendas and forged or coopted regulatory networks with counterparts from foreign jurisdictions. The Federal Reserve joined a network of European central banks to form the Basel Committee on Banking Supervision in 1975, while the Securities and Exchange Commission attended the first meeting of the International Organization of Securities Commissions in 1983. These US regulators did not consistently share views on the content or structure of the international architecture and often used regulatory cooperation with foreign counterparts to compete rather than cooperate with each other. Indeed, it is more appropriate to speak of regulatory factions within the United States rather than a single US position.

While regulators from the United States left the most pronounced imprint, regulatory structures in other polities also contributed to the character of international financial regulation—though often in less direct ways and usually when US internal fragmentation and decentralization undermined effective external action by US actors. In insurance, where the United States long lacked a federal regulator and the European Union made significant progress in harmonizing national regulation, EU Commission officials have been the primary drivers of cooperation through the International Association of Insurance Supervisors (Alexander et al. 2006; Davies and Green 2008; Quaglia 2014). However, in a more typical pattern, US authorities moved first and Europeans found themselves hamstrung by weak internal regulatory institutions. For example, securities markets in Europe were long overseen through various forms of industry self-regulation. As a result, some countries, like Germany and the United Kingdom, did not have counterparts to US statutory agencies and therefore obvious representatives who could be sent to transgovernmental meetings with the SEC. As the international financial architecture for securities regulation increasingly relied on such networks of public sector regulators, these countries found it difficult to participate. In turn, the disparity produced feedback effects for internal reform within Europe as firms and governments hoped to better represent their interests in the emerging financial architecture (Lütz 1998).[20]

The fragmented nature of international cooperation by subsector reflected internal domestic configurations in other ways. For example, regulators with established jurisdiction over one subsector such as commercial banking or securities markets resisted soft law that might encroach on their preserve and sought to expand into areas traditionally under another agency's domain (Coleman and Underhill 1995; Mügge 2011a). So again, the legacies of domestic regulatory institutions created pressures that worked against centralization in international regulation (Bair 2013; Lavelle 2013). In these ways, domestic turf wars solidified international fragmentation.

Finally, other internal factors extended beyond national borders to influence the creation and evolution of international financial regulation. Financial market authorities faced domestic pressures to liberalize the economy in general and the financial services sector in particular (Derthick and Quirk 1985; Vogel 1996). The Reagan administration sped up liberalization efforts and pressured regulators to ease oversight. The combination of fairly broad independence from legislators and industry and the new international environment gave regulators opportunities to push back against the deregulatory tide: cooperation with overseas counterparts was a way, within existing legal

[20] International Securities Regulation Report, "Calls for German SEC Grow," January 17, 1990, 7.

frameworks, to build legitimacy for an expanded role in governing international markets and sometimes do an end run around domestic political constraints. The UK's Thatcher government and the Single Market Project in Europe introduced liberalization measures at about the same time, unleashing similar motivations for national authorities to cooperate informally and use international cooperation for political ends. In the aftermath of the 2008 crisis, the UK Treasury under Gordon Brown likewise saw in FSB-centered international cooperation an opportunity to improve British leverage within EU regulatory contests and counterbalance EU–US bilateralism (wherein EU institutions were the main representatives) with a multilateral forum in which British officials had considerable status and influence.[21]

Another aspect of domestic financial arrangements also contributed to the particular contours of international fragmentation and, as discussed in Chapter 6, became especially relevant in the aftermath of the 2008 crisis. The degree of public reliance on industry self-regulation, especially in the United States, helped define which subsectors at the international level would have prominent private standard setters. Self-regulation by exchanges, accountants, and other service providers arose across borders, in large part because of the technical complexities of finance (Porter 2005a). Nevertheless, the particular balance and linkages between private self-regulation and direct public regulation varied tremendously cross-nationally and temporally and was often part-and-parcel of broader constitutional and political bargains. As finance internationalized, private transnational industry associations, carrying out multiple roles, proliferated. McKeen-Edwards and Porter (2013: 3) count 225. Yet the ones that became prominent standard setters, the IASB and the ISDA, covered regulatory areas that, under US domestic arrangements, were either heavily dependent on self-regulation (i.e. accounting standards and the private regulator known as the Financial Accounting Standards Board) or a domain with little direct public regulation (such as over-the-counter derivatives, which we discuss in Chapter 6). Thus, the quirks of US regulation, at the moment when finance was again internationalizing, played a critical role in the evolution of international financial governance both in terms of subsector fragmentation as well as the mix between private transnational and public transgovernmental soft law generators.

In the next sections, we review both the variance in development of soft law across several subsectors and the roles played by particular regulatory factions in shaping its content.

[21] Author interview with former FSF official, Basel, June 24, 2015; author interview with IOSCO official, Madrid, June 26, 2015.

The Basel Committee and capital adequacy for commercial banks

One of the earliest and most developed areas of transnational regulatory cooperation in finance is the Basel Committee on Banking Supervision (Kapstein 1994; Wood 2005; Singer 2007; Walter 2008). Originally bringing together regulators from a small core of ten economically advanced countries in 1975, the Basel Committee expanded in 2009 to twenty-seven jurisdictions (Goodhart 2011). As of 2014, the group meets three to four times a year and maintains a secretariat in Basel at the Bank for International Settlements. Member countries are represented by their central bank and other regulators of banks. The two main goals of the body are to prevent regulatory gaps as banks operate across multiple jurisdictions and to guarantee adequate prudential regulation and supervision across the member countries. In addition to developing principles and standards for prudential regulation and the division of responsibilities between home and host authorities, the body also works to facilitate information exchange between its members and to enhance the effectiveness of banking supervision.

Both the move toward financial integration within Europe and the breakdown of the Bretton Woods system increased the potential for systemic banking crises. The 1974 bankruptcy of Herstatt Bank epitomized the risks associated with such macro-structural changes when a banking issue in Germany temporarily froze the New York interbank market. The event exposed the lack of global governance mechanisms in place to deal with the problems of a reemerging international finance and is often identified as the proximate cause of banking sector cooperation.

In 1975, the Basel Committee agreed to the Concordat, which laid out a set of principles for assigning responsibility for the oversight of foreign bank affiliates active in a host market. While some consider the Concordat a relatively vague set of principles with an unclear impact, it began a conversation over issues of home vs. host regulation that have continued to plague banking supervisors in the twenty-first century (Porter 2005a; Wood 2005; Walter 2008; Goodhart 2011). Moreover, leading central bankers claim to have used the revised versions of the Concordat to set post-crises policies, a point we develop further in Chapter 6 (Tarullo 2014).

The Basel Committee's 1988 agreement on capital reserve standards expanded its ambit and greatly amplified the salience of the soft law it produced, turning it into what Büthe and Mattli (2011: 18–41) call a focal institution. The capital adequacy framework (known colloquially as Basel I, Basel II, and Basel III) sets out guidelines for the level of capital that banks must maintain as a buffer against economic strain that could produce banking crises.

Much of the existing literature on the emergence of the Basel Agreements has focused on the United States and the United Kingdom and their desire to balance rising competitive pressure from Japanese and German banks and stiffer US regulation following 1980s bank failures (Oatley and Nabors 1998; Singer 2007). Worried that lower capital requirements for Japanese and German banks might undermine the competitiveness of home banks and promote regulatory arbitrage, the US Federal Reserve and its British counterparts used the Basel Committee to achieve domestic aims, employing threats and other coercive measures to forge the agreement (Kapstein 1992; Oatley and Nabors 1998).

Competitiveness challenges no doubt played a role in motivating some form of international cooperation. Yet the cross-national focus ignores deep rifts within the US policy community over how best to address banking instability and misses how regulators used the Basel-based regulatory arena to shape the way the conflict played out. In brief, while US regulators generally supported clearer rules governing capital requirements, they disagreed on the best way to do it (Reinicke 1995; Ryan 2013). The stakes were high because different proposed resolutions would have far-reaching implications for the power of individual regulatory agencies as well as the types of capital held by banks (Thiemann 2014). The risk-based assessment system ultimately adopted as part of the Basel approach was not merely a cooperative solution to growing financial internationalization but also helped to settle an ongoing conflict between US agencies about the future of regulatory oversight.

As noted, the supervision of US banks has long been fragmented among regulatory agencies including the Fed, the FDIC, and the OCC (Khademian 1996; Konings 2011; Lavelle 2013). For much of the post-war period, the Fed had authority over only a limited number of banking institutions compared to the FDIC and OCC. In 1970, for example, the Fed had responsibility for roughly one thousand banks with assets of $117 million, while the FDIC oversaw over thirteen thousand banks with combined assets of over $500 billion (Norton 1988). Importantly, the agencies did not share the same priorities with regard to banking stability and had different longer-term agendas.[22] The FDIC, in particular, was the more conservative as it lived and died by its insurance mandate to protect savers in resolving distressed banks. The FDIC (along with the OCC), moreover, had long employed an on-site inspection system as part of its holistic qualitative assessment of financial health. This system relied on an army of thousands of bank examiners, who believed that the qualitative assessment system allowed for better integration of local and contextual circumstances (Khademian 1996). As the FDIC and OCC oversaw more small and medium-sized banks, the contextual approach sought

[22] Monica Langley, "Rival Bank Regulators Agree Only to Disagree on Most Major Issues—Fed, Comptroller and FDIC Have Bankers Uncertain How to Conduct Business," *Wall Street Journal*, January 23, 1984.

to address and often aligned with the varying interests of such banks (Reinicke 1995; Khademian 1996).

In terms of mission and staffing, the Fed had a distinct agenda. It focused much more on the nexus between the monetary system and bank financial health, which is why the Fed had long taken responsibility for the largest banks in the system (Reinicke 1995). At the same time, its vision for financial oversight relied on quantitative measures to determine the risks associated with a bank's assets. Rather than inspectors, the Fed primarily employed financial analysts (Khademian 1996).[23] And in order to implement quantitative assessments, the Fed weighted assets by the varying risks they posed (for example, sovereign debt being less risky than mortgage-backed securities), which ultimately changed the incentive structures for the types of assets banks held (Hemel 2011; Thiemann 2014).

In the 1980s, the Fed had faced a series of simultaneous domestic challenges to its role within the fragmented oversight system for banks. Congress, on numerous occasions, had sought to restrict, or eliminate, the Fed's jurisdiction. Both the Grace Commission established in 1982 by President Ronald Reagan to reduce regulatory burdens and the Bush Task Force on Regulation of Financial Services created later in the same year, for example, considered restrictions of or even the elimination of the Fed's role in bank regulation.[24]

The Fed used cooperation in the Basel Committee as part of its campaign to push back against challenges to its favored regulatory solution—risk-weighted assets—and its authority as a banking regulator. The Basel Committee proved a hospitable forum for a number of reasons. The FDIC and the OCC did not become members until 1982, and their representatives found themselves surrounded primarily by central bankers rather than bank regulators like themselves (Goodhart 2011). As a result, they did not receive the same deference and respect as their Fed counterparts, who belonged to the tight-knit community of central bankers (McNamara 2002). Similarly, the FDIC promoted its favored approach of a risk-based deposit insurance system, which cut against the grain of central bankers' thinking (Kapstein 1994). The approach would have used a variant of the FDIC's domestic assessment system to calculate an additional premium that banks would contribute to a deposit insurance fund to be used in the case of a crisis. The FDIC questioned the legitimacy and effectiveness of a quantitative system like that proposed by

[23] Bertlett Naylor, "Volcker to Propose Risk-Based Capital Rule," *The American Banker*, September 12, 1985.

[24] Jay Rosenstein, "Reagan Panel Urges Transfer of Fed's Duties," *The American Banker*, May 19, 1983; Jay Rosenstein, "Volcker Defends Regulatory Role for Fed, Calls Demands to Limit Power 'Unacceptable'," *The American Banker*, October 11, 1983; Gratchen Chell, "Garn Hits Idea of Continued Fed Regulation," *The American Banker*, February 7, 1984.

the Fed.[25] Only a handful of other Basel members at the time, however, had deposit insurance systems (Demirgüç-Kunt et al. 2005) and of those most were overseen by central banks or consolidated regulators. The timing of deposit insurance's development across Basel members rendered the proposal dead on arrival (Hemel 2011; Ryan 2013). Thus, the Fed-promoted expansion of the domestic regulatory battle to the transnational arena put the FDIC at a significant disadvantage.

In addition, in an early example of using the perceived legitimacy of international soft law for domestic purposes, the Fed made claims about the Basel Committee to augment its position at home. It argued that the Basel Committee's system of risk-weighted assessments—reflecting the Fed's reliance on quantitative assessment—represented scientific best practice (Mackenzie 2006; Hemel 2011). Paul Volcker, head of the Fed at the time, warned Congress against the credibility of the FDIC position. "There would be great drawbacks to basing premiums on the already difficult and inherently qualitative, judgments contained in bank examinations," he declared, adding, "Such judgments are fallible and our forecasting ability limited" (Volcker 1985: 18). Volcker went on to sign a bilateral agreement with the Bank of England that further elevated the importance of risk-weighted assessments (Kapstein 1994; Wood 2005). Given the FDIC's isolation within the Basel Committee and the agreement between the Bank of England and the Fed, the FDIC conceded the point in late 1986 and signed on to the Fed policy position (Seidman 1986).

The first Basel Accord, in addition to its economic distributional consequences across financial markets discussed in Chapter 5, had critical political distributional effects within the United States and globally. It contributed to the Fed's rise as the dominant voice on international banking regulation and sidelined the FDIC and the OCC as potential global regulators (Bair 2013). Moreover, the Fed later leveraged the legitimacy of the Basel Committee to bolster its authority even further in the domestic political arena (Hemel 2011), a point we return to in Chapter 6.

Internal regulatory fragmentation within polities with large international banking sectors influenced the Basel Committee's agenda in an additional respect: it shaped the committee's focus on commercial banking. IOSCO and private industry associations like the ISDA had primary responsibility for coordinating regulation of investment banks and non-bank broker-dealers. These lines of demarcation mirrored US arrangements: since the 1930s, separate regulators oversaw commercial and investment banking (reflecting the

[25] Bart Fraust, "Seidman Opposes Volcker on Risk Plan," *The American Banker*, November 21, 1985, 1; Nina Easton, "FDIC Study Says Risk-Based Plan Could Reduce Capital Overall," *The American Banker*, April 21, 1986.

prohibition of both activities within a single firm). And similar divisions existed within the UK: the Bank of England had considerable authority to regulate commercial banks but capital markets were largely governed through self-regulatory trade associations and the industry-owned-and-run London Stock Exchange (Coleman 1996). Throughout the 1980s and 1990s, the UK experimented with various regulatory structures and only gradually established well-resourced regulators in the area of securities regulation, since 2013 divided between the Bank of England's Prudential Regulation Authority and the Financial Conduct Authority. Similarly, Germany experimented with different forms before arriving in 2002 at a model that places banking, insurance, and securities regulation under the Bundesanstalt für Finanzdienstleistungsaufsicht (BaFin), the Federal Financial Supervisory Authority, which itself falls under the purview of the Federal Ministry of Finance.

As subsector market segmentation began to break down, the Basel Committee struggled in the 1990s and 2000s to address the mismatch between its members' authority and the need to create standards for changed realities on the ground. The problem proved difficult as the Basel Committee's efforts to expand its gambit beyond commercial banking met resistance from securities regulators organized in IOSCO, as discussed in the following section. One byproduct was an overly narrow regulatory focus—despite the above-mentioned complaints by the IMF and others. With primary jurisdiction over the commercial banking sector, the Basel Committee members tended to stick to micro-prudential systemic risks (minimized by supervisory quality and individual bank health) rather than macro-prudential ones (dampened by addressing interconnectedness and procyclicality) (Baker 2010, 2013).

While market complexities and competition pressures motivated regulators to expand the Basel Committee's scope and to minimize economic adjustment costs to their own industries, internal battles between regulatory factions were the more important driver of the scope and substance of the committee's soft law. These conclusions—that depict domestic regulatory politics deeply embroiled in the development of Basel Committee soft law—preview those in later chapters showing the implications of internal politics in soft law's second-order effects, first in the role of Basel rules in domestic reforms (a topic taken up in Chapter 4) and then in the determination of the Fed's rules in post-crisis United States (a topic taken up in Chapter 6).

The SEC, IOSCO, regulatory export, and bureaucratic autonomy

The area of securities regulation also demonstrates the importance of domestic subsector fragmentation and internal regulatory politics for international cooperation and the development of soft law. As in the example of the Fed and the Basel Committee, the US SEC used international cooperation to fight domestic battles, though in the case of the SEC, the threats emanated from Congress's and the Reagan administration's sweeping deregulatory campaigns as well as from banking regulators' encroachment into traditional SEC territory. The agency's strategy involving the creation of soft law through IOSCO mirrored its mission at home. Rather than emphasizing prudential standards as the Fed did in Basel, the SEC used IOSCO to export the US model for protecting investors and minimizing political interference in writing and enforcing market rules.[26]

Cooperation in the securities domain started in 1974 as the US SEC worked with the International Finance Corporation, an arm of the World Bank, to create the Inter-American Association of Securities Commissions (also referred to as Inter-American Conference of Securities Commissions). This body included securities commissions from the Western hemisphere and was geared to encourage new capital market formation. The early cooperation was thus built around developing financial systems in these countries rather than preventing cross-border crises (Sommer 1996).

Such capacity-building efforts demonstrate an attempt by the SEC to promote its regulatory model globally and to expand markets for US corporations (Bach and Newman 2010; Marcacci 2014; Kleibl 2015). As Michael Mann, the first head of the Office of International Affairs of the SEC, explains in a 2008 interview with the SEC Historical Society, "It was clearly in the interest of the United States to further its own system as opposed to other systems that existed for securities trading . . . the more they were like us, the better the cooperation, the better the possibilities for the markets intertwining."[27] He explains further in a 2005 interview, highlighting SEC efforts in Hungary:

> The concern was that as this market developed—both as a competitive market, but also as a matter of good governance—that it would be better to have the Hungarians looking to the United States for technical assistance, than looking to Europe, or somewhere else. There would be great advantage to support and develop those markets so that they would align with the American market; not just in terms of cooperation, but in terms of the whole legal scheme being developed.[28]

As Mann's comments suggest, the SEC's ambitions to create similar regulation in other countries expanded opportunities for US financial companies. Nevertheless, it would be wrong to place too much emphasis on competitive dynamics as the primary motivation behind the SEC's international agenda. Rather, the US agency intensified cooperation with other securities regulators

[26] Author interview with two FSB officials, Basel, June 24, 2015. One official emphasized that IOSCO's post-2008 turn to systemic risk issues was new and could not have happened before the crisis.

[27] SEC Historical Society: Fireside Chat on SEC Office of International Affairs, April 22, 2008, 10. Online.

[28] SEC Historical Society: Interview with Michael Mann, June 13, 2005, 29. Online.

in the 1980s largely to enhance its political legitimacy and clout at home. The SEC's domestic political maneuvering was also the main driver behind the development of transnational soft law.

Upon coming into office, the Reagan administration targeted the agency for budget cuts, arguing that its regulations threatened business competitiveness.[29] Facing mounting pressure at home to appear necessary amidst these rising demands for deregulation, the SEC sought to raise its profile by targeting bad apples in the US market.[30] Insider trading enforcement by the regulator became a politically savvy priority, playing well in the press by burnishing the SEC's consumer protection image and promoting general market health by identifying firms that tarnish the quality of the exchanges.[31] This campaign brought considerable attention to the enforcement unit at the SEC and helped the agency garner influence with Congress (Khademian 1992; Seligman 2003).

Even though relatively rare, insider trading cases with an international dimension fed into the SEC's populist strategy (Mahoney 1990; Khademian 1992). Foreign firms were a win-win for the regulator. The SEC raised its profile at home by increasing standards on foreign firms and simultaneously embarked on an expanded mission into international regulation. Under the chairmanships of David Ruder and Richard Breeden, the agency turned its attention to the globalization of financial markets and the SEC's international role, marked by the creation of the Office of International Affairs in 1989.[32]

Using Memoranda of Understanding (MoUs) to link with other jurisdictions, the SEC developed a regulatory framework in which it gained greater investigatory powers to address these new international problems. The best example is the relationship between early MoUs negotiations and a series of reforms passed in the United States during the late 1980s.[33] Formulated and drafted by the SEC, these new laws created broad exemptions for the SEC from the Privacy Act and other sunshine laws and new enforcement power (e.g. to employ rulings in foreign jurisdictions to bar brokers from US markets). In short, the SEC used international cooperation to circumvent basic due process regulations and bolster its powers. As Michael Mann, the head of the SEC international division during the period, explains:

[29] "Revamp SEC, Reagan is Told," *The New York Times*, January 23, 1981.

[30] Barbara Thomas, "Insider Trading: An Internal Problem with International Implications," Address by SEC Commissioner to the Conference of the International Faculty for Corporate and Capital Market Law, Paris, France, March 11, 1983. On file with the author.

[31] Kenneth Noble, "SEC Chief Plans Insider Trade Curb," *The New York Times*, October 26, 1981.

[32] See, for example, David Ruder, "Remarks to the Seventh Annual Washington Briefing on US Perspectives Hosted by the American Stock Exchange," Washington, DC, October 19, 1987. On file with the author.

[33] For example, the Insider Trading and Securities Fraud Enforcement Act of 1988; the International Securities Enforcement Cooperation Act of 1990. For more on MoUs see Zaring (1998); Raustiala (2002).

> When we sat down to negotiate... there was a recognition that we had to change the law. And what we decided, in the first instance, was that we should signal each other's cooperative intent; this was a MoU, statement of intent, after all. We would negotiate the framework for what we would want if we could change the law. And then we would go to our legislatures, and ask them to change the law. So rather than approaching it the way you do a treaty, which is: you negotiate the treaty, and then the treaty is ratified; we made this decision that, in fact, the better course would be to have a memorandum of understanding that created a framework, and then get the unilateral power—the organic power—under the securities laws to implement the memorandum of understanding.[34]

Mann thus argues that the MoU negotiations were really about the acquisition of new domestic powers. He goes on to say, "And if you look in the memorandum of understanding, at the very beginning it says: Neither authority has the power to actually implement this MoU, but we're both committed to go out and get it."[35]

Not only did these transnational interactions serve a domestic purpose in bolstering the regulator's image and justifying task expansion, they created a loose network of regulators interacting transnationally on issues of international financial governance. The SEC signed an increasing number of MoUs over the following decade, positioning itself at the hub of a regulatory network of similar bodies. And in 1983, a group of these regulators formed the International Organization of Securities Commissions (IOSCO), tasked with promoting information exchange and the development of soft law best practices.

IOSCO was a relatively sleepy organization during its initial years. Yet the SEC and Chairman Breeden sought to upgrade the organization so as to better position it vis-à-vis the rise of the Basel Committee and fend off encroachments from banking regulators at home and abroad.[36] In 1987, at the SEC's suggestion, IOSCO created a technical committee to coordinate and develop standards development. In 1990, at the IOSCO annual meeting in Santiago, Chile, Breeden introduced an SEC prepared Strategic Assessment document, which detailed a list of reforms intended to upgrade the organization's performance and decision-making. Among other things, it created a hierarchy within the technical committee (including a position of chair, which Breeden would occupy) and also a new requirement that technical committee members be represented by public officials (limiting participation of self-regulatory bodies or private actors).[37]

[34] SEC Historical Society: Interview, June 13, 2005, 16–17. Online.

[35] SEC Historical Society: Interview, June 13, 2005, 17. Online.

[36] Dennis Holden, "IOSCO's New Commandant," *Global Custodian*, March 1, 1991.

[37] International Securities Regulation Report, "US SEC Forges New Global Role within IOSCO: Breeden Chairs Strengthened Technical Committee," November 19, 1990, 1.

The SEC's privileged position during IOSCO's early years stemmed from core cross-national differences in institutions and capacities. At noted, several countries including Germany and the United Kingdom had traditions of self-regulation for the financial services sector (Coleman 1996; Lütz 1998; Deeg and Lütz 2000). They initially sent representatives from self-regulatory bodies, which did not have formal IOSCO membership. Even after these countries established independent agencies, they lacked technical expertise and staff compared to the SEC.[38] Japan similarly only adopted arm's-length regulatory structures in the 1990s and even then they were subjugated to the government's industrial policy (Moran 1991; Sobel 1994; Vogel 1996; Walter 2006). Up through the mid-1990s, few could challenge the bureaucratic capacity of the SEC as it promoted the US system in transnational networks. Sara Hanks, an SEC attorney involved in early IOSCO negotiations, describes the standards process:

> The SEC had the expertise and an infrastructure that nobody else had. The SEC had two thousand employees. Nobody else had anything like that. They didn't have the financial resources; they didn't have the institutional knowledge; they didn't have the principles . . . in my experience, it was very much, "you know, here's an interesting problem, let's all discuss it. U.S., what do you do? This is how we do it." And everyone goes: "Oh, okay. Well, we could do it like that."[39]

Not surprisingly, early cooperation to create soft law contributed to the dissemination of US regulatory approaches. Like the rest of its international program, the SEC's actions tell us as much about the United States as anything else. Two of IOSCO's first standards—promoting independent oversight and prohibiting insider trading—are embedded in the US regulatory architecture and the principle of investor protection, respectively. IOSCO's principles on proper market oversight emphasize the independence of the regulator (Bach and Newman 2010; Marcacci 2014).[40] Similarly, IOSCO's principles that proscribe insider trading reflect longstanding US priorities.

Such US-style market rules would support a functionalist explanation of soft law's content, if they could be shown to promote market capitalization, growth, or some other intended outcome. Yet scholarly debate casts serious doubt (Leland 1992; Kerner and Kucik 2010). Take the example of insider trading rules. Through much of the post-war period capital markets served a wide range of purposes across countries. In insider systems with considerable

[38] Lütz (1998: 162) argues, "Germany joined IOSCO in 1988, but was excluded from decision-making because it was represented by stock exchange delegates. In 1990, the Federal Ministry was asked to take over membership of IOSCO, but it lacked the technical expertise for dealing with the details of securities regulation. German representatives once more found themselves unable to collaborate."

[39] SEC Historical Society: Interview with Sara Hanks, Washington, DC, February 8, 2008, 7.

[40] These principles were codified in the 1998 Objectives and Principles of Securities Regulation.

concentration of ownership in a few families and firms, capital markets were largely alternative mechanisms for compensation and control (Zysman 1983). By contrast, the US system, requiring more transparency and public information, in principle prioritized decentralized investors over creditors and managers. In short, the rules promoted by the SEC reflect the US way of regulating rather than a proven welfare-enhancing approach for all types of financial systems. Although insider trading rules have distributional effects, their welfare consequences are unclear—obscuring the SEC's purported technocratic reasons for promoting these and other principles of arm's-length regulation and investor protection (Soederberg 2004; Davies and Green 2008; Baker 2010).

By the 2000s, most countries with ambitions to join the ranks of international financial centers had adopted SEC-style oversight structures, and the regulators participating in international discussions came to the table with relatively similar rule-making and rule-enforcement powers. The SEC could no longer claim the same level of institutional or resource superiority. The British Prudential Regulation Authority and the German BaFin employed thousands of workers and had over a decade of experience with arm's-length regulation under their belts. After the turn of the millennium, the politics within IOSCO changed dramatically as the SEC no longer dominated as it once had and representatives from the European Union and its member countries had taken on a more active role, an issue that we explore in greater detail in Chapter 4. That said, the effects of SEC influence on early IOSCO soft law remain important as the substance of IOSCO standards still reflects core assumptions of the US regulatory model for securities markets.

To return to the chapter's themes, the SEC promoted international cooperation as part of its reaction to Reagan's deregulatory campaign and used the creation of soft law as a tool to augment its domestic authority. These actions of a US agency are another early instance of the deep entanglement of internal and international regulatory politics. And they anticipate Chapters 4 and 6, where we show that regulators before and after the 2008 crisis made use of existing soft law to achieve domestic aims.

US regulatory fragmentation and a slow start to insurance soft law

In contrast to the subsectors discussed above, regulatory cooperation in insurance started much later and is relatively less developed (Singer 2007; Quaglia 2014). This pattern of cooperation is striking as the reinsurance industry, which insures many of the risks present in the other financial subsectors, is highly globalized (Cummins and Weiss 2000). In terms of US domestic arrangements, regulation of the insurance industry, unlike that of commercial banking and securities markets, has long been fragmented along state lines with weak federal institutions. As a result, the United States played a more limited role in developing international soft law in the subsector, where the European Union, especially after creating more centralized regulation, emerged as a key actor (Brown 2009; Quaglia 2014). Insurance is thus another case of differentials in domestic institutions shaping international cooperation and soft law.

The main reason for the later emergence of cooperation lies in domestic regulatory structures for insurance in the United States and Europe. Dating back to the 1869 Supreme Court decision, *Paul v. Virginia*, insurance regulation has been deemed a state and not a federal responsibility. Congress reaffirmed this in 1945 with the McCarran-Ferguson Act that created federal legislation delegating authority for insurance regulation to the states. Along with the more encompassing 1933 Glass-Steagall Act that separated banking, securities, and insurance activities, the 1945 law made insurance unique among the major financial services sectors in the United States. Even with the formal repeal of Glass-Steagall in 1999, insurance supervision remained under the jurisdiction of the states (Konings 2011).

To coordinate their oversight, state regulators formed a network in 1871. The National Association of Insurance Commissioners (NAIC) develops best practices and model laws for state insurance commissioners. Until the 2010 passage of the Dodd-Frank Act, NAIC retained responsibility for representing the collective views of state insurance commissioners and served as the primary international representative.[41]

The federated structure, however, made it difficult for the United States to participate actively in international cooperation processes. NAIC has limited resources to devote to international governance issues. Moreover, roughly a quarter of its insurance commissioner members are elected officials, giving them incentives to pay attention to local issues and sometimes to be cautious about technocratically derived best practices. Additionally, NAIC has frequently been outflanked by its larger and more powerful regulatory cousins, the Fed and the SEC.[42] NAIC was sometimes forced to have one of them represent its views in IOSCO or Basel Committee debates (Government Accountability Office 2016). David Snyder, assistant general counsel for the American Insurance Association, concluded, " . . . the state regulatory system is structurally incapable of representing US interests effectively, because it must defend the inefficient US regulatory system and it lacks the legal authority to bind the United States."[43] The 2010 Dodd-Frank reform attempted to address

[41] "National Association of Insurance Commissioners," naic.org, last accessed July 26, 2017, <http://www.naic.org/>.

[42] Author interview with NAIC official, Washington, DC, December 18, 2009.

[43] Meg Fletcher, "US Regulators Seek to Increase Visibility," *Business Insurance*, January 5, 2009, 3. An EU official responsible for insurance issues confirmed the difficulties of negotiating with

these institutional deficiencies by establishing within the Treasury Department the Federal Insurance Office (FIO).[44] The FIO has the authority to enter into agreements with other nations on insurance issues. Nevertheless, many of the standard inter-agency conflicts persist and state insurance regulators remain wary of ceding authority to the Treasury.[45] Meanwhile, the Treasury does not always see insurance as its primary regulatory responsibility and has only limited expertise in the area.

As a consequence of these US arrangements—and fragmentation in Europe along national lines—the IAIS was not founded until 1994 and emerged as an outgrowth of NAIC meetings. Starting in 1989, NAIC invited a few additional jurisdictions to attend its annual meeting.[46] It was through these interactions that the participants, mindful of coordination in banking and investment services, decided to form IAIS. But unlike IOSCO or the Basel Committee, IAIS's early work focused primarily on information exchange rather than uniform soft law standards (Braumüller 2007). Jonathan Spencer, former head of the UK Department of Trade and Industry's Insurance Directorate, offers this assessment of international cooperation in the early 1990s: "The existing arrangements between insurance supervisors, much less between insurance supervisors and other financial services regulators who may have a legitimate interest in particular organisations, are at best patchy and at worst non-existent."[47]

The work of IAIS accelerated dramatically in the late 1990s following the Mexican and Asian financial crises, not so much from either domestic competitiveness concerns or bureaucratic politics, but from pressure emanating from international financial institutions (IFIs) as they sought to create the new international financial architecture around the Compendium of Standards (Eichengreen 1999). While the Basel Committee and IOSCO both had made progress in developing standards, IAIS had barely started. As the IMF realized the state of insurance standards, it worked with the IAIS to refine and develop

NAIC and the state-based US system. Interview with European Commission official, Brussels, December 2009.

44 Mark Hofmann, "Federal Insurance Office Seeks International Cooperation," *Business Insurance*, November 17, 2010.

45 See the comments of NAIC President Ted Nickel in "US and EU Reach Agreement on Insurance Regulation," *Insurance Journal*, January 13, 2017: "After more than a year of secret meetings it's disappointing that in the waning days of the administration we are finally seeing the details of what purports to be a covered agreement between the U.S. and EU. As most state regulators were not allowed to participate in the process, the NAIC is coordinating a thorough review of the agreement to ensure consumer protections are not compromised through the preemption of state law, and we encourage Congress to do the same. Of great concern is the potential to use this agreement as a backdoor to force foreign regulations on U.S. companies."

46 NAIC, Annual Report (1989).

47 "Casting a Watchful Eye Over the World," *Reinsurance*, May 12, 1997, 9.

them. IAIS thus hastily released its first set of core standards in 1997, which were then revised in 1999, again at the behest of the IMF (IMF 2001).

Internal reform in the European Union, not the United States, intensified and accelerated international cooperation. Brussels' effort to harmonize and coordinate national regulation on the continent offered the first major step toward internal cohesion by either of the two financial regulatory giants and had a profound impact on international cooperation. Through the 1990s, as noted, insurance regulation in Europe, despite harmonization efforts, was also fragmented. Then, the subsector was included in the European Union's 1999 Financial Services Action Plan (Ayadi 2007), a legislative package designed to develop pan-European financial services markets on par with those of the United States (see Chapter 4). In 2003, to ensure coordinated implementation of new rules, Brussels created the Committee of European Insurance and Occupational Pensions Supervisors (CEIOPS), a network of insurance supervisors (replaced by the European Insurance and Occupational Pensions Authority after the financial crisis) (Vogelgesang and Kubicek 2007).

These internal reforms enhanced the European Union's external influence and ambitions, and by the 2000s, the polity's attempts to shape IAIS rules on capital reserves for insurance had altered the tenor of international debates.[48] Given the nature of the insurance industry, sector authorities needed to devise capital adequacy rules distinct from those promulgated by the Basel Committee. At IAIS, the European Union championed a unified and clearly articulated position based on its internal approach, outlined in legislation known as Solvency II. "The IAIS standards," according to an expert review, "more closely reflected the European Approach rather than the American approach."[49]

The insurance example, like those of banking and securities, highlights the interconnections between domestic factors and international cooperation. A central theme in the insurance case is the impact of domestic regulatory arrangements on the evolution of international cooperation and standard setting. Fragmented internal domestic regulation in the United States and delayed harmonization in the European Union combined to generate a comparatively underdeveloped transnational standard setter and body of soft law. In the absence of international leadership, the sequence of developments in regulatory cooperation—its timing and its rapid acceleration—was primarily driven by international, rather than internal factors; the IAIS's relative underdevelopment became a problem when IFIs, seeking to give international financial regulation more coherence, compared insurance to other subsectors. However, the importance of internal arrangements is evident in the effects of EU integration. The ability of Brussels to take on a leadership role in shaping

[48] "Solvency II: Setting a Global Standard," *Reactions*, July/August 2008.
[49] Brown (2009: 968).

soft law's substance—only after carrying out internal reforms—is similar to what we found in the securities case (when an SEC with more capacities than foreign counterparts was able to influence soft law's content). The insurance case thus also exemplifies the impact of complex domestic–international linkages on international cooperation and soft law.

Conclusion

This chapter has two purposes. First, it offers background, especially for readers new to international financial regulation. We stress the prevalence of soft law and the fragmented nature of international governance. By contrast to areas of the global economy governed by interstate treaties enforced through dispute settlement mechanisms, international finance is regulated through a hodgepodge of organizations, populated by public officials and private actors, grouped by subsector, and engaged in writing advisory prescriptions for influencing national rules and market behavior. It is the temporal effects of this soft law that will be the focus of the following chapters as we trace its disruptive impact on powerful regulatory factions within the European Union, the ecology of financial industry trade associations, and the politics of financial reform in the United States.

Second, the chapter identifies the origins and charts the evolution of international financial regulation and its architecture. We suggest that the prevalence of soft law, the compartmentalization by subsector, and the unevenness and content of the substantive agendas within each are not merely the product of rational design, of concerns about the competitiveness of national industries, or of technocratic processes. Rather, the chapter links the origins of these features to complex interconnections between internal regulatory dynamics and institutions, on the one hand, and international cooperation, on the other. Regulators launched international collaboration and created soft law as part of their strategies for fighting political battles at home; and the subsector organization and the substance of international soft law largely reflect internal arrangements, approaches, and the relative capacities of the leading countries. In a foretaste of what follows in Chapters 4 and 6, we even find echoes of soft law's second-order effects, as domestic authorities invoke the legitimacy of international standards to settle domestic conflicts over regulatory models.

A key takeaway is that the content, comprehensiveness, and precision of soft law varied considerably by subsector. In banking, soft law on capital requirements largely reflected an approach preferred by the Fed, which used international standards to outflank other domestic regulators (such as the FDIC) and elevate its own status globally. In securities, US domestic politics—this time, the SEC's campaign to stave off potential threats from deregulation—prompted the SEC to intensify its international engagements. In some examples (i.e. securities and insurance), the subsectors were at times marked by cross-border institutional differences and capacity asymmetries. In such circumstances, the more powerful US and EU regulators ended up with greater influence over soft law's form and substance—which tended to reflect the internal approaches and models of the more powerful regulator. The SEC's leadership thus resulted in international soft law about insider trading and arm's-length regulators. IOSCO devoted little soft law to areas that were not on the SEC agenda—such as public regulation of OTC derivatives markets (see Chapter 6) or rules governing competition among trading venues (see Chapter 4), because, respectively, the United States relied heavily on industry self-regulation or had not yet itself decided how to organize markets undergoing rapid technological change. In insurance, as in securities, levels of internal weakness and fragmentation in the European Union and the United States were a determinant of international soft law's development and substance.

This variance in origins and outcomes—which attests to the fragmentation and unevenness of international soft law by subsector—did not result from the innate qualities of banking, securities, and insurance regulation or any arising cooperation problems. Rather, it emerged from internal regulatory arrangements that gave rise to factional infighting as well as from other domestic political dynamics that drove authorities to participate and shape international cooperation processes. Those internal regulatory arrangements, moreover, derived from policy responses sometimes dating back to the Great Depression and the post-war recovery. Despite legislative trends to undo historical subsector divisions (such as the 1999 Gramm-Leach-Bliley Act that repealed provisions of the 1933 Glass-Steagall Act forbidding affiliations between banks and securities firms and the 2002 Conglomerates Directive that seeks to enhance supervision of financial groups active in different subsectors), the legacies and continued existence of powerful agencies with narrow missions in the United States and elsewhere have at various junctures reinforced bureaucratic and interest group pressure to maintain the fragmented nature of regulatory oversight by subsector at the international level.

As we demonstrate in the following three empirical chapters, this fragmentation is important not only because of soft law's differential temporal impact on internal and transnational regulatory politics, but also because of its methodological virtues. The subsector differences turn out to be a useful investigatory tool as we observe outcomes where soft law was present and relatively developed and where it was not. These differences help us assess the extent to which the outcomes support our argument about soft law's politically disruptive second-order effects.

4

Legitimacy Claims and Pre-Crisis Transatlantic Alignment

In the last quarter of the twentieth century, the European Union[1] underwent an economic and political transformation. Brussels built the legal foundations for the free movement of goods, services, capital, and people, largely completed its "single market," and successfully introduced a common currency (McNamara 1998; Egan 2001; Jabko 2006; Fligstein 2009). In the area of finance, the European Union initiated a massive reform program to establish the regulatory and supervisory framework necessary for Europe-wide markets. This program included the ability to control market access by foreign firms and to coordinate member country implementation and enforcement of joint rules.

The European Union's financial regulatory transformation set the stage for a new international dynamic. At the end of the Cold War, the United States, home to many of the world's largest and most liquid markets, was the undisputed financial hegemon (Simmons 2001). It had routinely used its position to set the terms of competition, projecting its domestic regulations globally and shaping multilateral efforts (Burley 1993; Bach and Newman 2010). With its new regulatory capacities, the European Union was able to harness the size of European markets (which as a whole often matched or exceeded those of the United States), thereby replacing US unipolarity with transatlantic bipolarity by the turn of the millennium (Bach and Newman 2007; Drezner 2007; Posner 2009a; Newman and Posner 2011; Quaglia 2014).

Despite its newfound clout, however, the European Union did not seriously challenge US financial regulatory approaches as it had in other sectors and as international relations theory expects (Posner and Véron 2010). From capital requirements for banks to accounting standards in corporate governance, the

[1] Prior to 1993, the European Union was called the European Community. For the sake of simplicity we use the term European Union throughout.

European Union and the United States negotiated in international forums with fairly compatible preferences and adopted similar approaches.

This remarkable alignment is all the more puzzling given the European repudiation of US models in other areas of global governance (such as data privacy and chemicals) and the historically different national financial systems within Europe. The United Kingdom and the Netherlands, for instance, placed a greater reliance on capital markets (the provision of financial resources via decentralized investors). Other countries, like Germany, France, and Italy, gave creditors including banks or the government a more central role in the distribution of capital. These "system" differences long gave rise to clashing regulatory approaches and conflicting proposals for pan-European standards and integration schemes (Zysman 1983; Story and Walter 1997).

Given these distinctions among the member states, it is particularly striking that Europe harmonized internally. Yet despite important outliers (e.g. company law, capital requirements for securities firms, and insurance), harmonization did take place and simultaneously made transatlantic alignment possible. And perhaps even more surprising, G20 financial regulatory commitments indicate that the alignment continues (again, with a few outliers as discussed in Chapter 6) even in the aftermath of the financial crisis. Rather than resisting it, European officials partnered with their American counterparts in reforming the international financial regulatory order (Helleiner 2014b).

In this chapter, we apply arguments about soft law's second-order effects developed in Chapter 2 to explain the European Union's curious financial regulatory passivity. We argue that the timing of internal European reforms vis-à-vis the emergence of international soft law shaped the trajectory of European policy and in turn led to transatlantic alignment. Echoing the scholarship on European economic integration (Sandholtz and Zysman 1989; Fligstein and Drita 1996), the chapter identifies a political contest between two main factions. The first consisted of reformists—including parts of the European Commission, internationally oriented business, and domestic regulators from Northern member states—who sought to harmonize European financial rules but were frequently divided over whether to use internationally oriented standards or a uniquely European approach to financial governance and integration. A second—status quo—faction included industries who perceived harmonization as a threat to their business models or an unwanted one-off adjustment expense as well as authorities fearful of losing regulatory turf and national control.

We show that where soft law was already more developed, internationally oriented reformists succeeded. They leveraged the perceived legitimacy of those standards as global "best practice" and politically neutral, winning support for reform and undermining claims that internally derived rules offered the only alternative. In this way, soft law's presence altered the financial regulatory status quo in Europe. And because of the prominence of US-based actors in the development of international soft law (see Chapter 3), these internal EU reforms had the consequence of aligning transatlantic preferences and approaches. In addition to highlighting soft law's disruptive impact in the European Union and on EU–US relations, the chapter probes the viability of the argument as an explanation for financial regulatory reforms in China and Japan, two other rising regulatory powers.

The Rise of Cooperative Bipolarity in Finance

At the turn of the millennium, the European Union together with the United States dominated financial rule-making at the international level (Posner 2009a; Drezner 2007; Quaglia 2013). The European Union's rise reflected the international face of a massive internal reform. Responding to competitiveness challenges from the United States and Asia and seeing the euro's introduction as an opportunity, EU policy-makers took on the daunting task of completing a long-sought regulatory framework to underpin pan-European financial markets and ultimately boost economic performance. The initiative aimed to deepen earlier efforts to harmonize national financial regulation and to revamp the rule-making and supervisory architecture. The Financial Service Action Plan or FSAP (a program that initially included more than forty pieces of proposed legislation) and the Lamfalussy process (the adopted rule-making procedures and coordination mechanisms) transformed financial regulation in Europe. While retaining its multi-level character, the sector's governance became much more of a Brussels-based, pan-European system (Posner 2007; Mügge 2010; Quaglia 2010).[2] One US official deeply involved in managing the international spillovers of the EU project described it as "breathtaking" and "a fundamental overhaul":[3]

> The EU aims to achieve what no market has ever tried: within a few short years adopt new rules on accounting, bank capital, securities market operations, auditing, and supervision of financial conglomerates and install new institutional infrastructure to ensure proper implementation. Imagine in the United States, Graham-Leech-Bliley, US General Accepted Accounting Practices, the

[2] Fritz Bolkestein, "One Currency, One Accounting Standard: Unless the European Union Adopts One Single Set of Rules, it Risks Losing the Benefits of the Euro," *Financial Times*, June 14, 2000, 23; Fritz Bolkestein, "Fragile Dream of a Single Financial Market," *Financial Times*, December 4, 2002.

[3] Author correspondence with US Treasury official, May 31, 2006. Also see Peter Chapman, "Launch of Finance Laws is Anything but Child's Play," *European Voice*, November 8, 2001.

> Securities Act of 1934, and Sarbanes-Oxley legislation being adopted within five years.[4]

As with the internal reforms of other areas of regulation, the effects of the European Union's financial governance transformation spilled over globally. Scholars depict the United States through the late 1990s as "hegemonic" and the "unconditional first mover" in the area of financial regulation (Simmons 2001). As Simmons writes in her 2001 study on regulatory harmonization, "The United States is 'hegemonic' in finance in the sense that it is costlier to alter its preferred regulatory innovation than to try to change the policies of the rest of the world. U.S. regulators can be thought of as *unconditional* [sic] first movers" (Simmons 2001: 595). The distribution of financial power was reflected in the international diffusion of US approaches and administrative structures via multiple mechanisms across national frontiers and in the terms of transatlantic financial regulatory cooperation that favored US firms (Moran 1994; Sobel 1994; Coleman 1996; Vogel 1996; Simmons 2001; Posner 2009b; Bach and Newman 2010).

The power constellation changed when the internal EU reforms (notably the expansion of centralized capacities to control foreign access through equivalence provisions and to limit differences in national implementation and enforcement of Brussels rules) enhanced the bargaining strength of European officials vis-à-vis their US counterparts (Newman and Posner 2011). Through the development of these regulatory tools, policy-makers leveraged the European Union's market size into regulatory power (Bach and Newman 2007; Posner 2009a; Quaglia 2013).

Like other regulatory areas such as food and product safety, data privacy, and anti-trust, finance witnessed an increase in the number of rule-making powers from one to two (Newman 2008a; Bradford 2012; Vogel 2012). In many of these other areas the European Union charted its own regulatory course, often reflecting European interests and stringent regulatory approaches that clashed with more laissez-faire US ones (Newman 2008b; Pollack and Shaffer 2009; Bradford 2012; Vogel 2012; Scott 2014).

In finance, however, US–EU approaches broadly aligned (Posner and Véron 2010). Despite some differences in legislation, the underlying regulatory principles demonstrated considerable compatibility. US and EU regulators were on the same page and that page for the most part belonged to the manual of industry-friendly oversight.

Recognizing the departure in Europe from the era of wide national variance in financial rules and systems, scholars note that change in EU regulation (more so than in the United States) brought about the alignment; European

[4] Author correspondence with US Treasury official, May 31, 2006.

reforms that had been occurring in fits and starts over several decades (Coleman and Underhill 1995; Posner 2005; Jabko 2006). As we document in the following section, European harmonization and transatlantic alignment had important early examples, including the European Union's 1989 milestone agreement on capital requirements for banks (Mügge 2010). As part of the 1999 FSAP, the European Union adopted a package of rules with a neoliberal character and with general affinities to the US and UK regulatory approaches. Daniel Mügge called the reforms since the late 1990s "a relatively stringent implementation of regulatory liberalism" that represents dogmatic as opposed to pragmatic policy-making (Mügge 2010: 186). Likewise, Posner and Véron deemed the reforms "in sync with US and British approaches" (Posner and Véron 2010: 401). Using Scharpf's categories, they classified the overall legislative program as an exercise in "positive integration" (i.e. regulatory harmonization) and "market-making" (as opposed to "market-correcting") (Scharpf 1999; Jabko 2006). In many instances, European rules moved away from national protection and state-directed market oversight to rules that increased firm discretion and promoted cross-border competition. The FSAP's accelerated pace of change and the European Union's rise as a regulatory power marked a turning point as the stakes of alignment increased dramatically.

Because of the transatlantic preference alignment, the new bipolarity altered the terms of cooperation. US unilateralism and European emulation and adjustment shifted to a more even relationship based on mutual accommodation. The regulatory compatibility meant that the new power distribution encouraged authorities to be pragmatic in their approaches to managing disputes and coordinating policies—rather than lead them to develop two sets of competing standards (Drezner 2007; Posner 2009a). The result was better channels of communication at several levels, less misunderstanding of the other's intentions, and improved dispute management with mutual adjustments and accommodations. Cooperative forms of interdependent decision-making developed because neither jurisdiction could impose its rules on the other nor achieve its goals without some kind of interaction (Posner 2009a, 2010a).

In fact, EU–US financial regulatory relations, organized loosely under the Financial Markets Regulatory Dialogue (FMRD), won approbation as a rare example of successful transatlantic regulatory cooperation. An analyst of a German-domiciled international bank, comparing the FMRD to other sectoral dialogues, characterized it as "one of the success stories of policy cooperation between the US and the EU" (Kern 2008: 3). As one US official wrote:

> To date the US–EU FMRD has been regarded a "success." It has contributed to managing or avoiding direct conflicts. Put another way, this means the absence of negative news and the presence of positive news. Substantive FMRD discussions

> have provoked changes in legislation. Most importantly, has been the FMRD's contribution to the deepening of professional ties between relevant supervisors.[5]

It is hard to exaggerate the substantive impact of the increasing similarity in EU and US approaches to financial regulation. In the pre-crisis years, banking, securities, and insurance markets in the transatlantic corridor were the world's largest by most measures including the assets of commercial banks, international and domestic debt securities, stock market capitalizations, foreign exchange transactions, international holdings of bank assets, insurance premiums, mergers and acquisitions sales and purchases, and OTC interest-rate, equity-linked, and foreign exchange derivatives transactions (Hamilton and Quinlan 2005). Moreover, finance between European and US markets was deeply interknit. For example, 51 percent of US foreign direct investment (FDI) went to Europe in 2005, and 70 percent of European FDI went to the United States (Hamilton and Quinlan 2008: 19). In 2006, as a percentage of foreign holdings, Europeans accounted for 41 percent of US long-term securities, 51 percent of US equities, 36 percent of US long-term debt securities, and 43 percent of US short-term securities.[6]

Against this backdrop of tight cross-Atlantic financial integration, the shared acceptance by EU and US regulators of increased self-regulation and greater firm discretion across financial markets is an underappreciated factor that enabled banks and other financial services companies to take undue and ultimately calamitous risks. The great power convergence thus sustained and abetted the trend toward industry-friendly financial regulation that failed so miserably in 2008. Had the EU turn-of-the-millennium reforms (discussed in detail below) given rise to a regulatory approach with greater divergence from the US one, the European Union might have challenged the United States as it had in the regulation of personal data, chemicals, food, and monopolies and the US-sparked crisis would have evolved differently.

A Puzzling Preference Alignment

In addition to the sheer real-world importance of this preference alignment, the pre-crisis similarity in transatlantic regulatory approaches poses a puzzle from a social science perspective. Given the increased number of great powers involved as well as their distinct domestic regulatory traditions, cooperation should be the exception not the norm.

[5] Author correspondence with US Treasury official, May 31, 2006.

[6] Federal Reserve Bank of New York and Board of Governors of the Federal Reserve System, "Report on Foreign Portfolio Holdings of US Securities as of June 30, 2013," April 2014, Tables 16a, b, c, & d.

The study of great power preferences sits at the center of international relations research dealing with cooperation and the distribution of power. Concerned with the prospects for an open international economy in the face of relative US economic decline, scholars have long asked whether state-to-state cooperation could be sustained in the aftermath of "systemic" change from a single great power to two or more (Krasner 1976; Gilpin 1987; Ikenberry 2001). Researchers originally posed the question when trade and monetary relations were the main areas of economic cooperation. Yet scholars have continued along the same lines of inquiry as regulation became a primary obstacle to deeper economic interdependence (Drezner 2007).

To simplify an important vein of a large body of research, state-to-state cooperation depends on both perceptions of potential joint gains (that is, that the participating parties all believe they will benefit from cooperation, an outcome of Pareto improvement) and agreement on how to divvy up those gains (that is, what the particular terms of cooperation will be or where on the Pareto Frontier). Thus even when it is, in principle, unproblematic to assume the parties see joint benefits, cooperation can easily prove difficult because the negotiating parties do not believe they will receive an even amount of those benefits (Krasner 1991). The greater the differential in preferred terms, the wider the gap in perceived benefits, and the more vexing cooperation is expected to become.

In theory, cooperation eases under hegemony, even when there are large preference differentials (Martin 1993). Given perceptions of joint gains, the hegemon enjoys the prerogative to establish the terms of cooperation either by using coercive diplomacy to win its preferred terms, by letting network effects or other impersonal constraints achieve the same outcome, or by accepting terms more favorable to the relatively weaker participants (Simmons 2001). In a world of two or more great powers, however, cooperation should prove more difficult—if preference differentials are large. Since no single power establishes the terms of cooperation, they must negotiate, and cooperation becomes restricted to limited areas of preference alignment—an outcome akin to Underdal's "law of the least ambitious program" (Helleiner 1996; Victor 2006).

Based on the findings of a robust comparative capitalisms literature (Zysman 1983; Berger and Dore 1996; Hall and Soskice 2001), EU–US financial regulatory bipolarity should yield such a pessimistic outcome. Despite decades of rising levels of economic globalism and of capital mobility, national forms of capitalism did not converge to the extent predicted by globalization theorists of multiple colors (Hay 2000). Nowhere is this more apparent than in financial systems—often identified as the institutional arrangements at the heart of national types of capitalism—where research stresses pronounced cross-national differences in the pre-crisis decades (Zysman 1983; Deeg 1999; Hall and Soskice

2001; Hardie and Howarth 2013) and finds them at the root of conflicting preferences over the terms of international cooperation (Story and Walter 1997; Fioretos 2010, 2011; Quaglia 2014).

Starting with Zysman's (1983) pioneering work, scholars of comparative politics highlight persistent differences in national financial systems in Europe and across the Atlantic. These differences include deeply embedded characteristics of countries' political economies such as the nature of government oversight, sources and access to capital, and rules concerning market entry. National financial systems did not, of course, remain frozen in the decades before the crisis, and change was not restricted to within-path trajectories (Deeg 2010). Rather, a new complexity of cross-jurisdictional differences emerges in the years before and after 2008 (Hardie and Howarth 2013; Hardie et al. 2013). In clarifying four possible dimensions to describe how banking became market-based, for example, Hardie et al. (2013) document a growing list of ways by which domestic models differ. Not only does finance vary considerably across capitalist jurisdictions but the differences also produce large adjustment costs for firms operating globally, an observation that leads scholars to predict preference divergence and regulatory confrontation within Europe and across the Atlantic (Story and Walter 1997; Fioretos 2010; Kalinowski 2013; Quaglia 2013).

For all these reasons, the history of financial system diversity diminishes the possibility of finding common ground in the European Union, and the new EU–US bipolarity should increase the potential for preference heterogeneity over the terms of international cooperation—not generate great power preference alignment. To use Drezner's nomenclature, the rise of the European Union as a financial regulatory power should complicate collective action in the "clubs" that develop transnational regulatory standards—rather than facilitate it (Drezner 2007). At a minimum, EU and US preferences over regulation should be farther apart and without a marked shift from stalemate to cooperation in the 2000s.

As noted, transatlantic preference alignment in finance contrasts with a large number of regulatory areas historically characterized by conflict that do follow the theoretical expectations of international relations and comparative politics scholars. In the areas of food safety and chemicals regulation, for example, the European Union actively promotes the precautionary principle, which creates a bias against introducing new products with uncertain effects and differs from the more permissive US regulatory approach (Pollack and Shaffer 2009; Vogel 2012). Similarly, the European Union continues to clash with the United States over comprehensive data privacy regulations, which give consumers a range of rights over how their data can be collected and processed (Newman 2008b). Financial regulation becomes an anomalous case only with the European Union's financial regulatory transformation. Until then, clashing models of finance within the European Union produced decades of policy stalemate (Zysman 1983; Story and Walter 1997; Quaglia 2010; Mourlon-Druol 2016). Transatlantic preference alignment and cooperation only became a possibility when EU decision-makers moved beyond many of these longstanding internal political standoffs.

The Limits of Regulatory Capture

Why were EU decision-makers able to overcome these conflicts? Why did this unexpected turn—which made the transatlantic preference alignment possible—happen at the turn of the millennium? The leading answer focuses not just on alignment but also on the finance-friendly content of transatlantic preferences. Transnational private actors, especially highly mobile firms, it maintains, pressure or otherwise influence policy-makers into adopting regulation that affords greater levels of firm discretion. Merging arguments about international class structures and relative asset mobility, advocates of this approach give pride of place to the role of transnational capital in systematically influencing rules (Gill and Law 1989; Kurzer 1993; Underhill 1995; Laurence 2001; Baker 2010; Lall 2012; Tsingou 2015). Multinational banks, asset managers, and other financial services providers promote policies that minimize oversight by public authorities. Financial firms possess a range of resources—critical technical knowledge, organizational capacities, and credible threats of exit—all of which allow them to steer the policy agenda and outcomes. Finance stands out as an area of transatlantic regulatory cooperation, by these arguments, because firms in the sector have more of these resources at their disposal. Financial regulation—at the local, regional, and transnational level—reflects the interests of internationally active firms.

Such firms and their associations no doubt play an important role in regulatory processes. Yet our evidence, along with recent scholarship, reveals severe deficiencies in arguments that cast industry lobbies as the prime shapers of regulation. First and foremost, firm influence varies widely over time and across issue areas—even during periods when capital mobility levels are consistently high (Büthe and Mattli 2011; Young 2012; McKeen-Edwards and Porter 2013; Pagliari and Young 2014). We also show, again consistent with the empirical work of others, that arguments attributing causation to firm lobbying often underestimate the role of politics, ideas, and institutions in structuring industry preferences (Berger 1983; Woll 2008; Posner 2009b).

Put differently, globally oriented firms made up an important part of the regulatory factions that sought to reform European rules (Sandholtz and Zysman 1989; Jabko 2006; Mügge 2010). In some cases these actors failed; in others, they succeeded. The rest of this chapter demonstrates that the availability of international soft law goes a long way to account for when international firms and other reformist faction members achieve their goals.

Soft Law as Disruptor and Alignment Mechanism

In line with the argument presented in Chapter 2, this section highlights the importance of soft law in bringing about the US–EU financial regulatory preference alignment. Reformist coalitions in Europe used newly available soft law to win domestic political contests, even though doing so did not always constitute their primary aim. In instances where soft law existed, EU member countries overcame internal political stalemate and adopted a harmonized regulatory approach similar to that of US regulators. Only one of our four cases where soft law was unavailable had the same outcome. After documenting congruence between the presence of international standards and transatlantic alignment, we show, through a process tracing exercise, that the two are causally linked. The evidence also helps to explain why state power expectations of diverging great power preferences were rarely realized and why industry pressure arguments are insufficient.

The logic of congruence: soft law and alignment

This section establishes a congruence between international soft law, internal EU political contests, and transatlantic policy positions. We show through a matching exercise that European reforms undertaken when international soft law already existed resulted in transatlantic alignment.[7] We examine a wide range of core financial regulatory issues (capital reserves, accounting standards, financial conglomerates, insurance, company law and financial instruments) that feature prominently in previous studies of financial reform within the European Union (Mügge 2010; Quaglia 2010, 2014).

We find alignment with US approaches in the three areas where international soft law existed prior to EU regulatory modernization (capital reserves for commercial banks, accounting standards, and conglomerates) and alignment in only one (financial instruments) of the four where it did not (capital reserves for investment banks, insurance, company law, and financial instruments). And variance in the timing of congruence (i.e. whatever the date of soft law's creation, EU modernization and transatlantic alignment follow), moreover, suggests that the pattern holds in different temporal contexts.

[7] For more detail on congruence analysis see Mahoney (2000).

The European Union transposed and implemented the 1988 Basel I and 2004 Basel II agreements producing similar cross-Atlantic policies regarding capital adequacy for commercial banks (see Chapter 3).[8] In 2002, the European Union adopted legislation[9] requiring that companies listed on EU stock exchanges use IAS/IFRS developed by the IASB by 2005. Like the US GAAP, the IAS/IFRS catered to the informational needs of investors (Perry and Nölke 2006; Nölke and Perry 2008; Büthe and Mattli 2011). Finally, the 2002 Financial Conglomerates Directive[10] mandates that a single regulator must oversee all components of large financial conglomerates with the goal of reducing regulatory arbitrage. The blueprint for the directive, like the two previous examples, followed the creation of transnational standards (the 1999 Joint Forum on Financial Conglomerates, in this instance). These same standards produced analogous reforms in the United States.[11]

We find considerably less transatlantic alignment in cases with weak or no transnational rules including capital adequacy for investment firms, company law, and the regulation of the insurance sector. In the case of capital adequacy rules for investment houses, the European Union went ahead with internal rules without international standards. The European approach differed from those in the United States and resulted in years of disagreement (Singer 2007). Likewise, the transnational network of insurance regulators known as the International Association of Insurance Supervisors (IAIS) had just been founded and had no consensus standards concerning solvency rules when the European Union underwent its modernization.[12] In the absence of international guidance on insurance regulation, the European Union's Solvency II Directive[13] follows a homegrown approach at odds with US practices (Quaglia 2014). Insurance has been a critical area of prolonged and intractable international financial regulatory conflict. In company law, an area largely devoid of transnational regulatory cooperation, deeper integration failed as EU governments, each with their own traditional model, failed to agree on a common policy response (Callaghan and Hopner 2005; Fioretos 2009). Transatlantic

[8] The Second Banking Directive (89/646/EEC) incorporated Basel I standards. The Capital Requirements Directive, incorporating Basel II standards, includes the Directive 2006/48/EC and Directive 2006/49/EC.

[9] Regulation (EC) no. 1606/2002 of the European Council and Parliament, July 19, 2002.

[10] Directive 2002/87/EC of the European Parliament and of the Council of December 16, 2002 on the supplementary supervision of credit institutions, insurance undertakings, and investment firms in a financial conglomerate and amending Council Directives 73/239/EEC, 79/267/EEC, 92/49/EEC, 92/96/EEC, 93/6/EEC, and 93/22/EEC, and Directives 98/78/EC and 2000/12/EC of the European Parliament and of the Council.

[11] Joint Forum of Financial Conglomerates, "Supervision of Financial Conglomerates," BCBS/IOSCO/IAIS, February 1999.

[12] Fragmented US regulatory authority hindered early transnational cooperation in the sector, see Singer (2007).

[13] Directive 2009/138/EC of the European Parliament and of the Council of November 25, 2009 on the taking-up and pursuit of the business of Insurance and Reinsurance (Solvency II).

Table 4.1. Congruence between international soft law and transatlantic preference alignment

	International soft law exists prior to EU harmonization efforts?	**EU harmonizes?**	**Transatlantic alignment?**
Capital reserves for commercial banks	*Yes*	*Yes*	*Yes*
Accounting standards	*Yes*	*Yes*	*Yes*
Conglomerates	*Yes*	*Yes*	*Yes*
Financial instruments	No	Yes	Yes
Capital reserves for investment banks	No	Yes	No
Insurance	No	Yes	No
Company law	No	No	No

authorities have had to make exceptions where necessary to overcome incompatibilities between American and European national company law.[14] These cases provide important evidence of the limits of arguments that focus on the material benefits of cooperation, since despite substantial potential benefits to financial services firms with multinational operations, the European Union and the United States failed to align. Table 4.1 summarizes the congruence between soft law, EU reform, and transatlantic alignment.

The one anomaly to the pattern is the European Union's 2004 Market in Financial Instruments Directive (a revision of a 1993 directive, the Investment Services Directive or ISD, aimed at liberalizing cross-border trading of financial instruments and investment services provision). While not contradicting our argument about the role of soft law, this case indicates equifinality in the sense that more than one causal path may produce the same outcome. Despite the absence of international soft law concerning the core issue (i.e. how to structure cross-border competition of securities trading and investment services),[15] the European Union eventually adopted more permissive rules mirroring the direction of US reforms (Mügge 2010: 125–42; Quaglia 2010: 83–90). Overall, the congruence pattern thus provides encouraging evidence linking the preexistence of international soft law to EU harmonization and transatlantic preference alignment.

Soft law, legitimacy claims, and internal EU reform

Having established a pattern of congruence between soft law, EU reform, and alignment, we now apply the method of process tracing to explore the extent to which soft law disrupted internal reform battles across the three positive

[14] On exceptions made to accommodate Germany's dual board system, see Tafara (2004: 8).

[15] IOSCO's 1998 "Objectives and Principles of Securities Regulation" lacks guidance on the issue. See Mügge (2010: 66).

cases—capital adequacy for banks, accounting standards, and conglomerates rules—and one case of non-alignment—capital adequacy for investment firms. The exercise offers support for our claims by documenting causal linkages: reformers used international soft law to legitimize their arguments and to overcome policy stalemate over EU regulatory harmonization. Because the area of capital adequacy has within-case variation (allowing for controlled and granular comparison), the analysis also reveals how the absence of soft law contributes to transatlantic preference clashes.

By the late 1990s, a group of reform-minded European policy elites, spearheaded by the European Commission and supported by multinational banks, actors in the UK, in other Northern member countries, and in the European Parliament, formed in favor of rapid integration that would complete the long-sought single market in financial services (Posner 2007; Mügge 2010; Quaglia 2010). Despite the anticipated material benefits, this reformist faction faced many of the same obstacles that had vexed previous harmonization efforts: barriers stemming from differences in the political economy of finance across Europe. Key to the political bargain of the late 1990s was that EU financial integration, unlike monetary union, continued the historical pattern of encompassing all member states, including the UK with its leading international financial center. Even without Britain, numerous sticking points among continental members (for example, resistance to the creation of supranational financial authorities), not to mention among EU political institutions (Buerkle 2002; Pollack 2003), persisted. With the UK's involvement, the reform process faced many difficulties similar to those of previous eras: the governments and EU political institutions had to find common ground between the continental countries, especially the heavily banked and embedded German and French financial systems, and Britain with some of the world's largest capital markets and with its unembedded light-touch regulatory regime (Mügge 2010: 31–50).

The FSAP legislative package attempted to break these ongoing and unsettled political battles over the rules of finance. Many proposals revised previous legislation from the 1980s (European Commission 1983, 1985; Posner 2007). Neatly captured by Story and Walter's phrase "battle of the systems," the earlier efforts failed when confronted by incompatible national preferences. And as a whole, they yielded weak and porous legislation, which could not form the foundation of pan-European financial markets (Story and Walter 1997; Lamfalussy 2001; Pollack 2003).

How did the reform faction accomplish its goals? The answer is neither monocausal nor deterministic as each piece of legislation has an idiosyncratic political story. In some areas, member states engaged in significant regulatory reforms. In others, the shift in policy preferences of the largest financial firms brought German and French governments closer to longstanding British (and market-friendly) positions (Mügge 2010: 31–49). A theme across cases, however, is that the presence of soft law increased the probability that negotiators would find agreement and tilted outcomes in favor of reformist coalitions.

CAPITAL REQUIREMENTS

Focusing on capital requirements, this section provides evidence of enterprising reformists disrupting EU policy battles through the invocation of soft law. The European harmonization of capital requirements for commercial banks is remarkable given the initially stark contrast in regulatory practices across the member states and the ineffective preexisting rules (e.g. the 1977 First Banking Directive) (Dale 1984; Zavvos 1988). This instance of harmonization also stands out because it began a decade before the FSAP and Lamfalussy Process that triggered the European Union's rise as an international financial regulatory power.

Because of natural internal variation (in the sense that international standards existed for some banking activities but not others), the capital adequacy case helps to reveal how soft law (and its absence) influenced patterns of reform. For the historical reasons described in Chapter 3, international capital standards for banks and investment houses fell under the auspices of two different soft law bodies: the Basel Committee on Banking Supervision and IOSCO, respectively. The Basel Committee moved early in this domain and agreed to its first body of soft law (the 1988 Basel I accord) just before Brussels forged ahead with new banking legislation (the 1989 Second Banking Directive). So capital adequacy soft law for commercial banks existed prior to and, as we show, played an important role in the politics of European harmonization and the shaping of transatlantic compatibility. In the case of investment houses, by contrast, IOSCO's efforts ran contemporaneously with European reform and ended without an international consensus. In the end, Europe moved ahead with its own distinct regulatory trajectory.

The European Commission had long sought to harmonize banking regulation. Already in the 1970s, it drafted ambitious legislation that attempted to create a comprehensive banking union, which among other things would have mandated common capital and solvency requirements (Mourlon-Druol 2016). This supranational project, however, quickly met with fierce resistance from the new member states of the United Kingdom and Denmark, which feared over-regulation. Giving up on its grand vision of banking union, the Commission turned to piecemeal steps to integrate the markets. The 1977 First Banking Directive captures the weakness in this strategy, as it followed what would become the typical "battle of the systems" pattern that undermined strict harmonization (Story and Walter 1997). George Zavvos (1988: 268), a key Commission official responsible for banking integration, concluded that "the meticulous harmonization efforts—judged by their results—have proven to be impractical and cumbersome in many respects . . . the member states' banking and financial systems are frequently the product of different economic, political, and legal developments, which does not make it feasible to achieve a high degree of harmonisation." While the First Banking Directive set minimum standards for "own funds," it left discretion to the member states for deciding how to reach these capital requirements and thus, for practical purposes, failed to resolve the issue of pan-European prudential harmonization.

As the European Commission and internationally oriented business worked to reenergize the single market project in the 1980s (European Commission 1985), they once again faced serious barriers to cooperation over banking rules (Story and Walter 1997; Quaglia 2010). Countries had different levels of capital requirements, with some member states highly capitalized (the British) and others less so (the French). Moreover, the member states differed over the types of assets that might count toward such capital requirements, with Germany holding an exceptionally conservative position (Goodhart 2011). Yet the Commission's goal of European banking integration by way of a single passport for financial services would not be possible without agreement on prudential rules, especially capital requirements.[16]

Basel I presented a solution. Even in the early discussions, European reformists found useful tools for advancing their agenda to harmonize at home (European Commission 1983: 17; Story and Walter 1997: 281–3). They saw potential in enmeshing the European Banking Advisory Committee, a network of national supervisors in Europe, and the Basel Committee, which created working groups to examine technical differences (including the European ones) and propose practical solutions (Goodhart 2011). Relying on different tiers of capital, for example, responded to German concerns about the quality of capital (Goodhart 2011). Moreover, several European banking authorities were early adopters of the risk-based assessment system, which the Basel Committee would later adopt. The Bank of England, in particular, used the Basel process (as well as the US–UK Agreement described in Chapter 3) to shape the emerging international standards both to facilitate European harmonization and to head off alternative pan-European approaches (Kapstein 1994; Solomon 1995).[17]

While Commission officials had studied various alternatives to the capital adequacy question in the previous decade, they struggled to find a workable solution. With Basel I, they possessed a new political resource. They could subsequently argue for the incorporation of soft law as an attractive solution

[16] Guy de Jonquières, "Big Doubts Face EC Drive to Unify," *The Financial Post*, February 29, 1988, 11.
[17] Don Munro, "UK–US Pact Questioned," *The American Banker*, January 30, 1987, 3.

for harmonizing the vast differences in national capital requirement approaches.[18] Zavvos continued:

> The need for equivalent standards on an international scale becomes increasingly important as banks conduct their operations on a global basis . . . The Commission believes that the development of common standards of capital adequacy in relation to assets at risk is one of the essential areas of harmonisation necessary for the achievement of mutual recognition and the completion of the internal market in banking services . . . Work on banks' capital and on solvency ratios is proceeding in parallel in the Community and in the G-10 Supervisors' Committee in Basle. On 10 December 1987 the Committee of the Governors of the Central Banks, on the suggestion of the Committee of Banking Supervisors, endorsed the proposal for bank capital adequacy standards. (Zavvos 1988: 285)

As the other cases examined in this chapter indicate, this type of framing (where the European Commission harnessed the perceived legitimacy of soft law by presenting its own agenda in terms of compliance with it) would become a prevalent strategy of the Commission across financial services reform (Jabko 2006: 78; Kudrna and Müller 2017).[19]

The Basel accord did not merely lend legitimacy to the European reform process but specifically limited the attractiveness of an inward-facing European solution. European-based standards would likely have generated rules much less compatible with the standards of the United States and other international financial centers. As Peter Cooke, chair of the Basel Committee concluded:

> From the Community's point of view, maximum consistency between the two approaches [Europe's and Basel's] would mean there was less danger of the Community regime coming into conflict with the systems in non-Community countries, thus avoiding setting the EC bloc at odds with the rest of the world on matters which everyone recognized should, for good practical reasons, be dealt with in the same way in what was one single global marketplace.
>
> (Cooke 1990: 317)

Pointing out the risks of devising conflicting rules (Jabko 2006: 76), reformists like Cooke strengthened the Commission's argument that it was necessary to transpose the ready-made Basel solution into EU legislation (Mügge 2010: 57). The successful use of a multilateral template disciplined member state positions and limited changes in the agenda (that would have necessitated further global negotiations) (Matthews 1992, 2009; Hemel 2011).[20]

[18] Mark Milner, "Stepping Towards Financial Harmony," *The Guardian*, October 31, 1989.

[19] John Duffy, "Europe Warming up to Risk-Based Capital Plan," *The American Banker*, May 2, 1988, 1.

[20] David Lascelles concludes: "the Solvency Ratio Directive . . . are closely modeled on last year's international Basel Agreement so as to avoid creating a further set of rules for banks." David

The 1989 precedent of using Basel rules in EU legislation was repeated in subsequent banking legislation[21] when the European Commission listed revision of EU capital adequacy rules as among the goals of the FSAP's financial regulatory overhaul of 1999 (European Commission 1998, 1999). Again, a reformist European Commission looking for ways to overcome internal divisions over how to integrate Europe's national banking industries made use of transnational processes and their aura of political neutrality and technical soundness to legitimize its aim. Commission officials argued that harmonizing in accordance with Basel II standards was essential to maintaining international competitiveness:

> Core elements of existing EU bank capital requirements are now being re-examined to bring them up-to-date with supervisory practices and banking trends [as discussed in the Basle Committee on Banking Supervision]...The EU should take a leading role in tackling issues to maintain a level playing field (taking into account the heterogeneous structure of the EU banking sector). The Union must also take steps to adapt its legislation as swiftly as the regulators of the US, Canadian and Japanese banks. (European Commission 1998: 19)

The European Union's adoption of international soft law did not complete the global harmonization process, as domestic pushback against US Basel II compliance and disagreements over Basel III within the European Union demonstrate. Yet it brought Europe and the United States closer on the ground rules for capital adequacy standards. The European Union's incorporation of Basel soft law also contributed to the transformation of national financial systems within Europe, particularly in those countries with more traditional continental banking arrangements. The risk-weighted approach encouraged investments in mortgage-backed securities and other new asset classes, which both undermined old business models and created new vulnerabilities exposed during the global financial crisis of 2008 (Thiemann 2014). In short, international soft law played a major role in aligning European rules with those in the United States and transformed European industry at the same time.

The evolution of capital adequacy rules for commercial banks in Europe contrasts sharply with what transpired for investment banks. Here too, the European Commission felt tremendous pressure to achieve harmonized rules or risk the viability of the single passport in financial services.[22] Yet differences in approaches across the member states complicated reform. For the UK,

Lascelles, "Single Banking Licence Opens Road to a Wider Market," *Financial Times*, June 21, 1989, 4. European policy-makers implemented Basel I rules in the Own Funds Directive [Council Directive 89/299/EEC] and the Solvency Ratio Directive [Council Directive 89/647/EEC]. These accompanied the Second Banking Directive [Council Directive 89/646], December 15, 1989.

[21] See the 1993 Capital Adequacy Directive (93/6/EEC) that accompanied the Investment Services Directive.

[22] Richard Waters, "The Quest for a Capital Adequacy Directive," *Financial Times*, April 5, 1991.

investment services made up a distinct and large segment of the financial sector, while in other countries like Germany, there were few pure investment banking houses. The universal banks of the continent typically held on to securities as long-term investments and, unlike dedicated investment banks stayed out of the full range of capital market services, especially those focusing on short-term proprietary transactions. Anticipating the continued growth of capital markets, German and other continental banks worried that European or global capital requirements for investment banks might give an advantage to dedicated investment houses and limit the future ability of universal banks to engage in the subsector.[23] Accordingly, continental banks pushed for common capital adequacy rules that applied to both commercial and investment banks.

British authorities saw things differently. The 1989 Second Banking Directive established a European passport for universal banks, which could use it to sell investment services throughout the European Union, but not for dedicated investment houses. British regulators wanted to level the playing field by introducing a similar passport for the latter and doing so implied a need for Europe-wide investment bank capital requirements. British authorities were particularly concerned that Brussels would forge ahead on the basis of the German-inspired approach, which they thought would put UK-based investment banks at a competitive disadvantage vis-à-vis US and other non-EU rivals (Mügge 2010).[24]

The main British regulator at the time, the Securities and Investment Board (SIB), reached out to its peers in IOSCO to forge a global deal with the goal of heading off European rules. Starting in 1989, the SIB worked exhaustively through IOSCO to generate capital adequacy rules for the investment sector, repeatedly raising the specter of European rules and their potential to drive divergence across the Atlantic.[25] As Peter Rodgers of the *Independent* reported, "British representatives believe a firm line by IOSCO on capital adequacy would prevent the European Commission sticking rigidly to its proposals and open the way to a compromise in Brussels."[26]

[23] David Frank, "'German Question' Holds up Securities Regulators' Talks," *The Independent*, September 22, 1989, 26.

[24] Peter Rodgers, "Britain in Row over Securities Capital," *The Independent*, January 25, 1992, 17; Richard Waters, "EC Directive on Capital Rules Could Hit UK Firms," *Financial Times*, December 22, 1989.

[25] Peter Rodgers, "Government in Row with EC over Securities Capital Regulation," *The Independent*, January 25, 1992, 17.

[26] Peter Rodgers, "Government in Row with EC over Securities Capital Regulation," *The Independent*, January 25, 1992, 17. See also Rod McNeil, "Compromise on Capital Adequacy Directive Represents a Political Breakthrough for EC," *Thomson's International Banking Regulator*, June 29, 1992. In the article that author argues, "The battle cry from the British Bankers Association to tie progress on the CAD [Capital Adequacy Directive] with the Basel/IOSCO discussions could go unheeded." At the same time German representatives attempted to stall IOSCO discussions.

Through the early 1990s, however, IOSCO lacked a coherent position on the issue. Although the US SEC had played a central role in the organization's early years, it had become disinterested by the mid-1980s. As detailed in Chapter 3, in 1987 when David Ruder became the agency's chair the SEC again reengaged with the international organization but its involvement continued to be intermittent. The SEC initially demonstrated interest in harmonizing global capital adequacy rules when Ruder's successor Richard Breeden backed an IOSCO committee that looked into the issue (Singer 2007).

Yet the timing of European Commission efforts drove a wedge between the SEC and the SIB, derailing consensus. According to one anonymous banker, "There is a sort of competition between Brussels and Basle[27] to regulate us first, and Brussels is winning."[28] While the SIB attempted to negotiate with the SEC at the global level, it also had to move forward on the European front to ensure investment banks would have a European passport (Coleman and Underhill 1995). British negotiations attempted in vain to slow the European legislative process so as to synchronize with an IOSCO deal.[29]

The SEC pushed for a stringent set of regulations based on its own uniform net capital rule, a source of pride to SEC officials who believed it had worked well in the 1990 collapse of Wall Street investment bank Drexel Burnham Lambert.[30] SEC officials considered British and continental approaches too oriented toward preserving insolvent banks and insufficiently attentive to investor protections. For their part, many of the continental authorities, with only minor investment services sectors in their jurisdictions, feared a US-led approach would prove incompatible with domestic markets. Jean Saint-Geours, president of France's Commission des Opérations de Bourse, argued, "The United States would like to influence what happens in Europe. I would like us to complete our [directives] in Europe before starting negotiations aimed at coordination with the United States."[31] Without US support in IOSCO, the SIB struck a relatively lax deal within Europe in the form of the Capital Adequacy Directive. A key component of the European agreement was to distinguish between the types of investments used by commercial banks and those used by investment banks through the use of the "trading book."[32]

See Richard Waters, "German Action Threatens Capital Adequacy Accord," *Financial Times*, September 21, 1989.

[27] The banker refers to Basel as IOSCO and the Basel Committee had been working together to finalize IOSCO standards. Maggie Fox, "Bankers, Regulators look to Commission on Capital Rule," *Reuters*, January 31, 1992.

[28] Maggie Fox, "Bankers, Regulators look to Commission on Capital Rule," *Reuters*, January 31, 1992.

[29] Maggie Fox, "EC Faces 'Messy' Capital Adjustment," *Reuters*, June 24, 1992.

[30] Author interview with former SEC official, Washington, DC, May 20, 2004.

[31] International Securities Regulation Report, "Differences on Equity, Technical Details Suggest Long Wait for Global Capital Rules," February 1, 1992, 5(5): 7.

[32] "A Passport to Strife," *The Economist*, April 28, 1990.

One result was that Europeans allowed commercial banks to maintain their practices, while setting rules for investment houses at a lower level. The European deal, in turn, generated tensions with the SEC, which resisted lowering its standards to those proposed in new European rules.[33] A public row resulted between the European Commission Vice President, Leon Brittan, and SEC head, Richard Breeden, both arguing that their regulatory regime offered a better solution.[34] In the absence of international soft law on capital requirements for investment banks, both the SEC and European reformists saw advantage in following different regulatory trajectories and set the path for transatlantic clashes.[35] At the same time, the failure of IOSCO to resolve the capital adequacy issue for investment banks proved a major blow to the organization's reputation (a point we return to in Chapter 5).

ACCOUNTING STANDARDS

Early efforts to develop common accounting rules played out much along the lines of the "battle of the systems" logic. In particular, the directives from the 1970s and 1980s (known as the Fourth and Seventh Directives) allowed for so much variation in terms of compliance that little harmonization existed. In short, Europe entered the late 1980s with a diversity of accounting rules reflecting national traditions (Hulle 1993).[36]

This national diversity posed a challenge for the European Commission, which hoped to push forward the single market agenda, as well as for internationalizing European companies, who sought to raise funds on foreign stock exchanges most notably those in the United States (Glaum 2000). Far from mere academic details, the differences in accounting standards had material consequences for firms seeking cross-border opportunities. In a famous example, Daimler-Benz faced a major revaluation of its positions (from a DM168 million profit to a DM949 million loss) as it listed on US markets and shifted from using German accounting standards to US GAAP (General Accepted Accounting Principles). For their part, European authorities became increasingly concerned as they watched a growing number of European firms voluntarily switch reporting practices to US GAAP (Botzem 2012). The Commission feared that Europe might lose control of standard setting to another

[33] "The Regulators are at Odds and the EC's Directive adds to the Confusion," *The Banker*, June 1, 1993, 143 (808).

[34] Robert Peston and Tracy Corrigan, "Sir Leon Brittan Joins Row Over Capital Adequacy," *Financial Times*, October 29, 1992, 28. See also "Capital Spat," *The Economist*, October 31, 1992, 100; International Securities Regulation Report, "SEC Letter to IOSCO on Capital Adequacy," November 3, 1992, 11.

[35] Tracy Corrigan and Robert Peston, "IOSCO Setback over Common Capital Requirements," *Financial Times*, October 27, 1992, 33.

[36] Mary Keegan, "Whose Standards Should We Bear? The Problem Posed by Multiple Accounting to European Unity," *The Independent*, July 19, 1994, 30; Peter Holgate, "Problems Remain over Accounts Harmonisation," *Accountancy*, February 7, 1990, 27.

country (Kaya et al. 2016). A diverse coalition including the Commission, global corporations, and large accounting firms hoped to harmonize standards across Europe as a way both to facilitate market competitiveness with the United States and to preserve a European voice in accounting practices.

Despite interest in harmonization, however, resistance existed toward the most readily available reform strategies. The traditional legislative tool, the EU directive, had proven ineffective. National biases generated opposition to a directive that would choose a single "European champion" from the diverse array of member state standards. Small to medium-sized firms in continental countries were particularly opposed to reporting requirements that might generate additional burdens, such as those contained in the adoption of foreign standards.[37] Accounting professionals from these countries similarly saw little benefit from a shift to harmonized standards that would primarily facilitate integration with international markets. The directive process also required extensive back and forth between the Council and Parliament, which was likely to generate too many veto points to allow for a successful revision of existing directives. As the European Commission explained:

> No further progress has been made at EU level in harmonising the basic rules on accounting and financial reporting. There is disagreement between Member States about the usefulness of the Directive [which needs to be implemented by national governments] as an instrument for accounting harmonisation... Some Member States might seek to renegotiate parts of the Directives they do not like. The preparation and negotiation of such an important revision of the Directives would take a long time. (1995: 3–5)

The intensity of the struggle between the reform and status quo camps is reflected in the fact that policy change took over two decades.

Similar to the capital adequacy case, Europe's accounting battles had an additional dimension. Within the reform faction, a split developed between advocates of pan-European standards, which would have likely limited future transatlantic convergence, and promoters of international standards, which laid a foundation for US–EU compatibility. Starting in the late 1980s, the European Commission promoted a strictly European approach. Hermann Niessen, the head of the accounting unit in DG Internal Market, along with his second in command, Karl Van Hulle, shopped around a proposal to various stakeholders for the creation a European accounting standards board. This board would be a sanctioned body of private experts similar to the Financial Accounting Standards Board (FASB) in the United States (Camfferman and

[37] Karl Van Hulle, a European Commission official responsible for accounting standards, argued in 1989, "We cannot speak internationally about harmonization while the member states are still defending their own national positions." "Commission's Cold Comfort Farm," *Accountancy*, July 1, 1989, 13.

Zeff 2007). The Commission believed that Europe needed to develop its own perspective on accounting standards to anchor the internal market project but also to defend its interests and approaches globally. Van Hulle concluded in 1989, "There is also a need for a European voice in the area of standard setting. We should not be afraid to admit we are European and that our first duty lies with Europe. Only then can we play a valid role internationally . . . let us not try to escape this responsibility by announcing an international commitment without a strong European base established."[38]

The Commission faced resistance to its scheme from member states and the private sector, wary of delegating too much authority to Brussels. Member states, including those within the reform camp, feared Commission domination of a pan-European accounting standards body,[39] while the accounting profession, also in favor of harmonization, voiced concern that such a body would weaken the authority of national advisory bodies that they controlled.[40]

The fate of both the more decentralized (a new directive) and centralized (a European board) strategies, however, was determined substantially by the existence of international soft law generated by the International Accounting Standards Committee. Formed in 1973 by a group of accounting experts from the United Kingdom, Canada, and the United States, among others, the IASC sought to generate a set of common standards that could be used by firms hoping to exploit the opportunities emerging in newly internationalizing markets (Camfferman and Zeff 2007; Botzem 2012). Led by Henry Benson of the Institute of Chartered Accountants of England and Wales, the initial work of the organization was carried out by a number of high profile, internationally focused accounting professionals.

Its creators also saw the new organization as a possible alternative venue to regional standard setting. With British accession to the European Union in 1973, accountants from the United Kingdom became particularly worried about how internal regional developments might drive substantive debates. Given the very different national rules in the United Kingdom, which emphasized investor protection, from those on the continent, which often focused on creditors, standards harmonization could involve sizable switching costs (Perry and Nölke 2006; Botzem 2008; Djelic and Quack 2010; Posner 2010a). For UK experts, early transnational collaboration was a strategy for managing continental ambitions. Anthony Hopwood, an expert on British accounting and founder of the European Accounting Association, explained:

> The British accountancy bodies were worried by the potential consequences of what they saw as the imposition of continental European statutory and state

[38] "Commission's Cold Comfort Farm," *Accountancy*, July 1, 1989, 13.
[39] See "EC Directive Review Sparks Spectre of 'Euro-ASB'," *Accountancy Age*, February 16, 1995, 1.
[40] "Accounts Harmonisation—which is the way forward?" *Accountancy*, February 7, 1990, 9.

> control on much more discretionary relationships between corporate management and auditor in the UK... Wanting to have a more institutionalized manifestation of British commitment to a wider transnational and Commonwealth mode of accounting, with the cooperation of its partners in the primarily English language audit community, the IASC was established. Its creation was intended to give a strong signal of Britain's role in what no doubt was perceived as a global accounting community rather than a more narrowly circumscribed European one. (Hopwood 1994: 243)

In the early years, the IASC (renamed the International Accounting Standards Board or IASB in 2000) attempted to please a broad swath of constituents by producing catchall standards, encompassing basic principles that allowed diverse national implementation through optional treatments. While useful for developing countries as they crafted new accounting regimes, the Core Standards Project allowed too much variation to facilitate serious harmonization (Camfferman and Zeff 2007).

During the 1980s, however, the IASC began to refine and detail its soft law standards. In part, the turn resulted from an important interaction with IOSCO and indirectly the US SEC. IOSCO and the SEC had an interest in facilitating foreign listings on domestic stock exchanges. Diverse accounting standards were an obstacle. IOSCO then engaged with IASC in a multi-year compatibility and improvement project, which streamlined IASC standards and brought them new credibility (Camfferman and Zeff 2007; Kaya et al. 2016). Importantly, IASC was composed of sector experts rather than national representatives, and a majority came from global accounting firms that were familiar with and specialized in accounting practices of countries with large capital markets like the United States and the United Kingdom (Perry and Nölke 2006). The IOSCO–IASC project produced a distinct set of standards, compatible with US GAAP.

The IASC and its standards played a key role in overcoming resistance to harmonization and in stymieing those within the European Commission behind the pan-European alternative. Pointing to a ready-made set of global standards, the pro-IASC reformers undermined the notion that a Commission-led solution was the only alternative and highlighted the speed of adopting international standards when compared to having to create new European ones from scratch.[41] They also appealed to the desire (shared throughout the European Commission) to avoid fights among member states typical of European policy-making that relied on directives. Rather than picking a national winner, Commission officials and their supporters could promote IASC standards

[41] Van Hulle explains, "It is actually the resistance of several member states to a higher level of harmonization which is the root cause of the failure of a European alternative" and thus the necessity of IAS. Interview with Karel Van Hulle, *Accountancy and Tax*, 2004.

as neutral relative to existing member state positions.[42] In addition, the reformists leveraged the purported technical superiority of standards that had received IOSCO recognition (Kaya et al. 2016). In the words of Hermann Nordemann, president of the Fédération des Experts Comptables Européens (FEE), which was the leading European accounting standards trade association: "Given the prior existence of standards at both a national and worldwide level, it is no longer necessary to have an intermediate layer of European standards . . . Indeed, such an intermediate layer, by contributing to the already very real problem of standards overload, can only lead to confusion and extra burdens on the financial reporting community . . . FEE believes the best force for achieving this harmonization is the IASC."[43]

The pro-IASC reformists argued that international soft law met the core harmonization objectives of the Commission, allayed member state concerns over further centralization of Commission authority, and overcame member state fears that reforms would be based on one member state's rules over another (Kudrna and Müller 2017). National standard setters including the UK's David Tweedie echoed this position ("We have got to be sure that we do not end up with three sets of standards for companies to be burdened with"[44]). In the words of Hans Hoogervorst, former chairman of the International Accounting Standards Board, the international standards presented themselves "as an off-the-shelf solution to the problems caused by the lack of accounting harmony in Europe."[45] The overwhelming support for international standards eventually led Karel Van Hulle and other proponents within the Commission of a pan-European solution to conclude, "Stakeholders considered that European standards would create confusion and more complexity with the possible co-existence of national, European and international standards. The IASB's existing standards seemed the best and quickest solution for the EU."[46]

In 2002, the European Union adopted Regulation 1606 on the application of international accounting standards, which required companies listed on European markets to use IASC's standards, known as International Financial

[42] "Van Hulle backs IAS," *The Accountant*, January 1, 1999.

[43] Quoted in "Commission's Cold Comfort Farm," *Accountancy*, July 1, 1989, 13.

[44] Quoted in "EC Directive Review Sparks Spectre of 'Euro-ASB'," *Accountancy Age*, February 16, 1995, 1.

[45] Hans Hoogervorst, former chairman of the International Accounting Standards Board, *Europe's Future in Global Markets* (Brussels: ICAEW, 2014). Paul Cherry, who chaired the IOSCO working party on accounting standards at the time, concluded, "If the IASC and EC do not work together to develop international accounting standards, we face the prospect of regional blocks which would likely destroy any real prospect of significant global harmonization," in International Securities Regulation Report, "EC Moves could Doom Global Accounting Harmony," January 17, 1990.

[46] Karel Van Hulle, *Europe's Future in Global Markets* (Brussels: ICAEW, 2014).

Reporting Standards (IFRS), for their consolidated reporting.[47] The European Union decision had its own far-reaching second-order consequences beyond Europe's adoption of international standards. It forestalled the development of a uniform set of European standards, which would have made transatlantic alignment much less likely. While IFRS and US GAAP are not perfectly convergent, they became increasingly compatible, as demonstrated by the US SEC's 2007 decision to allow IFRS for reconciliation by foreign issuers.[48] The European decision to resolve its internal harmonization dilemma through the use of IFRS, moreover, turned the IASC into the world's standard setter (Posner 2010a; Newman and Bach 2014). While only a handful of countries adopted IFRS prior to the European Union's action, by 2015 they were required in over 100 jurisdictions for all or most accounting purposes.[49] The European Union also increased its influence over the decision-making process of IFRS. Thus, the reformist coalition that invoked the legitimacy of international soft law not only disrupted the politics of company reporting requirements within Europe but also set the course for transatlantic alignment and international harmonization (Posner 2010a).

FINANCIAL CONGLOMERATES REGULATION

The set of rules for financial conglomerates is similar to both capital adequacy for commercial banks and accounting standards in that the preexistence of international soft law helped reformers to disrupt a longstanding political contest, restructure internal bargains, and brought the European Union into closer alignment with the United States. The key issue in the case of conglomerates was to establish a point regulator responsible for firms that had complex affiliates and subsidiaries spanning subsectors and national jurisdictions. Despite high profile scandals like the massive failure of the Bank of Credit and Commerce International (BCCI) in 1991, regulators and firms resisted efforts for consolidated supervision (Corrigan et al. 1992; Quaglia 2010). Regulators facing turf battles, and firms who used the fragmentation to improve their position vis-à-vis authorities, also opposed such reforms. In Europe, rather than creating a consolidated supervision structure across sectors, each sector ended up with its own directive (Coates 2001; Gruson 2004).

The Financial Services Action Plan reignited the debate, as it hoped to expand cross-border operations in Europe and further integrate market activity across sectors. The adoption of a single national regulator for all financial services sectors in the United Kingdom (1997) and Germany (2002) prompted

[47] Regulation 1606/2002 of the European Parliament and of the Council of July 19, 2002 on the application of international accounting standards.

[48] SEC, Final Rule Release No. 33-8879, December 21, 2007, <http://www.sec.gov/rules/final/2007/33-8879.pdf>.

[49] <http://www.ifrs.org/Features/Pages/Global-reach-of-IFRS-is-expanding.aspx>.

their governments to take the lead in the new legislative effort. Nevertheless, reformists continued to face head winds from member states without unified supervision.

The availability of the 1999 Joint Forum's principles for supervision of financial conglomerates facilitated Europe-wide agreement. The Joint Forum's principles concerning coordination of authorities and supplementary supervision (atop of existing "silos") offered the pro-reform faction arguments for overcoming the political impasse rooted in sectoral differences (Gruson 2004). Both the European Commission and reformist Members of the European Parliament (MEPs) used the legitimacy of the international soft law to bolster their arguments in favor of harmonization. From its earliest proposals, for example, the Commission framed its arguments around the Joint Forum (European Commission 1999: 30). Reformist members of the European Parliament did the same. In urging MEPs to adopt Commission-proposed conglomerates legislation, the rapporteur used similar rhetoric. "It [the proposed legislation] is not an isolated initiative taken at Community level," he argued. "Its principles have been internationally agreed within the G10 Joint Forum. Parallel initiatives to implement the recommendations of the Joint Forum are presently underway in countries like Australia, the US and Switzerland."[50] The new approach won over the resistance of Mediterranean countries and some of the new member states, which had not adopted the single regulatory model at the national level and were reluctant to alter existing domestic arrangements (Quaglia 2010: 63). By writing legislation based on perceived international best practice and including provisions that required foreign firms—especially US ones—operating in London (and elsewhere in Europe) to have equivalent supervision or be subject to the European Union's regime, the reformers satisfied British concerns (Quaglia 2010: 64).[51]

The adoption of the Joint Forum soft law was not politically neutral. It eased agreement in the narrow area of consolidated supervision but sparked new conflicts. Within Europe, by borrowing the Joint Forum's emphasis on coordinating mechanisms, the directive aggravated a simmering battle over oversight and led to the extension of the Lamfalussy architecture to banking, insurance, and conglomerates.[52] This, combined with the fallout from the 2008 financial crisis, generated new impetus for regulatory centralization at

[50] Rapporteur Alain Lipietz's comments in COM(2001) 213. C5-0159/2001. 2001/0095(COD), A5-0060/2002 Final, February 27, 2002, 32–3.

[51] David Green, "A European Regulatory Perspective," FSA Speech, Annual Washington Conference of the Institute of International Banking, March 4, 2002, <http://www.fsa.gov.uk/library/communication/speeches/2002/sp92.shtml>.

[52] Tom Buerkle, "European Disunion," *Institutional Investor*, July 1, 2002.

the European level as fragmented regulatory networks were centralized into more coherent supervisors. The European Union became a much more coordinated actor both internally and globally (Quaglia 2014).

The European Union's adoption of Joint Forum soft law also set off a conflict with the United States, which, paradoxically, prompted transatlantic alignment. The EU Conglomerates Directive required equivalent supervision of US and other foreign firms operating in the European Union, and, as documented below, Washington officials (responding to complaints by Wall Street banks and apparently unaware that the European Union had modeled its law on Joint Forum principles) pushed back. Yet after an initial transatlantic spat, the SEC introduced a new holding company rule also designed to meet the international principles (Posner 2009a: 672–3 and 683–8; Lo 2012: 2–3 and 31–6). The conglomerates case further demonstrates how European reformists leveraged the legitimacy of international soft law to disrupt internal political stalemate and harmonize national regulation within the European Union, thereby fostering transatlantic alignment.

Alternative Arguments

Do counter arguments better explain great power alignment? Accounts highlighting the number and preferences of great powers face a host of challenges. As noted, these models assume that existing internal regulatory structures prior to global cooperation determine great power preferences. Given differences in financial regulatory styles across the Atlantic and within Europe, these arguments generate an expectation of transatlantic preference divergence. Our cases find internal policy paralysis within Europe that then gives way to internal reform and transatlantic policy alignment—in the majority but not all instances (i.e. not in capital requirements for securities, insurance, and company law). Thus the power-based approach not only incorrectly predicts the probability of transatlantic alignment but also offers no mechanism to explain subsector variance.

Is the great power preference alignment better conceived as a function of organized international firms? Evidence runs counter to such arguments. First, the firm influence account has difficulties in explaining variance in transatlantic alignment across subsectors as organized international firms have constant incentives during the period under study. Second, leading political actors in Europe were not captured by industry. Even Daniel Mügge's careful study, which emphasizes the importance of the largest international banks in Europe's financial regulatory overhaul, supports our claim. With its attention to transnational public–private alliances, Mügge's argument maintains that the policy entrepreneur behind the FSAP, the European Commission, "had already reached its position in favour of further integration" (Mügge 2010: 93–4). Third, at the time of the EU reforms, cross-Atlantic private sector coordination hardly existed. Once EU policy-makers decided to move ahead with the legislative agenda, US banks were first to lobby (Wicks 2005)—a fact that triggered angry reactions from their poorly organized European counterparts. Unable to sway EU policy-makers to their satisfaction, US banks turned to the US Congress, Treasury, and the SEC for help.[53] When the extraterritorial effects of EU and US legislation sparked regulatory conflicts, US and EU firms were sometimes on opposing sides.

Finally, the public–private alliance between the biggest banks, the European Commission, and "Northern" governments comprised the anchor of the broad European coalition of reformers in longstanding political battles over financial regulation. Clearly, this camp did better than the competing one.[54] The evidence from our study, however, shows that the reformists did not win every battle; and that international soft law played a significant role across cases in bolstering their relative bargaining power. In the absence of soft law, it is hard to imagine that the European Union would have gone nearly as far in the direction as it did.

In sum, at the end of the millennium, the European Union faced a number of pressures to modernize its financial architecture. Nevertheless, reformist policy-makers managed entrenched institutional and sectoral differences (e.g. universal versus fragmented banking, fair value versus historical value accounting, anti-trust versus competition policy, and interlocking directorates versus independent boards to name a few), which generated preference heterogeneity across the member states and frequently sham standards or policy failure internally. How this reform program was resolved and on what terms played a critical role not only for Europe but also for cooperation globally. While hardly a monocausal pathway, as demonstrated by the case of financial instruments, our evidence strongly supports the claim that the availability of international soft law increased the probability of reform. Standards created in earlier periods with significant input from US regulatory actors, provided reformist factions in later periods with important leverage in domestic debates. This pattern holds whether the soft law was created in the late 1980s or at the turn of the millennium. In appealing to the legitimacy of soft law, reformists navigated the delicate politics of member state divisions while at the same time (sometimes unintentionally) promoting preference alignment globally.

[53] Author interview with senior staff, US House of Representatives, Washington, DC, May 6, 2004.

[54] Quaglia identifies two main coalitions: a market-making coalition that more or less corresponds to Mügge's and a market-shaping coalition (2010).

International soft law as a vehicle of US regulation and influence?

One lingering question is whether US regulators intentionally used international soft law to bring about EU convergence to US approaches. Such a proposition, which depicts soft law as merely a US tool for transforming European financial arrangements rather than a source of independent, temporal effects, too often engages in ex post analysis and, in important cases, makes incredulous assumptions about the ability of actors to strategize into the future.

Starting with the Basel I accord of the late 1980s, US policy-makers sought to require foreign banks to hold similar levels of reserve capital as US banks. Yet although scholarly accounts mention German banks, the primarily target were Japanese (Kapstein 1994; Solomon 1995; Oatley and Nabors 1998; Solomon 1995). More to the point, as described in Chapter 3, US authorities had a range of motivations for spearheading the risk-weighted assessments contained in Basel I. Chief among them (especially for the Fed) was the possibility of outflanking domestic regulatory rivals.

A decade later, when the European Commission first proposed the FSAP, no one in Europe, let alone across the Atlantic, anticipated the concatenated factors that would produce the most comprehensive episode of regional harmonization and transatlantic alignment. The project commenced at a time when US financial regulatory strategy vis-à-vis transnational bodies was not focused on Europe. US authorities during this period supported the enhancement of transnational standards and bodies as tools for reforming "crony" financial systems of Asian and other "emerging" markets in the wake of the Asian financial crisis (Blustein 2003).

The lack of US attention to Europe is understandable, given the record of regional integration failures. European policy-makers had launched a remarkably similar legislative program in 1985, which fell woefully short of the "single financial market" goal (Story and Walter 1997). In 1995, when the European Commission proposed EU adoption of international accounting standards, for example, US officials had good reason to doubt the plan would ever come to fruition. Two earlier pieces of EU accounting standards legislation (the Fourth [1978] and Seventh [1983] Company Law Directives) had accomplished little. For much of the 1990s, pressure from the New York Stock Exchange to maintain US market competitiveness, not the prospect of EU emulation, drove intermittent SEC interest in IOSCO and IASC. SEC officials assumed that it was a matter of time before US GAAP would become the global standard (Levitt 2001).

US officials misjudged and misperceived EU reforms in other ways in the late 1990s. The European Union's Financial Conglomerates Directive is a case in point as explained by a US Treasury official:

> The atmosphere surrounding the initial meeting was charged with suspicions by some market participants that EC officials wanted to "push back"...The initial

> meeting between the US and EU experts did not confirm these concerns, but dispelled them.[55]

The lack of strategic action on the part of US authorities notwithstanding, it is still possible that soft law functions as a subtle mechanism diffusing US structural power. The evidence from careful process tracing suggests a more complex picture. A theme across the chapters of this book is that the United States (like other countries and the European Union) does not operate as a unitary polity in transnational regulatory bodies, and "American" positions often reflect one side in unsettled domestic political battles. In the case of Basel II, a split developed between commitments made by US representatives in international negotiations and an opposing coalition of the FDIC and small and medium-sized banks. Moreover, political battles over regulation continue both inside the United States and in transnational bodies. For example, the SEC won a major fight over the IASB's governance structure in 1999 (Martinez-Diaz 2005), yet FASB and IASB are different standard-setting organizations and have different degrees of autonomy from political influences. Nothing guarantees that IFRS will reflect the SEC's preferences in the future; and transnational standards do not change in lock step with US reforms.

Is the European Union a Special Case?

The core of the chapter focuses on the interaction between international soft law and internal politics in the European Union. While it is beyond the scope of the book to conduct fully fleshed out case studies of other countries, the interaction between the Basel Committee and Japan and China supports the more general significance of our argument. The scholarship examining the relationship between global capital adequacy rules and Japan has circled around questions of compliance. Most of the earliest research emphasized the coercive pressure deployed by the United States and the United Kingdom to force competitive adjustment by Japanese banks (Kapstein 1994; Oatley and Nabors 1998). More recent evidence, however, suggests that because of deft Japanese negotiation tactics as well as mock compliance behavior the competitive effect of Basel was initially much less than US or British firms and governments had expected (Tamura 2005; Chey 2014). In particular, Japanese authorities successfully negotiated to allow banks to count 45 percent of unrealized capital gains on securities holdings as reserve capital. Given Japanese accounting rules, which relied on purchase price rather than market value,

[55] Author correspondence with US Treasury official, May 31, 2006.

Japanese banks were well positioned in the late 1980s to meet Basel rules with little adjustment (Tamura 2003).

While international pressure contributed to Japanese adoption of Basel rules and compliance, it was probably less than the United States and the United Kingdom had hoped. A second vein of research suggests a critical interaction between international soft law and domestic politics (Pempel 1999). Reminiscent of the EU case, reform-minded factions within Japan used the Basel process to transform the financial regulatory infrastructure. For much of the post-war period, Japanese finance was organized around a tightly regulated semi-cartel. Known as the convoy system, the arrangement had high barriers to entry and other rent-generating protectionist mechanisms, underpinned by a Ministry of Finance guarantee against bank failure. In short, rents inherent to the system were distributed across competitive and non-competitive banks with an implicit bailout guarantee offered by the state (Rosenbluth 1989; Amyx 2004). Politicians supported the system because it sustained small and medium-sized banks in their districts and thereby patronage politics (Rosenbluth and Thies 2001).

The convoy system worked quite well during the period of global capital controls and Japanese reconstruction as it helped to dampen competition and allow for long-term investments in the industrial revival (Zysman 1983). With the internationalization of finance, however, Japanese firms began to take on additional risks, exacerbating the Ministry of Finance's exposure to moral hazards.[56] Regulation of the convoy system had relied on administrative procedures and lacked prescriptive capital adequacy rules. Moreover, the system's politicized nature complicated the Ministry's ability to supervise banks. In fact, through the 1970s and early 1980s, the Ministry repeatedly attempted to press for legislation that would formalize capital requirements but found itself continually rebuffed by the ruling Liberal Democratic Party (LDP) (Amyx 2004).

In line with our argument, the Ministry of Finance used the Basel process to nudge Japanese financial regulation away from the relational approach associated with the convoy system toward an arm's-length, rules-based one. The Ministry argued that the Basel rules had altered the reversion point for Japanese banks as they would face new global regulation and cautioned that there would be reputational consequences without reform (Tamura 2003: 236). The Ministry used the reputation of Basel to justify its regulatory agenda. As Tamura explains, "The Basel Accord legitimized the MoF's domestic effort to give Japanese capital rules a legal basis" (2003: 236). The Ministry's effort led to the 1992 revision of the Banking Law, which for the first time included

[56] Robin Pauley and David Lascellee, "Banking Regulations Accord May be Delayed," *Financial Times*, November 7, 1987, 20.

statutory capital requirements. Equally important, it put the Japanese regulatory system onto a new trajectory that while not completely converging with US or European rules, altered the relationship between banks and their governors (Walter 2006). Regardless of Japanese compliance with Basel rules, it is clear that a regulatory faction used Basel to disrupt the domestic politics of banking.

A brief assessment of existing research on China, a newly rising financial power, also suggests policy entrepreneurs outside the European context have used soft law in similar ways. Because of the inwardly focused and statist financial sector, Chinese officials had little interaction with the Basel process until the end of the twentieth century. With China's WTO accession and its central role in global supply chains, the Chinese financial sector confronted the limits of the state-run system in which political considerations largely determined capital allocation (Naughton 2007). As Shih (2008) argues, two general factions tussled: one wanting to continue using state-owned banks to drive short to medium-term growth and the other seeking reforms to bring about medium- to long-term stability within a financial sector increasingly plagued by cronyism and corruption.

The creation in 2003 of the China Banking Regulatory Commission (CBRC) marked the rising relevance of the reformists. Until then, the central bank, the People's Bank of China (PBC), had been the primary bank regulator but had prioritized monetary policy over bank regulation. With the creation of the CBRC, the government gave greater weight to bank surveillance and compliance (Pearson 2005; Naughton 2007). Not an independent agency in the transatlantic tradition, the CBRC delicately balanced competing political interests. On the one hand, state banks, state-owned enterprises (SOEs), and local governments had interests in maintaining control over the allocation of capital and independence from centralized oversight. On the other hand, a reform-minded faction within the Central Party, concerned about the growth of non-performing loans and the potential destabilizing effects of banking crises, saw the dangers of excessive credit allocation and continued politicization of the financial services sector.

The CBRC used the Basel process and capital adequacy rules to elevate its standing and to improve the chances of realizing its agenda. Participation and eventual official membership in the Basel Committee helped to give the Commission the stature of other prominent political actors within China. The CBRC also used the legitimacy of the Basel Committee's soft law and processes to promote capital adequacy requirements. Such rules, which the reformist faction supported as an important mechanism to root out corruption by local governments and SOEs, injected new levels of reporting and transparency into the domestic financial system. As Chao Xi (2014: 87) concludes:

> Basel III, portrayed as international best practices in banking regulation and an international agreement that binds China, would lend to the CBRC the authority and legitimacy necessary for it to fulfill its regulatory mandates. But for Basel III, the CBRC would find it very difficult to put in place and enforce capital rules that apparently are not in line with powerful, organized vested interests... Capital standards favored by the CBRC would presumably face a lesser degree of domestic resistance should they be endorsed and adopted by Basel III and become 'international banking standards'.

By arguing the Basel rules were politically neutral and international best practice, these Chinese reformists, echoing claims made in Europe a few years before, enhanced their hand in the contentious politics surrounding the domestic regulatory system (Shih 2008; Foot and Walter 2010; Walter 2010). While debate continues as to the extent of Chinese compliance with Basel rules, the evidence indicates that soft law has nonetheless had a decisive role in domestic transformation.

Conclusion

This chapter addresses a core question in political economy: What explains regulatory preference alignment (or fragmentation) in a world of rising economic powers? Given differences in models of capitalism across the advanced economies, such alignment should be particularly difficult and indeed has proven so in many domains—yet not in pre-crisis finance. The chapter thus illustrates the book's major theoretical themes about the second-order consequences of soft law over time. When the European Union sought to reform internal governance, reform-minded actors borrowed extensively from the existing palette of soft law and used it as a political resource to legitimize their positions and overcome blocking factions. Where reformists were successful, their actions supported transatlantic alignment.

This chapter also highlights the interaction between soft law and regional integration in Europe. Many existing studies on soft law focus on national stories, e.g. the Bank of England or SIB versus the US FRB or SEC (Oatley and Nabors 1998; Singer 2007). The evidence here demonstrates how European integration itself played a decisive role—by forcing reform-oriented actors to navigate among national, international, and regional alternatives. European actors had to weigh the costs and benefits of national divergence, unique European approaches, and harmonized international rules. The uncertainty and potential for international regulatory fragmentation from homegrown European rules enhanced the attractiveness of international solutions. The Commission and others routinely fueled these fears, underscoring the critical role of regional-level dynamics in fostering transatlantic alignment (Coleman and Underhill 1995). Thus the success of bodies like BCBS, IASB, or IOSCO, often unintentionally, depended on the timing of reforms within the European Union and ultimately on the rhetorical skills of policy entrepreneurs. The European Commission, for its part as the leading reformist, found itself, on the one hand, empowered to break long-running stalemates among member states but, on the other hand, pressured to abandon much of its own rule-development authority in areas like accounting standards.

The chapter's findings also serve to broaden our understanding of what soft law is and does. They do so by illustrating important effects beyond those emphasized in the literature. Extensive research argues that transnational financial regulatory networks are better understood as ideologically charged purveyors of neoliberal ideas (Nölke and Perry 2008; Mügge 2011a; Tsingou 2015). Much of the soft law generated by financial standard-setting bodies during the period under study certainly reflects a dogmatic version of regulatory liberalism (Mügge 2011a)—but not all of it. And in cases where the standards are not particularly finance-friendly, international soft law still generates the kinds of policy feedback discussed above. For example, international soft law concerning capital reserves for banks had similar effects inside Europe before (Basel I) and after (Basel II) the neoliberal turn (see Chapter 5). In one of our seven cases, moreover, the Joint Forum principles for supervising conglomerates are not especially neoliberal.

Likewise, scholars often depict international soft law as a technical and functional solution to cross-border coordination problems. Our findings support research that reveals the deeply political context of transnational rule-making and the interlinkages between international soft law and domestic regulatory conflicts. Jurisdictions do not necessarily adopt soft law primarily out of concern for smoothing the regulatory bumps to cross-border finance. Rather, the creation of soft law—a reflection of but not reducible to US regulatory approaches—gave rise to an important and largely unintentional second-order effect, which reduced preference heterogeneity between the United States and the potential challenger. The reason? When the European Union sought to reform internal governance, policy entrepreneurs borrowed the perceived legitimacy of existing soft law to win longstanding regional regulatory battles. In short, international soft law offered a politically expedient solution to an internal political conflict.

5

Arena Expansion and the Transnationalization of Business Advocacy

This chapter considers international soft law's second-order effects on another set of powerful actors: associations of financial services companies. Any discussion of financial regulation would be incomplete without mentioning the power and influence of these organized business interests. Since the 2008 financial crisis, the point seems obvious. Documentaries, political campaigns, and media exposés[1] have all cast the spotlight on big corporations, especially banks, and their lobbyists, depicting them as the main culprits behind faulty domestic financial regulation in the United States and Europe. The specter of industry influence has been used to justify every conceivable reform from greater stakeholder input, to more invasive supervision, to the substitution of independent regulators with increased market competition. As for the scholarship on financial regulation, much of it revolves around the concept of "regulatory capture," a widely used label describing the success of businesses in shaping the rules to reflect narrow industry interests over those of the broader public (Stigler 1971; Pagliari 2012b; Carpenter and Moss 2013).

Accusations of regulatory capture have certainly sparked contentious debate about the influence of transnational financial lobbies over international soft law. Most analysts agree that private sector actors have resource advantages—rooted in expertise, international mobility, cozy government ties—and play an outsized role in shaping international soft law (Underhill and Zhang 2008; Seabrooke and Tsingou 2009; Culpepper 2015). While the extent to which these resources amount to "structural" versus "instrumental" power remains controversial (Andrews 1994; Culpepper 2015; Fairfield 2015), financial services lobbies are not just another interest group. Nonetheless, mirroring findings of the broader political science literature on regulatory

[1] See, for example, the movie *The Inside Job* (2010) or Matt Taibbi, "The Great American Bubble Machine," *Rolling Stone*, April 5, 2010.

capture (Vogel 1983; Baumgartner et al. 2009), scholars differ over the extent to which international soft law merits the label of regulatory capture, with some showcasing it as an exemplary case (Underhill and Zhang 2008; Lall 2012; Tsingou 2015) and others finding a more complex pattern of business influence over rule-making (Mattli and Woods 2009; Young 2012; McKeen-Edwards and Porter 2013).

This chapter takes a different tack, cutting across the competing positions on regulatory capture and using the Basel Committee on Banking Supervision (BCBS) and Institute of International Finance (IIF) as the prime illustration. Our temporal focus raises important, puzzling, and largely unexplored questions. What explains change in the priorities of business associations and why does the importance and influence of particular lobby organizations rise and fall over time? What accounts for new layers of industry representation and contestation at the transnational level and what are their political effects?

For answers, we build on the ideas developed in Chapter 2, arguing that the development of transnational regulatory arenas alters the ecology of interest group representation and the purpose, organization, and power of individual industry associations. Transnational arena expansion undermines traditional two-level politics whereby firms organize and lobby within territorially bounded jurisdictions and then national (and regional in the European Union's case) public officials negotiate an international regime (Putnam 1988; Evans et al. 1993). The political effects, we argue, are often disruptive and include new complexity, including simultaneous and interacting national and transnational sites of contention (Abbott et al. 2016). International soft law and the arenas where it is created reorient lobbying organizations and provide opportunities for those industry associations able to engage directly in the new transnational political arena. These new sites of contention produce asymmetries among industry associations, as some will be better positioned to adjust and to shape and engage in transnational arenas (Farrell and Newman 2014, 2016).

Turning to the chapter's empirical illustrations, academic interest to date has centered on the industry-friendly imprint of the IIF (frequently singled out as the most important contemporary global financial services lobby[2]) on the 2004 (and to a lesser degree 2013) Basel Committee accords (Tsingou 2003; Underhill and Zhang 2008; Lall 2012). By contrast, we investigate the transformation of the IIF and its agenda between the 1988 and 2004 Basel accords—a development that altered the ecology of financial services industry associations and the nature of financial regulatory politics. The IIF went from primarily providing economic data to commercial banks, to concentrating on

[2] McKeen-Edwards and Porter (2013: 38) write, "Its sheer size and global representation make it the most important TFA (Transnational Financial Association) in the world today."

regulatory policy at the transnational level. What, we ask in this chapter, explains the transformation of the IIF from a struggling organization with no regulatory agenda, lobbying skills, or access to the negotiations preceding the 1988 Basel accord, into the world's most influential financial industry advocate, directly engaging transnational forums fifteen years later?

By demonstrating that the disruptive effects of arena expansion (the move to multiple competing rule-making settings at the domestic and transnational level) account for the crucial case of the IIF's transformation better than competing explanations, the chapter's evidence gives important support to the book's arguments about soft law's second-order effects. In brief, a multitude of factors contributed to the IIF's ascendance and its new access to transnational rule-making. However, the evidence presented here highlights the primary causal role played by second-order effects of the 1988 Basel accord, one of the first uses of financial regulatory soft law. In reaction to the perceived importance of the early Basel process and the BCBS's need for private sector expertise and relationships, the IIF leaders saw an opportunity to reverse the organization's decline. They understood that the IIF was well positioned within the field of industry associations to become a "neutral" vehicle for meeting the particular informational needs of the new rule-makers. With the reorientation toward Basel underway, IIF's leadership reformed the organization's mission, purpose, and bylaws to attract investment banks and other new members. A resuscitated organization with replenished resources and new capacities, the IIF became the Basel Committee's most important industry interlocutor and the leading transnational industry lobby, advancing the interests of its new membership-base of investment and money-center banks. In short, soft law's second-order effects catalyzed the expansion of regulatory politics to the transnational level, becoming a primary cause of the IIF's transformation into a transnational advocacy organization focused on regulation.

These findings are based on a structured temporal analysis that examines event chains, evaluates the merits of alternative explanations, and uses an empirical record rooted in original interviews and primary documents. The chapter also probes beyond the case of the IIF as a preliminary assessment of the argument's explanatory potential.

Arena Expansion and Three Propositions about the Structuring of Business Representation

A long line of research demonstrates the importance of *national* institutions shaping industry representation (Berger 1983; Vogel 1983; Pierson 1993). Chapter 4 illustrates the structuring effects of soft law—an international institution—on internal political battles over financial regulatory legislation in second-mover polities. In this chapter, we ask whether international soft law also has disruptive effects on powerful financial services interests. Our evidence suggests in critical cases it does.

The narrative presented in this chapter gives substantial support to three logical expectations, derived from Chapter 2's theoretical framework, in answer to the following question: What are likely temporal effects on industry lobby associations of creating international soft law? First, some industry associations will reorient themselves toward the new level of contestation; the advent of international soft law thus spurs a shift from nationally oriented advocacy organizations filtered through domestic political institutions to direct transnational lobbies. Second, in terms of the timing, soft law catalyzes the transnational organization of business representation. Rather than the reorganization of industry representation preceding soft law's creation, the latter prompts the change in representation. Third, and finally, business associations that do well in the new rule-making arena undergo internal changes to facilitate interactions with transnational rule-makers, improve capacities to supply the type of information and expertise demanded, and otherwise enhance their ability to influence the agenda set out by soft law generating bodies. We expect transnational business associations to take on the agenda of soft law bodies, rather than generate it, and to make reforms in accordance with the procedures, norms, and needs of the rule-makers.

Arena expansion is the label we use for these hypothesized mechanisms by which soft law has second-order effects. In the remaining sections of the chapter, we examine the extent to which the logic of arena expansion explains the IIF's transformation and whether such an explanation does better against the evidence than two leading and competing alternatives: arguments attributing the organization of industry interests to structural power and material interests of business (Lindblom 1977; Andrews 1994; Block and Piven 2010; Culpepper 2015; Fairfield 2015), on the one hand, and to the hegemonic power of the United States, on the other (Simmons 2001; Drezner 2007).

The IIF is a crucial case. In terms of real-world importance, a theoretical framework must be able to explain the IIF's transformation because it is regularly identified in existing scholarship as the leading industry lobby shaping transnational rule-making (Underhill and Zhang 2008; McKeen-Edwards and Porter 2013). And the Basel accords, for their part, offer the most important example of international financial soft law (Kapstein 1994; Oatley and Nabors 1998; Wood 2005; Singer 2007; Claessens et al. 2008; Lall 2012; Young 2012). If soft law is having the effects we attribute to it, therefore, we must be able to show in the empirical record a link between the Basel accords and the IIF's transformation. Of course, the empirical evaluation of a single instance of arena expansion has obvious theoretical limitations. Within the chapter's narrative, we thus explore the argument's validity in a few significant shadow cases, including industry representation in the securities domain and the International Swaps and Derivatives Association (ISDA).

Backdrop to the IIF's Transformation: The Creation of International Soft Law

The emergence of direct transnational lobbying by financial industry associations—and the IIF's transformation and ascendance, in particular—begins with the creation of international banking soft law. As discussed in Chapter 3, soft law's origins in this domain fit a typical pattern. With the rising internationalization of finance, governments and regulators began to cooperate to limit contagion from failing banks and manage cross-border regulatory friction. For reasons of political expedience, tied to internal US dynamics, cooperation took the form of common capital adequacy requirements devised by the Basel Committee.

Capital adequacy rules regulate the size of financial reserves that banks must have on hand in case of a crisis. While capital reserves offer an important rainy day fund, more than one approach exists for determining appropriate levels and, in the late 1980s, the decision to use one approach over another had political ramifications. The Basel I accord by and large reflected the Federal Reserve Board's preferred risk-weighting assessment model, as opposed to its US rivals' competing firm-inspection approach, and thus should be seen, at least at one level, as an extension of a US policy conflict and a political victory of sorts for the Fed. The adoption in Basel of the risk-weighting approach also created incentives for banks and other financial firms to adopt unintended and sometimes perverse risk-taking behavior.

The creation of the Basel I standards was political in another sense. Capital reserve requirements have sizable implications for financial industry competitiveness. In a world where many banks, regardless of the location of incorporation, compete for the same customers, the firms from jurisdictions with lower capital requirements have more funds available for generating revenues than those from markets with higher standards. US firms became increasingly squeezed between stricter domestic regulations and global, particularly Japanese and German, competitors, who enjoyed relatively lower capital adequacy rules (Oatley and Nabors 1998; Singer 2007).

Regulatory harmonization using soft law, in the form of the Basel Committee's 1988 Basel accord (Basel I), provided a mechanism for managing the perceived dangers posed by regulatory arbitrage in the newly interdependent banking markets. It established common standards for capital adequacy that were then to be adopted across the advanced industrial economies (Wood 2005; Tarullo 2008).

The creation of new standards raised two issues for banks. First, there was the issue of whether to level the playing field, which pitted stringently regulated banks against laxly regulated ones. Lenders, particularly from countries with high levels of regulation, hoped to harmonize rules to protect their competitive position. Second, there were fights about the appropriate level, which was often a battle between profit-minded banks and stability-minded authorities. Although harmonization offers an appealing goal for firms seeking one set of rules, most banks sought to limit the cost of adjustment. While scholars have argued that Basel I represents an attempt by the United States and the United Kingdom to level the playing field to protect their banks from the new Japanese and German challengers, British and American bankers voiced deep concerns about the agreement and fiercely opposed many of its provisions.

The old politics of banking regulation: interdependent markets but national politics

During the lead-up to Basel I, the organization of United States, European, and Japanese banking interests fragmented along national lines despite the increased internationalization of credit markets. Rather than lobbying the Basel Committee directly, banks interacted with their respective national supervisors, who in turn represented the country in the committee. This period of regulatory politics reflects a two-level game frequently depicted in Open Economy studies of trade, in which national interest groups engage their national domestic political institutions to shape the bargaining position of national negotiators (Evans et al. 1993; Lake 2009). Singer (2007: 20), for example, describes global financial cooperation of this period as a domestic game. Officials faced the regulator's "dilemma" balancing stability—and the threat of punishment by their political principals—against competitiveness—and the threat of lobbying by domestic interest groups. The influence of industry lobbying over global cooperation, according to Singer, should be understood by focusing on domestic-level politics and contestation.

Two noteworthy observations pertain to the relative absence of direct industry lobbying of the Basel Committee during this period. The first is that, despite having internationalized their businesses by the late 1980s, the large money center banks lacked the transnational organization that might have helped them to engage the process. National trade associations, whose constitutions, mission statements, and traditions remained focused on domestic governments and members, were not positioned to work across countries to engage the transnational rule-making process and still saw advantage in historical ties to local authorities (Grossman 2004).[3] Contrary to prominent power and material interests of business arguments, the organizational forms of industry representation did not automatically adjust as banking revenues internationalized. As the CEO of Commerzbank, Klaus-Peter Müller mused in 2007, "I believe that the influence of the IIF can only be understood if you go back into the founding years of the Institute when we simply had not a single voice speaking on behalf of the international banking community. We had national banking federations and associations . . . but for the global community of financial institutions there was no voice."[4]

The second reason for firms to concentrate on national lobbying, as established in the secondary literature, is that Basel's network of central bankers and other supervisors still preferred to deliberate in a setting cordoned off from direct industry interactions. "We don't like publicity," Huib Muller, a former Basel Committee chairman, explained in a 1988 speech. "We prefer, I might say, our hidden secret world of the supervisory continent."[5] This position is a reflection of the bureaucratic politics of the Basel Committee, whose members guarded interactions with their respective national banks and did not yet have a set of procedures through which direct private sector input could be delivered to the committee as a whole, without giving the impression of regulatory capture.[6]

This image of Basel I as a nationally mediated event receives support from a number of different perspectives. At the transnational level, the Basel Committee did not directly engage private sector interests through open and transparent consultations. Moreover, the committee's proposals were internally developed and avoided significant external input during the agenda-setting phase. In his far-ranging history of the Basel Committee, Goodhart concludes that "there is no evidence at all that the BCBS, as an international institution, was captured by the large international banks in these years (1975–97)" (Goodhart 2011: 417). Critics of the network characterized this period of governance as the pure technocratic phase, in which a narrow group of public sector officials from core markets (particularly the United States and the United Kingdom) steered the outputs of networks (Underhill 1995). Structured input from the banking community was instead ushered through domestic channels whereby national supervisors consulted directly with their respective banks (Wood 2005: 78; Goodhart 2011: 413).

[3] Author interview with former IIF StaffA, Washington, DC, 2016.

[4] Quoted in IIF (2007: 139).

[5] Huib Muller, "Address to International Conference of Bank Supervisors," May 16, 1988. Quoted in Porter (1993: 66).

[6] Author interview with former IIF StaffA, Washington, DC, 2016.

The internal politics of the United States provides additional evidence of the two-level game at work. As the initial Basel proposal was put on the table, a core group of money center banks in the United States conducted a fierce yet unsuccessful campaign to alter the agreement. They feared that its requirement that banks raise additional capital would put them at a competitive disadvantage vis-à-vis international competition and regional US banks. For example, the leading US banks warned the Federal Reserve of "betraying" the industry's interests (Reinicke 1995: 178). Charles Schumer, representing a New York district with ties to Wall Street, was among the banks' advocates and led a series of hearings that decried the proposed accord as "plac[ing] American banks at a competitive disadvantage to their foreign counterparts" (Reinicke 1995: 176). Nevertheless, US regulatory authorities used the two-level politics to their advantage. As Reinicke observes, "The importance of the international dimension of the agreement, and the degree to which domestic policy maneuverability had become limited in order to maintain the agreement, became evident... The protests by U.S. banks and Congress had little effect and only a few minor changes were made" (Reinicke 1995: 178–9). Regulators successfully used the two-level nature of the negotiations to bolster their position as they could argue that revisions at this point would threaten the delicate nature of the international bargain that had already been struck.

Writing in 2008, Daniel Tarullo, former member of the National Economic Council and Governor at the Federal Reserve Bank, captures the point:

> The negotiation itself followed a familiar pattern: Countries exercised available sources of leverage to prod other countries into agreement on the basic contours of their proposal; certain compromises for particularized national interests were made along the way; and the interests of banks were, to a greater or lesser extent, mediated through their own countries' supervisors on the Basel Committee.
>
> (Tarullo 2008: 100)

A declining organization

The politics of banking regulation changed radically in the period surrounding the 2004 Basel accord, and a key component of the change is the emergence of transnational interest groups lobbying the Basel Committee directly, with the Institute of International Finance as the most important in the field. On the surface, the IIF was an unlikely candidate for becoming the leading transnational financial services association.

Founded in 1982 in response to the developing country debt crisis, the IIF originally provided economic data, surveillance, and forecasting to commercial banks that felt they lacked sufficient information to evaluate sovereign debt. At the time, much of the information on sovereign debt produced by the

IMF and BIS was not made readily available to the private sector.[7] Commercial banks, including smaller ones, sought an independent third party for information regarding sovereign debt. The IIF describes the situation: "Many of the larger, money-center banks . . . are perceived as being guarded with their information . . . The smaller banks, which do not have the same resources available for in-depth economic analysis, may feel led astray by the larger banks."[8] Filling the need, the IIF's core function was the collection and processing of sensitive public and private sector financial data including sovereign budgets and economic figures regarding the health of banks and banking sectors across the globe.[9] By contrast to the business power argument, the IIF did not engage significantly in regulatory policy issues or advocacy during the run-up to Basel I. Rather than identifying common member bank interests and pressing for transnational rules to facilitate cross-border exchange, the IIF's changes to its membership and priorities only came later, in response to the Basel I process.[10]

By the early 1990s, the IIF faced a serious organizational challenge. The Brady Plan of 1989 had resolved much of the debt crisis and many small commercial banks had left the organization or merged with larger banks.[11] As the IIF explains (2007: 142):

> The successful implementation of the Brady Plan ended the debt crisis of the 1980s. It also posed formidable challenges to the leadership of the IIF, which until now had seen resolution of the debt crisis as a raison d'être of the Institute. There was a need to review the organization's mission, which was made all the more pressing by declining membership.

At the same time, the IMF and BIS gradually opened up information to private actors, undercutting the value of IIF surveillance activities. US bank representation fell from forty banks in 1987 to eighteen by 1993. Overall membership declined from 167 full members in 1987 to 135 members in 1991. By the IIF's own account, the organization faced a crisis in the late 1980s as its primary mission had evaporated (IIF 2007).

The Endogenous Sources of Organizational Transformation

The following sections explain the transformation of the IIF from a near defunct organization to a powerful transnational business lobby. We attribute

[7] Author interview with former IIF StaffB, Washington, DC, 2016. See also IIF (2007: 3).

[8] Institute of International Finance, Annual Report. Washington, DC, 2002.

[9] Paul Taylor, "Banks to establish 'commercial IMF' to monitor lending," *Financial Times*, October 26, 1982.

[10] Author interview with IIF StaffA, Washington, DC, 2016.

[11] As a former staff member(B) of the IIF explained to the author, "When you solve a problem like the Latin American Debt crisis, what do you need the IIF for?" Author interview with former IIF StaffB, Washington, DC, 2016.

the IIF's change to an endogenous process that the Basel Committee and its original accord sparked and shaped. The IIF leaders, hoping to revive the organization, saw in Basel I the opportunity to expand its membership and resources. Tapping into investment and money center banks' complaints about Basel I and their desire to shape future revisions through direct lobbying, IIF's leadership changed its mission from economic surveillance to advocacy of transnational banking regulation, created capacities to generate expertise, and overhauled its internal organizational structure to bolster its effectiveness as a transnational lobby. Unlike other industry associations like the ISDA with its brazen lobbying style, the IIF was able to gain access to the Basel process by presenting itself as a trusted and capable source of information. The IIF thus transformed itself as an organization, using the Basel agenda to enhance its own relevance. By creating a political lobby that could directly interact with the Basel Committee without going through national political processes and banking supervisors, the new IIF also altered the nature of contestation, the politics of banking regulation, and the ecology of business interest groups.

A strategy for organizational revival

In the face of organizational decline, the IIF leadership recognized that they had to increase revenues by expanding membership, and in so doing, behaved as policy entrepreneurs might be expected to do in competitive ecologies of organizations (Fligstein 2001; Sell 2003; Posner 2005, 2009b). That said, the evolving effects of the Basel I accord shaped the IIF leaders' three main strategies for organizational revival: the targeting of large investment and money center banks as potential members; a comprehensive reorientation toward transnational regulatory policy efforts; and a reinvention and reorganization of the IIF to become the leading private sector interlocutor to the Basel Committee. In a nutshell, the Basel Committee's encroachment into new domains made large investment and money center banks with investment banking businesses obvious potential members. The enterprising IIF leaders, including the then chair of the organization, Barry Sullivan, and managing directors, Horst Schulmann and Charles Dallara, seeking to make IIF attractive to these banks, took a radical transnational and regulatory turn and instituted an internal overhaul to meet the Basel Committee's informational needs and align with its agenda. In the rest of this section, we describe each of the three Basel-induced IIF strategies for organizational revival.

First, the new direction of BCBS activity in the wake of the Basel I accord explains why of all potential members in the expansive financial services industries IIF leaders homed in on investment and money center banks. Given the sectoral nature of international financial regulation, the 1988 accord applied primarily to commercial banks. While a main purpose of the accord was to level the playing field, the leveling, whatever its faults, occurred more within the commercial banking sector than across different financial services sectors. Capital adequacy requirements harmonized behavior of commercial banks but not investment banks and non-bank financial services companies. With this limited reach of capital reserve rules, commercial banks had an incentive to move financial activities into investment vehicles that were not technically considered part of commercial banks. In this way, Basel I spurred the growth of less regulated financial products traditionally offered by investment houses and non-banks such as securitized mortgages and Collateralized Loan Obligations (Thiemann 2014).

These new market trends prompted a reaction from the Basel Committee itself. Concerned about the new risks associated with the entrance of commercial banks into less regulated markets traditionally occupied by investment banks, the Basel Committee proposed a set of amendments to the original accord (Wood 2005; Thiemann 2014). It started to chip away at the regulatory walls between commercial banks and investment firms. In doing so, Basel-based standard setting became important to investment banks, money center banks, and other financial services companies engaged in these markets, sparking a heightened demand for direct representation, access, and influence in Basel. Investment banks had another reason for wanting greater influence over transnational rule-making. The US Securities and Exchange Commission, which had long resisted international capital adequacy rules for the securities sector, did not formally sit on the Basel Committee (Coleman and Underhill 1995; Singer 2007). Given the lack of representation of their regulatory supervisor, investment banks found that traditional two-level game models of representation left them relatively weak. Recognizing that the Basel accord had created a pool of potential new members, IIF leaders focused their attention on making their organization attractive to these international banks.

The evolution of the Basel rule-making arena also explains why the IIF leaders adopted their second strategy for organizational revival: reorienting the IIF toward the transnational level and regulatory policies. This followed directly from the first. Having identified investment and money center banks as their primary new member targets, IIF's leaders sought to enhance the organization's relevance to these banks' new concerns about the Basel Committee's expanding regulatory agenda. The strategy meant that the IIF engaged the new transnational rule-making arena directly and added a regulatory advocacy dimension to its traditional functions.[12]

[12] Author interview with former US Treasury Department Official, Brussels, 2008.

In 1990, under the leadership of managing director Schulmann, the IIF formally altered its mission statement to broaden its goals, hoping to appeal to the larger set of firms. Banking regulation advocacy became a new core pillar of the organization alongside national economic surveillance. The executive committee of the organization further emphasized this change with the appointment of Charles Dallara, a longtime US Treasury Department official, as the managing director. He saw the Basel accord and global banking regulation in general as a key way to "grow the company."[13] As a 2007 IIF history explains:

> The Board recognized at this time that such a bold regulatory thrust may have a particular appeal to some of the very large banks that had still not joined the Institute. These banks were perceived as important 'targets' to recruit. A broader agenda of IIF activities and events was seen as part of the strategy to attract these banks…The challenge to the new Managing Director was to find more effective ways to keep the IIF relevant, to expand its influence and to revitalize its membership. Dallara's response came quickly. In the fall of 1993, following intensive discussions with the IIF's Board of Directors, he forged a new agenda for the Institute that would involve increased advocacy… (IIF 2007: 144)

Importantly, the drive to alter the mission and membership of the organization came from the interaction between the IIF's survival instincts and the activities of the Basel Committee, rather than pressure from the industry's material interests, as the business power argument would expect. The IIF continues (2007: 56):

> The BIS and related organizations, including most notably the Basel Committee on Banking Supervision, were the official sector's focal point for global coordination of banking and related regulatory issues. The far-reaching reforms that have ensued have had a profound impact on the Institute's membership. There has been a growing recognition of both the need for, and the potential value to be gained from, enhanced consultation and cooperation on regulatory and supervisory issues between the official sector and the banking community. These developments converged to bring the Institute to the center stage of the global regulatory and supervisory debate.

The IIF's leadership recognized that the shift from economic surveillance to regulatory policy had to happen in order to remain relevant in the ecology of financial services associations. This shift to regulatory advocacy was not anticipated by the organization, as the IIF's history makes clear:

> Unlike its economic work, which was enshrined in the Institute's Articles of Incorporation and envisaged by the "Ditchley Group" as its *raison d'être*, its regulatory policy work was not explicitly anticipated by its founding fathers.

[13] Author interview with former IIF StaffA, Washington, DC, 2016.

> Rather, it developed as a response to the evolving global financial environment and market trends as well as a new Management and Board vision formed in the early 1990s. The Institute's regulatory policy work was first conceived in terms of individual advocacy projects. Despite initial hesitancy on the part of the regulators, especially in Europe, to engage with regulated institutions, growing demand by IIF members for such work spurred the development of a new core activity for the IIF. (IIF 2007: 55–6)

The final strategy for organizational revival centered on deep internal organizational changes. Like the other strategies, the evolution of the Basel rule-making determined the particular changes adopted by the IIF. In 1994, its leaders amended the IIF's bylaws to allow both investment banks and securities firms to become full members and serve on the IIF Board. According to the IIF (2007: 60–1):

> The Institute anticipated that the proposed amendment to the Basel Accord would begin a broader process to align national as well as global banking regulation and supervision with market realities. It also realized that the exercise itself and the resulting changes in the regulatory and supervisory framework would have important implications for the Institute's membership structure. In particular, the proposed amendment gave the Institute a new and greater relevance to the investment banking community. This prompted the Institute to offer access by investment banks to full membership . . . thereby opening the way to their representation on the IIF Board.

To facilitate the new emphasis on Basel-oriented advocacy and to make it easier to impart expertise, information, views, and preferences, the IIF underwent an internal institutional isomorphism in the 1990s, aligning its own organizational structures and policy priorities with those of the Basel Committee.[14] This reform started with the creation in 1991 of the Working Group on Capital Adequacy, the first working group created under the new widened mandate on banking issues. Contrary to an argument emphasizing the material interest of industry, the IIF's shift in agenda reacted to Basel I rather than in anticipation of it. IIF's leaders' aim in revamping the internal organizational structure was to make the IIF a more valuable interlocutor with Basel, a source of expertise and other resources, and a more effective industry advocate—all of which would make it more attractive to its new members.

One of the IIF's chief resources was the information of its member banks.[15] Figuring out how to meet the particular informational needs of the Basel Committee—without revealing proprietary information of competing member

[14] IIF (2007: 69), "Given the significance of the proposals, the IIF developed a formal project structure for this work that paralleled that of the Basel Committee itself." For more on institutional isomorphism see DiMaggio and Powell (1983).

[15] Author interview with former IIF StaffB, Washington, DC, 2016.

banks—turned out to be the single most important achievement of the IIF's internal reorganization. Through its work on economic surveillance, the IIF had demonstrated that it could collect and maintain confidential and sensitive information of its members. It leveraged this reputation to position itself as a valuable resource both to the Basel Committee and its members. Because of the Basel Committee's adopted approach of determining capital requirements through risk-weighted assessments and the general move toward quantitative finance (in which firms used complicated models to manage risk), the committee needed industry data on risk modeling processes and exposures. National sovereignty concerns, bureaucratic politics, and competitive fears of banks prevented Basel Committee members from obtaining easy access to such information. The IIF filled the gap by turning itself into a transnational conduit between the private sector and the Basel Committee.[16] In doing so, the IIF also became the Basel Committee's most important private sector adviser, giving the IIF advantages in the dissemination of its reports and recommendations.

The three-pronged strategy worked. The IIF emerged in the early 1990s as a substantively new organization with a growing membership comprised increasingly of investment banks and non-banks (IIF 2007: 56). In terms of resources, the restructuring led to a near doubling of members and revenue increased by a factor of five (see Figure 5.1). These changes increased the resources available to the organization.

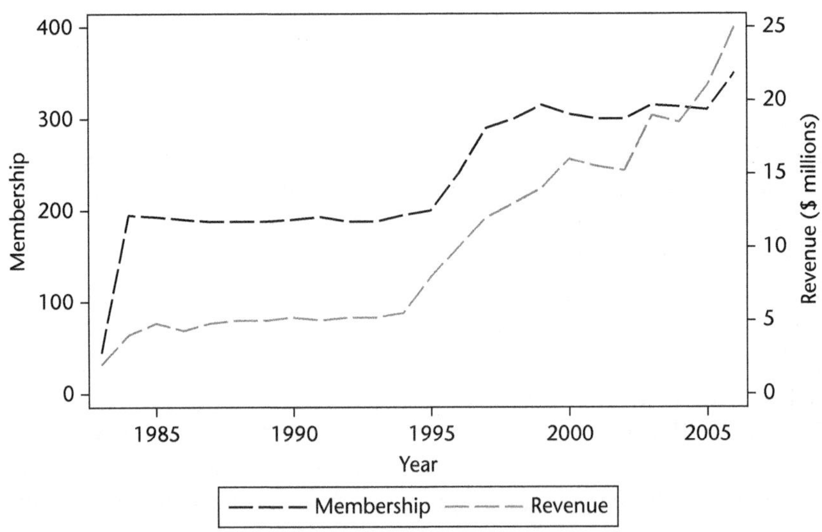

Figure 5.1. IIF membership and revenue, 1983–2006
Source: Institute of International Finance 2007.

[16] Author interview with former IIF StaffA, Washington, DC, 2016.

Enmeshing itself into the new banking regulatory environment created by Basel I, the IIF found a new lease on life. To attract investment banks and other financial firms, the IIF reoriented its activities and reinvented itself as a banking industry association. It assumed a new mission to lobby on regulatory policy at the transnational level and an organizational structure that paralleled the Basel Committee's and enabled it to convey sensitive—but needed—member bank information. The result was the IIF's climb to the world's leading transnational financial services lobby—a transformation attributable to the structuring feedback of the Basel Committee's actions, more than to any other causal factor.

A Story about US Influence?

Upon a superficial examination, it might be tempting to reduce the IIF's strategies and the resulting transformation to the long arm of US hegemonic influence. After all, IIF managing director Dallara was a former US Treasury official, raising questions about whether the IIF Board selected him as part of a general strategy to reorient the organization toward the United States. A closer inspection of the evidence, however, reveals little support for this alternative explanation. Two of the most important reforms—the change in mission and institutional isomorphism—predate Dallara's tenure. They began under the term of Schulmann, a German national, whose career featured stints at the World Bank and the German Bundesbank, rather than any connection to the US government (IIF 2007: 149). Moreover, according to interviews with former IIF staff, the IIF was very serious about serving as the counterpart of the Basel Committee, not the US government, and took great lengths to brand itself as the "neutral" intermediary between the committee and global financial firms.[17] Aligning too closely with the United States would have threatened this role both in the eyes of the Committee and within its global membership.[18]

Two other types of evidence raise serious doubt about the US alignment argument. First, the IIF and the United States had divergent positions on key provisions of Basel II. For example, US regulators sided with BCBS in rejecting IIF's proposals concerning full internal credit risk models (Young, 2012: 11–12) and the Operational Risk Pillar 1 Capital Charge (Young 2012: 15–17). Second, the ex ante preferences of US authorities split on key provisions of Basel II, with the Federal Reserve Board typically closer to the IIF and other industry associations, and the Office of the Comptroller of the Currency and Federal Deposit

[17] Ibid. [18] Ibid.

Insurance Corporation more in line with foreign regulators (Young 2012: 11–12). Finally, and perhaps the most important evidence against the US hegemony proposition, Dallara's professional network does play a vital role in turning the IIF into the leading industry association. Yet it is precisely because his network was broader than US officials and included such foreign authorities as former BCBS chair Tommaso Padoa-Schioppa (Lall 2012: 11) that Dallara and the other IIF leaders were able to grasp the Basel Committee's needs and preferences and make the appropriate internal adjustments.[19]

Soft Law's Uneven Second-Order Effects

The IIF achieved this status and role while other domestic and transnational industry organizations did not. In the ecology of financial services industry associations, the widespread perception of the Basel Committee's new salience altered the terms by which organizations became relevant and effective. It is beyond the scope of the chapter to detail why IIF's competitors were less successful in responding to the new terms. Nevertheless, a theme across associations mentioned in the secondary literature on Basel I and II[20] is that none met the challenge as well as IIF. National associations such as the British Bankers Association faced organizational barriers to operating in transnational space. Their mission statements oriented them toward engaging with respective national governments in two-level game arrangements.[21] They also had difficulty attracting the support and trust of firms from other countries. Similarly, existing transnational associations, especially the International Swaps and Derivatives Association, were unable to reorient toward the Basel Committee as successfully as the IIF. One of the first organizations to engage the Basel Committee and seek to shape its agenda, ISDA also played an important role in the creation of Basel II (Young 2012). Yet the secondary literature is quite clear that the IIF, not ISDA, emerged as the Basel Committee's leading interlocutor (McKeen-Edwards and Porter 2013: 38–41). By contrast to IIF, ISDA had already established itself as a lobby organization, promoting model legislation and standards that facilitated swaps and derivatives markets (Flanagan 2001; McKeen-Edwards and Porter 2013: 43–6). However, its lobbying approach, developed for other political arenas, failed to meet the particular informational needs and concerns of the Basel Committee. Insensitive to the

[19] Ibid.

[20] The list includes America's Community Bankers, European Securitization Forum, Second Association of Regional Banks, and the ISDA. See Lall (2012); Young (2012).

[21] Author interview with former IIF StaffA, Washington, DC, 2016.

Basel Committee's fear of appearing to be captured by industry lobbies, the ISDA leaders' hard-hitting style indicates a leadership less adept at adjusting to the new environment.[22]

In sum, the chapter offers considerable evidence confirming the three expectations of our argument. First, the Basel process provided the prime focus of the IIF's reorientation. This point cannot be exaggerated. Basel became the new reason for the IIF's existence. The Basel Committee's importance explains the association's transnational and regulatory turn and its strategy for attracting new members. By contrast, and contrary to the US hegemony and the business power and interests approaches, respectively, the IIF leadership was careful not to position itself with US positions and did not have ex ante regulatory priorities and agendas that structured the contours of the new transnational rule-making arena.

Second, the timing and sequence are clear. Basel rule-making catalyzed and shaped the IIF's reforms and, in so doing, the transnational organization of business representation, not the other way around. Such evidence runs counter to the standard business power and interests argument. Finally, and again contrary to the business power expectations that material interests give rise to organizational forms, the observed internal changes—new provisions in the bylaws, the isomorphism with the Basel Committee, and the transformation into a "neutral" conveyor of proprietary information—reflect the IIF leaders' efforts to revitalize the organization by turning the industry association into the Basel Committee's main interlocutor.

Looking to other subsectors, we find additional evidence for the structuring effects of international soft law on business representation. In the field of investment and financial services, the focus of trade associations remained national well through the 1990s (Posner 2009a). This domestic focus reflected both national legacies of business representation as well as the relatively underdeveloped nature of soft law in securities (Kempthorne 2013; Kalyanpur and Newman 2017). By contrast to the Basel Committee, IOSCO experienced several difficult blows in its early years, especially with the failure of its capital adequacy standards (Singer 2007). Daniel Mügge (2010: 102) describes the situation of the most powerful industry association in Europe, the London Investment Banking Association (LIBA), which even in the face of Europe's pre-crisis regulatory overhaul (described in Chapter 4) had difficulty reorienting itself to the transnational level:

> To the frustration of its members who favoured integration (Interview 070406), the organization in the mid-1990s remained absorbed in domestic issues in the UK (Interview 300306). In later years, certainly after the re-launch of EU legislative

[22] Ibid.

> activity in 1999, LIBA shifted its focus towards European matters...That said, its status in Brussels as the de facto mouthpiece of the investment banking industry remained tarred by the "L" in its acronym.

This national focus frustrated the ability of the securities industry to engage in transnational advocacy.[23]

Indeed, the investment and financial services industries spent much of the first decade of the new millennium reorganizing in response to fast-moving development of soft law. The emergence of the international financial architecture elevated the role of IOSCO and gave birth to the FSF and, in the wake of the 2008 crisis, took on a more comprehensive structure. Regionally, for example, the London Investment Banking Association merged in 2009 with the Securities Industry and Financial Markets Association (Europe) to create the Association for Financial Markets in Europe (AFME). The *Financial Times* (2009) concluded that the new regulatory architecture created incentives for such a reorganization "driven by demand from the larger industry players, who wanted the debt and equity market participants to speak with one voice," noting that "it also involved cost savings for members of both associations."[24] The reorganization has prompted AFME to rebalance priorities between the interests of London firms (LIBA's traditional focus) and those of continental ones (which had better representation in SIFMA-Europe) (Patel 2013).

A similar reorganization occurred at the transnational level, responding to changes in the international soft law environment. At the same time that SIFMA-Europe and LIBA merged, there was also an effort to create an umbrella organization like the IIF but for the securities subsector. Founded in 2009, the Global Financial Markets Association (GFMA) with its headquarters in New York combines three regional bodies: AFME, SIFMA in the United States, and the Asia Securities Industry & Financial Markets Association (ASIFMA) (McKeen-Edwards and Porter 2013). Blythe Masters, GFMA chair (and JPMorgan commodities executive) explained the relationship between soft law and the merger: "In the past, there were fragmented trade associations reflecting particular regional issues, or issues in certain asset classes or within sub-parts of firms...but now the regulatory agenda in particular is more global."[25] Echoing the point, the *Financial Times* wrote, "Plans to boost the prominence of the GFMA come as the two international regulatory bodies—the Financial Stability Board and the Basel Committee on Banking Supervision—move forward with their agenda to set tougher standards on a global basis for

[23] Peter Jenkins, "Global Body to Represent Big Banks," *Financial Times*, January 26, 2012.

[24] Jeremy Grant and Brooke Masters, "Banking Lobby Groups to Unveil Merger," *Financial Times*, May 5, 2009.

[25] Ibid.

the world's banks."[26] The growth of international soft law shaped not only the organization of industry representation but also its substantive focus. As the GFMA chief executive argued, "We plan to shape ourselves around the GSIBs (Globally Systemically Important Banks, a category of FSB-created soft law) constituency and their concerns."[27] While certainly not a comprehensive analysis of change in the ecosystem of securities industry associations, these observations suggest that our argument travels to other subsectors.

The New Politics of Banking Regulation

The IIF's transformation turns out to have been the first event in a sequence of disruptive effects that had wide-ranging results for the politics of global finance. In particular, the IIF is credited with significantly shaping the agenda of key provisions of Basel II. As Tsingou concludes (2008: 62), "These rather informal private-sector exercises led to intensified and arguably institutionalized policy functions for private actors in the development of the accord, as exemplified most strikingly through the influence of the IIF: indeed, the organization played an active consultative role in drafting, revision and final version of Basel II... The end result has been that IIF preferences for market-generated standards and market-based oversight solutions have been internalized in the Basel process, and that consequently, large sophisticated banks are the best placed and best suited to the ensuing proposals." Baker (2010: 650) comes to a similar conclusion, "The IIF not only wrote the final version of what became the Basel II agreement, which established a reliance on internal risk management systems based on state-of-the-art value-at-risk models for the biggest banks, but also engaged in continuous consultations with the BCBS, effectively allowing the IIF, as the regulated body, to 'write the entire Basel II policy script.'"

By the mid-2000s, the presence of a transnational lobby had radically changed the politics of banking regulation beyond the issue of industry influence over the content of the Basel II agreement. The best example comes from the United States. The country's representatives used their relative leverage to shape Basel I standards and the soft law was implemented smoothly into US rules and practices. The politics of Basel II, by contrast, extended well beyond its June 2004 passage and became an explosive political struggle between two factions, one composed of domestically focused banks and the FDIC, and

[26] Ibid. [27] Ibid.

the other of multinational banks, the Federal Reserve, the Treasury, the SEC, and like-minded foreign counterparts. The Basel II agreement became a new resource for the latter faction in an ongoing domestic political contest, altering the US regulatory reversion point (albeit temporarily) by diminishing the bargaining power of the FDIC in its efforts to resist the adoption of more flexible capital reserve requirements for the largest banks and forcing the domestic coalition into a rearguard campaign that successfully targeted and delayed US implementation of Basel II (Foot and Walter 2010; Bair 2013; Lavelle 2013). The politics of Basel II further demonstrates the interaction between transnational and national efforts.

Finally, the Basel Committee transformed its internal rule-making procedures so as to increase transparency surrounding transnational lobbying. By the late 1990s, the relationship between Basel rule-making and interest groups no longer reflected the closed and secretive standard-setting environment of the 1980s. The Basel Committee adopted reforms to improve participation, most notably a notice and comment system (Zaring 2004; Kingsbury et al. 2005). Legal scholar David Zaring (2004: 577) concludes, "The most interesting aspect of the second accord for lawyers is how procedurally different it is from the first one." Tony Porter (2001: 437) goes even a step further arguing that such participation in Basel suggests "significant progress in making the institutions that constitute the emerging international financial architecture more democratic."

The effect of such access has been disputed. Some argue that notice and comment systems enhanced access for the most powerful firms (Underhill and Zhang 2008; Baker 2010). The Fed first published Basel II regulatory proposals as concept documents followed by an open comment period. Analysis of these comments demonstrates that the voices of large international banks comprised the greatest portion of perspectives to engage the process (Barr and Miller 2006; Lall 2012). These interests found voice through multiple channels. Large international banks such as Barclays, Citigroup, and BNP Paribas submitted individual comments, and their aggregated position was presented by the IIF. The comments universally supported positions that advanced market-friendly measures such as using internal firm models and employing credit rating scores to securitize products to differentiate risk pools. Others, however, argue that these firms already had significant influence in the Basel process because of the transformation of the IIF and its ability to serve as a transnational lobby through informal access (Young 2012; Thiemann 2014). From this perspective, the notice and comment system may have even given smaller, domestically oriented banks and political actors direct access to the Basel Committee and to some extent reduced asymmetries between the IIF and other lobbies (Goldbach 2015a). While it is difficult to evaluate the exact influence and its distribution across actor-types, it is clear arena expansion has broadened the types of groups participating in transnational contestation.

Conclusion

Firms play an important role in transnational governance. They are often the primary target of such rules and analysts credit them with considerable influence over the process. Yet this chapter demonstrates the relationship is not as straightforward as a backroom cabal whispering into the ears of policy-makers. International public policy plays a big part in shaping business interests and their organizational forms.

The chapter shows the disruptive structuring effects of soft law in the politics of banking regulation. The Basel I accord was a gravitational force pulling financial services firms and associations toward the transnational rule-making process. It became the arena around which opportunistic and skilled actors transformed the Institute of International Finance into a transnational business lobby. Long siloed into separate national political debates and constrained by representation through their respective domestic supervisors, financial services companies pursued their interests within national channels and in line with the two-level game metaphor. Rather than a regulatory policy lobby, the IIF itself had been a source of information and data about credit risk. The 1988 Basel Accord and subsequent rule-making became IIF's prime focus, organizing principle, and raison d'être. Seeking to reverse the IIF's decline, its leaders used the Basel regulatory arena and its new soft law to reconfigure IIF's mission and membership. With a redirected and restructured organization and new capacities, they turned the IIF into a trusted source of proprietary information—a perfect fit with the Basel Committee that increasingly required detailed firm-level data for its adopted risk-weighted assessment approach for determining capital adequacy. By meeting the needs of the international soft law generating body, the IIF's transformation gave the association direct access and greater influence than other industry associations and fostered a new more complex politics of global banking regulation.

To return to the book's themes, these findings supply further evidence that international soft law does more than resolve cooperation problems related to cross-border economic integration. It transforms powerful international actors. Soft law's second-order effects have potential not only to bring about great power alignment by disrupting the internal politics of rising powers, as we saw in Chapter 4, but also to shake up the industry lobby landscape. In the latter case, the sequence of events surrounding the IIF's transformation highlights the penetrating impact of arena expansion on the ecology of business associations and on particular industry organizations. Our conclusions mirror a long line of domestic-level research stressing how domestic institutions shape, condition, and transform business influence and interests (Berger 1983; Thelen and Steinmo 1992; Hacker and Pierson 2002). Yet they also adapt these historical institutionalist arguments for the transnational setting, showing how arena expansion alters which business voices are heard and which are influential.

6

Disruptive Soft Law and Post-Crisis US Reform

After the worst financial crisis since the Great Depression, the United States passed sweeping legislation aimed at reforming the sector. The 2010 Dodd-Frank Wall Street Reform and Consumer Protection Act (DFA) tightened standards and expanded regulatory authority in the banking, investment services, insurance, derivatives, and other financial subsectors. Eight years after its passage, the law has had a profound impact on regulation, markets, and politics inside and outside the United States, even if its effects on financial stability as well as economic growth remain controversial (Baily et al. 2017).[1]

The DFA is a quintessential example of crisis response (Young and Park 2013; Woll 2014). Policy-makers came under extreme electoral pressure to do something in the face of regulatory failure and did (Carpenter 2010, 2011; Culpepper 2010; Pagliari 2013). The bill's main provisions turned on how, not whether, the United States would ratchet up financial regulation. Given the size and centrality of US markets to international finance, at least some of the post-crisis policy response promised to ensnare foreign market participants and jurisdictions. The chapter focuses on this external dimension of the US reforms, in particular, the degree to which the changes prioritized international coordination, the principle by which the reforms attempted to integrate US and foreign markets, and the discretion (over these two international aspects) that the new law gave to regulators.

As with any financial reregulation, Washington faced demands from industry to minimize competitive disruptions and from regulators to limit the possibility of regulatory arbitrage.[2] However, that still left open the question

[1] Ben McLannahan, "Did Dodd Frank Really Hurt the US Economy?" *Financial Times*, February 13, 2017.

[2] For example, following the scandal surrounding the Enron Corporation, the United States created the Public Company Accounting Oversight Board (<https://pcaobus.org/>) and encouraged the European Union and other jurisdictions to establish similar ones. See, more generally, Simmons (2001).

of whether to address these demands by creating US rules in conjunction with foreign jurisdictions or by unilaterally raising standards at home and then attempting to export them abroad. Which integration principle should regulate market access to foreign companies also remained a contentious issue. In some areas of finance, the United States insists on direct regulation by US agencies, while in others it recognizes the authority of foreign counterparts. Such issues of international coordination and integration, moreover, depended on the authority given to US regulatory agencies. The politics of finance only starts with the adoption of legislation. As a law moves through rule-making and implementation, regulatory discretion plays a critical role filtering industry demands, managing global frictions, and channeling the preferences of oversight agencies.

At first blush, the reform's responses to these questions—about foreign coordination, market integration principles, and regulators' discretion—appear to follow no coherent pattern. In terms of coordination, for instance, subsectors appear all over the map, even though regulators generally had wide legislative latitude to interact with foreign counterparts. Reforms seeking to curtail unwanted risks through capital requirements promoted global coordination (Turner 2012; Zaring 2015a). Other areas of banking reform (including rules aimed to resolve ailing systemically important financial institutions) and the new regulations targeting over-the-counter derivatives and dealers tended to encourage speedy unilateral US action (Coffee 2013; Johnson 2013; Zaring 2015a; Gravelle and Pagliari 2018). Similarly, US reforms concerning market integration principles also seem confusing and contradictory: banking authorities managed resistance to their territorial approach, but derivatives regulators found themselves less well able to contain conflict even though they adopted a more permissive integration principle.

However enigmatic the pattern, the US reforms have had global repercussions. To continue with the derivatives example, US regulators in key cases (i.e. rules about US persons and trading venues) sought to externalize the costs of adjustment by creating rules with extraterritorial reach. The strategy backfired (for the CFTC and its Brussels counterpart which attempted the same in the case of central counterparties) setting off several high profile transatlantic conflicts (Deutsch 2014; Knaack 2015; Buxbaum 2016; Gravelle and Pagliari 2018; Knaack 2018). Meanwhile, as the European Union and the United States hashed out the rules through power politics instead of technically oriented deliberation, upwardly mobile Asian financial centers exploited the rifts to their advantage (Li 2018) and transatlantic swaps trading began to fragment, with US and EU dealers migrating toward home platforms (Helleiner 2014a; Gravelle and Pagliari 2018; Knaack 2018).

How can we make sense of these seemingly random, paradoxical, sometimes contradictory yet consequential outcomes of the US reforms? We make no pretense of explaining every feature of the Dodd-Frank Act or of monocausal social science. Like most US legislation, especially when it involves an omnibus bill, sheer unpredictability is a central theme of Dodd-Frank's creation (Carpenter 2011; Lavelle 2013). Nonetheless, we argue that the uneven development of soft law left a lasting imprint on the US regulatory response to the financial crisis and explains much of the ambivalence toward its international interface.

As was the case in the pre-crisis EU reforms discussed in Chapter 4, legislators, regulators, and other policy-makers did not always share a common view of the appropriate policy response. Instead, at least three discernible factions hoped to steer the reform process: one deemed international coordination as part and parcel of bolstering stability, investor protections, and regulatory authority; another prioritized stiffer domestic regulation over international coordination and integration; and a third supported international cooperation like the first but with market-friendly, "light touch" rules.

As the factions battled over reforms, the prior development of international soft law was palpable—because it provided a valuable contemporary political resource and because it had already structured the orientation and policy preferences of many key players, especially regulators, who for political, institutional, and practical reasons were at the center of the decision-making. From the drafting of legislative proposals and texts through the implementation stages, policy activists used soft law (and its absence) to legitimize their cause and justify their preferred policy. And in areas that already experienced extensive arena expansion (see Chapter 5), the US policy entrepreneurs were enmeshed in transnational standard setting. The chapter shows in detail how these second-order effects of soft law—through the mechanisms of legitimacy claims and arena expansion—shaped the external dimension of US financial regulatory reforms and, specifically, the approaches to international coordination and foreign firm access and the relative autonomy of regulators.

These findings emerge from a comparison between reforms to banking and derivatives regulation. We selected the two subsectors because of their economic, financial, social, and political salience. Both are giant internationalized markets, often identified as key contributors to the crisis (Cohan 2009; Sorkin 2010). They also offer useful analytic variation as the soft law terrain differed across and within the subsectors. Banking officials inside the Treasury and the Fed (including Fed Chair Ben Bernanke, Treasury Secretary Tim Geithner, and Fed Governor Daniel Tarullo) were engaged in and committed to a well-developed soft law environment in the Basel Committee. In some instances (e.g. capital requirements), they deployed the perceived legitimacy of ongoing standard-setting processes to promote international coordination of US regulation. In others (e.g. resolution rules) where no standards existed, they used the Basel Committee's principles to temper reactions to a controversial integration principle that moved US policy in a territorial direction and strengthened the Fed's authority.

Just as the preexistence of soft law shaped outcomes in banking, so too did its absence and underdevelopment in derivatives. Without an obvious transnational arena or rehearsed working relationships between US and foreign officials, industry and Republican calls for simultaneous international coordination and permissive integration principles were relatively easy to counter, especially in the critical months before and after Dodd-Frank's passage. Gary Gensler, a key Obama administration adviser responsible for the subsector's reform and then Chair of the CFTC, was skeptical of London's (and the European Union's) commitment to match the stringency of US rules or of the prospects for building a new transnational arena and pushed hard for unilateral action. Determined to bring rigorous direct regulation over OTC derivative markets, Gensler and his faction pressed Congress for a prescribed regime, which they hoped would survive future industry challenges. This short leash also gave the officials license to act swiftly and then, in key instances, seek international coordination through coercion—attempting to exchange US market access for foreign acceptance of CFTC's rules, an approach sometimes mirrored by Brussels and resulting in contentious conflicts.

In many ways, the US post-crisis response is this book's "hardest" case—in the sense that theory and evidence have long cast the country as an international financial rule-maker and its internal legislative processes as a domestic affair (Helleiner 1996; Simmons 2001; Drezner 2007). With respect to soft law specifically, the general presumption among scholars is that the causal arrows go from the United States to the international level and not the other way around; according to this logic, if soft law is significant in the United States, it is as a tool for US officials to influence the behavior of others, not a contributor to US domestic regulation. We demonstrate that the presence, absence, and uneven development of soft law, even when compared to other factors, played a decisive and disruptive role in the drafting, negotiating, and implementing stages of the Dodd-Frank reforms—a process that would go on to influence the distribution of authority at home and the global coordination and integration of US regulation and markets.

International Soft Law and Post-Crisis US Regulatory Reform

The US response to the financial crisis—an enormous political undertaking that includes the Dodd-Frank Act itself, the preceding legislative process, the detailed rule-making by agencies, and international coordination—runs counter to the recent historical trend. For thirty years, with a few notable exceptions,[3] Washington eroded the 1930s regulatory arrangements that segmented the financial services industry, limited national consolidation, and promoted consumer protection (Coleman 1996; Vogel 1996; Mügge 2009; Schwartz 2009; Lavelle 2013). This trend was epitomized in the 1999 Gramm-Leach-Bliley Act, which tore down most of the remaining subsector divisions. The Dodd-Frank Act took financial regulation in the other direction. It imposed new restrictions on the activities of banks, stricter capital and leverage requirements, a more rigorous regime for systemically important financial institutions, direct regulation of over-the-counter derivatives markets and dealers, and a renewed emphasis on consumer protection (Coffee 2011; Baily et al. 2017).

In the remaining sections of the chapter, we lay out the case for soft law's substantial role in shaping the reform and its global consequences. We start here by juxtaposing the relative lack of attention to international factors in existing accounts of the US reform, with the observable rise of international references in the text of US legislation.

There are a number of reasons to be skeptical about the impact of soft law on the US reform. Unlike the European Union's Financial Services Action Plan, the Dodd-Frank Act occurred at a time of high public salience. Some areas of contention such as the issue of consumer protection or systemic risk played out in the full view of the public and received more journalistic and scholarly attention than others (Young 2013; Orban 2016; Kastner 2017).[4] Yet even highly technical domains, which generally garnered less attention, took dramatic turns under an occasional spotlight.[5] Theory and history show that public salience politicizes financial rule-making—bringing a wider range of actors into the process beyond the regular insiders of regulators, academics, and industry associations—and forces politicians to explain their positions to voters. Constituents, in turn, tend to care more about domestic, as opposed to

[3] Perhaps the most important exception is the 2002 Sarbanes-Oxley Act, which, among other things, created the Public Company Accounting Oversight Board.

[4] There were extensive public debates on consumer protection (resulting in the Consumer Financial Protection Bureau); systemic risk (that gave rise to the Financial Stability Oversight Council in spite of proposals to give new powers to the Federal Reserve Board); the relative powers of regulatory agencies (that bolstered the Fed's position, preserved the CFTC and SEC over calls for a merger, and closed the Office of Thrift Supervision); as well as the structure of the banking industry (that limited proprietary trading under the Volcker Rule and derivatives trading under the Lincoln Amendment). Martin Crustsinger, "Geithner Stresses Need for Consumer Protections," *Associated Press*, March 3, 2010; Paul Wiseman, Paul Davidson, and Pallavi Gogoi, "Wall Street Feels the Wrath of Man on the Street," *USA Today*, October 23, 2009.

[5] For example, the basic outline of reform for derivatives regulation, as written in the Treasury's original proposed bill, remained largely intact throughout the process, yet when scandal erupted over the revelation of a Goldman Sachs financier's emails, Congress added a whole new section on conduct of business. Zachary Goldfarb, "Goldman executives cheered housing market's decline, newly released e-mails show," *Washington Post*, April 25, 2010.

international, issues (Pagliari 2013), raising doubts about an account that might privilege international soft law.

Moreover, academic research on the decade before the crisis suggests that the United States continued along a much-observed trend of legislating unilaterally and expecting others to adjust. The 2002 Sarbanes-Oxley Act, for example, contained a number of extraterritorial provisions concerning corporate governance, which seemed to be the product of an inwardly focused Congress (Romano 2004; Shirley 2004; Posner 2009a). In an examination of ten financial regulatory areas, Posner and Véron (2016) show the pre-crisis United States to be less transnationalist than the European Union, by which they mean that Washington was less supportive of international standard setters and less adherent to international soft law.

Finally, recent analysis of the Dodd-Frank Act has not given international factors much weight (Carpenter 2010, 2011; Patashnik and Zelizer 2013). For example, Woolley and Ziegler (2012) mention that the coalition of Wall Street and the Washington financial elite supported coordination through the G20 agenda (Woolley and Ziegler 2012: 31). But the authors do not examine whether such international developments represent something new and important. Nor do they offer analysis of domestic–international linkages. In fact, one can easily conclude that the international financial architecture and international soft law processes had little impact on US financial regulatory reform. Many observers have noted the attenuated influence of international banking interests at key moments. While participants in the legislative process have gone as far as to label international banks as "toxic" (Geithner 2014: 620), scholars emphasize how public salience forced the financial lobbies to adopt less direct strategies (Culpepper 2010; Young 2013; Pagliari and Young 2014).[6]

A central goal of the chapter is to resituate the US reform within global financial regulation and thereby build on a new wave of scholarship attentive to the complex connections and interactions between US financial policymaking and international institutions (Lavelle 2013, 2014; Kempthorne 2015; Zaring 2015a; Wilf 2016). Rather than merely setting rules that others followed, US domestic reforms, we contend, were themselves shaped significantly by international soft law. Before documenting our main evidence based on a detailed examination of Dodd-Frank banking and derivatives reforms, we offer preliminary support for the argument found in a text analysis of international references in the 2010 law and the 2002 Sarbanes-Oxley Act.

Sarbanes-Oxley serves as a good comparator for three reasons: at eight years apart, the two laws are relatively close in time (which helps to keep many variables constant); both emerged in response to financial regulatory failures

[6] Edmund Andrews, "Battles over Reform Plan Lie Ahead," *New York Times*, March 27, 2009; Tim Ryan, "Wall Street is a Willing Partner in Financial Reform," *Financial Times*, June 9, 2009, 11.

and when levels of public salience were relatively high; and, while Dodd-Frank was much more comprehensive and responded to a deep recession, both laws included a range of financial regulatory areas. The idea behind the comparison is that the frequency by which words like "foreign," "cross-border," "global," and "international" appear in the texts indicates the extent to which members of Congress incorporated non-domestic factors into their decision-making. As described in Chapter 3, between those years, there was a general proliferation of international financial regulatory soft law including the Basel Committee's 2004 passage of a second capital reserve requirements accord, the widespread acceptance of the IASB's reporting standards, and the maturation of the FSF's role as international financial regulatory coordinator. If domestic policy entrepreneurs are conditioned by soft law and use it for political purposes as we maintain, then we would expect to see greater evidence of such processes as the body of soft law grows; and at least some of that evidence might be expected to manifest in the text of US laws.

The findings from our content analysis (see Figure 6.1) suggest that Congress was more attentive in 2010 to non-US factors than in 2002. Because the overall word count of Dodd-Frank is more than ten times larger than that of Sarbanes-Oxley, we focus on the frequency of these terms,[7] counting the times that the following words were used: "foreign," "international," "cross-border," "home country," "global," and "multilateral." We find that Congress used these words almost two times more frequently in the 2010 Dodd-Frank Act (0.00128) than in the 2002 Sarbanes-Oxley Act (0.000678).

We are cautious about these findings for obvious reasons: the analysis is not sufficiently granular to decipher what it means that Congress used such

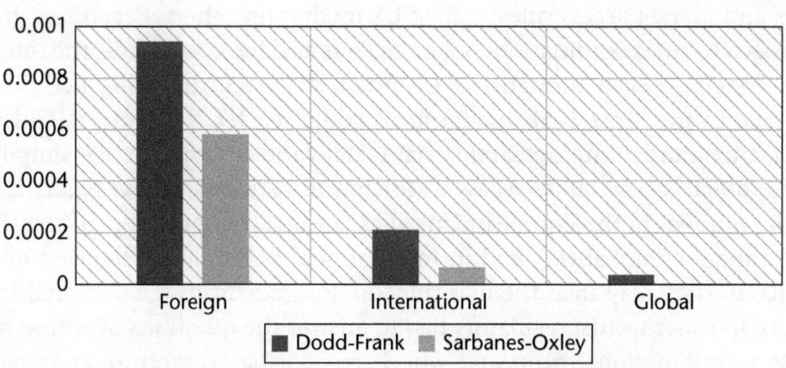

Figure 6.1. Indicators of legislative internationalization
Source: Authors.

[7] Following standard procedures we computed a ratio by dividing the raw number of times a term is used (the numerator) by the total number of words in the law (the denominator).

words. Yet the temporal pattern substantiates a trend that other scholars have picked up—that US financial rule-making is more intertwined with international developments than in the past. It also gives us confidence that even some of the best existing analyses of the Dodd-Frank Act and post-crisis reform efforts underestimate the extent to which international factors such as soft law penetrate US rule-making processes.

Differing Reform Trajectories: International Coordination, Integration Principles, and Regulatory Discretion

To move beyond preliminary evidence, we examine change in two policy subsectors. Banking and derivatives regulation govern enormous financial markets, figure centrally in the Dodd-Frank Act, and vary considerably in terms of the international institutional context and regulatory reform trajectory. For each, we seek to explain three elements of US regulatory reform: coordination with foreign rules, international integration principles, and agency discretion.

The first and second are the approaches concerning foreign firms and jurisdictions that regulators adopted during the implementation stages. In a world where capital moves and financiers choose where to execute transactions, authorities seek to prevent regulatory arbitrage and ensure a level playing field for their own industries through the promotion of cross-border rule similarity. US authorities considered two ways to ensure cross-border coordination: devising US rules as part of an international (or bilateral) process or forging US rules unilaterally and then trying to combine first-mover advantages and market access rules to foist US models on others. Regardless of the approach to rule coordination, policy-makers also have to address the integration principle. Even though the US financial system has long been international in the sense that foreign firms could reach US customers and vice versa, cross-border interoperability has taken various forms. In oversimplified terms, officials may allow access to foreign firms whose home regulation is similar (known in the European Union as "mutual recognition," in the US as "substituted compliance," and in international bodies as deference arrangements) or they may treat them as they do domestic firms (i.e. national treatment). In other words, regulators had to answer the questions of whose rules apply to international firms and who is responsible to monitor compliance with them.

The third element—the discretion of implementing regulators—concerns the degree and type of autonomy that Congress gave to regulatory authorities for rule implementation and international cooperation. In particular, we look in the text of the Dodd-Frank Act for levels of prescription (how detailed and long are Congress's instructions to regulators), the implementation deadlines (how much time Congress gave regulators to complete the tasks), and the type of instructions and powers for cooperating with foreign jurisdictions. These dimensions combine to direct and hem in the discretion of regulators.

The three elements of regulation are not independent of each other. As part of the implementation process, regulators' approaches to international coordination and integration are sensitive to how much and what kind of discretion they have. The selection of integration principle can also hinge on the degree of coordination. Yet we treat them as analytically distinct because it helps us identify the a priori preferences of actors and how various factions were or were not able to shape the policy process.

What do we observe in the empirical record? Very different reform paths emerge when one takes a close look at the ins and outs of the adopted approaches to coordination, integration, and regulatory discretion. Starting with banking, the legislation demonstrates important within- and cross-case variation. In terms of agency discretion, it leaves regulators considerable autonomy over capital reserves and leverage levels despite new mandated minimum requirements and thus encourages early and simultaneous international coordination (Geithner 2014: 645–7).[8] It introduces a fairly prescriptive regime for systemically important financial institutions (SIFIs), including foreign ones operating in the United States. In part reflecting the difference, the Federal Reserve and other banking regulators coordinated extensively with foreign counterparts to develop new international capital and leverage standards, but the Fed was less sanguine when it came to timely coordination of standards for systemically important firms and adopted a more territorial approach (compared to its pre-crisis one) by giving access to large foreign financial companies on the basis of the national treatment principle. As we will see, even though the territorial approach was less lenient than the one used for derivatives firms (and therefore less favored by foreign firms and governments), the Federal Reserve has not faced the kind of scorched earth resistance from industry or the European Union that the CFTC did.

Turning to the new regime of direct regulation of OTC derivatives, the DFA is relatively prescriptive and the timeframes are short, even compared to the text covering SIFIs. In terms of approaches to coordination and integration, the CFTC ultimately pursued the ambitious goal of preserving the international character of derivatives markets through substituted compliance arrangements, in which foreign oversight systems could be deemed equivalent to US oversight. This style of mutual recognition was in line with the expectations and preferences of the dominant market participants and the

[8] While the Dodd-Frank Act imposes new required minimum levels for all banks, known as the Collins Amendment, banking authorities retained powers to set the minimums.

European Union. However, efforts to achieve this goal (without compromising the hoped-for rigor of new US rules) only came after the CFTC prioritized rapid home implementation (e.g. of rules concerning US persons, central counterparties, and trading venues). The lack of simultaneous coordination produced inevitable differences between US rules and those of the European Union, leaving the CFTC (and its Brussels counterparts) without an easy pathway to recognize the other's rules as equivalent. This sequence repeatedly gave rise to ill-fated attempts to export US standards abroad in exchange for substituted compliance (e.g. in the US persons and trading venues cases). The result was several years of stormy CFTC relationships with industry groups, highly contentious bilateral bargaining with the European Union (which also adopted extraterritorial principles and strategies), and, arguably, a more fragmented international market than either the US or the EU officials purportedly wanted (Helleiner 2014a; Gravelle and Pagliari 2018; Knaack 2018).

To summarize, despite similar industry interests in support of early coordination and permissive integration principles and regulatory officials with broad delegated authority to cooperate, the two subsectors diverge with early robust coordination in some areas of banking regulation (capital adequacy rules) but not in others (resolution rules), nor in most areas of derivatives regulation.[9] Banking regulators enjoyed more discretion and managed resistance to the imposition of a territorial integration principle; whereas derivatives authorities were unable to contain the fallout from its extraterritorial strategy despite adopting a more permissive integration principle. Indeed, conflicts over regulatory differences became much more politicized in the case of derivatives.

Explaining the Reform Trajectories in Banking and Derivatives

International soft law's second-order effects—via the mechanisms of legitimacy claims and arena expansion—go a long way to explain these divergent regulatory trajectories. The following narrative provides our evidential support. It begins with a description of relevant political context, featuring the key actors. For political, practical, and institutional reasons, regulators ended up as the central players behind the divergent reforms. Yet in making decisions, they had to wade through a battlefield of three key factions—those

[9] The ongoing case of margin requirements for non-centrally cleared derivatives may prove the exception (FSB 2016). In this area of derivatives regulation (a November 2011 addition to the G20 program), the European Union and United States along with Japan sought to coordinate through a BCBS–IOSCO collaboration, before implementing home rules.

pressing for international coordination, domestic stability, and light touch regulation. The uneven pre-crisis development of soft law explains how policy-makers maneuvered among competing factions and the decisions and policies they ultimately adopted.

Regulators and factions: coordination, domestic first, light touch

Regulators and administration officials played an outsized role in the reform process (Carpenter 2010).[10] The Obama administration turned to subsector regulators and campaign and White House insiders (some of whom later became regulators) to develop much of the draft law and many of these individuals would lead the implementation effort. Even though the double role of regulators (of both policy activists and designers and then implementers) is not unusual, per se, the political context of a new Democratic president, supported by Democratic majorities in both houses of Congress, and the particular aims and strategies of the Obama administration resulted in expanded opportunities for the policy influence of regulators. As Tim Geithner (2014: 607–8) explains:

> Whatever their flaws, regulators were much better equipped than politicians to determine, say, the precise amount of common equity a bank should have relative to its risk-weighted assets, or the amount of cash it should hold to meet potential withdrawals. History suggested that Capitol Hill would be too easily swayed by the clout of the financial industry and the politics of the moment; we didn't think that was the place for the intricate work of calibrating the financial system's shock absorbers. The Fed was not a very popular institution at the moment, but it had a lot of technical expertise as well as political independence, and we thought it was much better suited for the job.

In this way, regulators were given the opportunity to participate in the writing of the original language and the possibility to steer the text in ways that would later define the extent of their independence and support their preferred approaches to implementation and international interactions.[11] Adding to the complexity of regulators' roles, some of these very same agencies had sometimes been blamed for the crisis and targeted for reforms (including loss of powers and even dissolution). Part of their agenda was to find ways to justify their authority in the post-crisis regulatory arrangements (Carpenter 2010).

[10] Stephen Foley, "Lobbyists and Agency Rivals Fight to Shape the New Wall St," *The Independent*, June 7, 2009.

[11] Regulators became even more important in the drafting stage as the Treasury was not yet fully staffed and it relied on seconded staff from the agencies to draft critical portions of the legislation (Bernanke 2015: 436–66).

Similar to the EU case of the 1990s, factions existed even within administration-associated policy activists who otherwise shared a commitment to more and better regulation. First, a coordination faction centered around Tim Geithner and his Treasury[12] but drew also from the Fed whose regulatory officials saw collaboration with foreign counterparts and preservation of international financial integration as necessary parts of improving domestic regulation. Second, a domestic stability faction including Gary Gensler and the CFTC under his leadership, consumer protection advocate and future Senator Elizabeth Warren and groups like Americans for Financial Reform,[13] former Fed Chair Paul Volcker, and members of the FDIC, who prioritized domestic market stability and investor and consumer protection. This group was either hostile toward international finance or saw coordination and integration as issues to address only after improving regulation at home.[14] Woolley and Ziegler (2012) have described this as "two-tiered politics," one representing the old guard of financial insiders who historically had set financial policy in relative obscurity, the other reflecting a grassroots mobilization. Others have depicted these factions as having staked out positions against a mass public that had woken up to the real pocketbook costs of under-regulation and industry concerns that over-regulation would harm long-term competitiveness (Orban 2016; Kastner 2017).

During the legislative stages, a third group of voices opposing over-regulation and advocating competitiveness concerns were muted. But they returned to full volume during implementation and arguably comprised a faction of their own—of industry groups, pro-Wall Street think tanks, and law-makers and regulators such as Republican CFTC Commissioner Scott O'Malia (Farrell and Quiggin 2017). They argued that sound regulation could not be achieved without international coordination and ease of access

[12] Indeed, an entire chapter (of five) in the administration's plan, *A New Foundation* (Department of the Treasury 2009: 80–8), is devoted to improving international coordination. While one of the aims (and the primary reason industry lobbies supported this part of the administration's package) was to ensure a level playing field for Wall Street firms, arguably the Treasury's more immediate motivation (as implied in the chapter title, "Raise International Regulation and Improve International Cooperation") were concerns about the potential for regulatory arbitrage. "We also thought these problems [related to improving the stability of the financial system] demanded global solutions," Geithner writes in his memoir. "This was a global crisis, and we had been hurt by weak regulatory standards overseas, not just by our failures at home. If we had unilaterally imposed strict new limits on risk, without encouraging higher standards globally, we simply would have reduced the market share of US firms around the world, without making the global system more resilient" (Department of the Treasury 2009: 607–8).

[13] "Americans for Financial Reform," ourfinancialsecurity.org, last accessed July 26, 2017, <http://www.ourfinancialsecurity.org>.

[14] Robert Kuttner, "Wall Street Meets its Match," *American Prospect*, December 1, 2009; Stephen Taub, "CFTC Boss Gary Gensler Wants to Clamp Down on Wall Street," *Institutional Investor*, May 28, 2010.

to US markets but aimed to prevent many of the industry constraints in Dodd-Frank from ever being implemented.[15]

Even during the legislative process when this light touch faction could not take a public role, it was influential. The leading policy activists of the other two factions always anticipated a future decrease in public salience and increase in the sway of a financial industry that would benefit from predicted Democratic losses in the 2010 and 2012 elections. And these expectations along with the overriding post-crisis political imperative to shore up financial governance severely limited regulators' goals and approaches to foreign coordination and international integration.

From the point of view of regulators, international cooperation involved tradeoffs—that were not generally expressed in high-level Treasury pronouncements about the G20 program. Industry benefited from having similar regulation across borders and regulators benefited when incentives for regulatory arbitrage were low. There were also the possible costs of cooperation, as regulators must sometimes make compromises in levels of consumer protection or risk-abatement to find common ground with foreign jurisdictions. In 2009 and 2010, these potential costs were especially problematic for US regulators, who, as a result, were less flexible and accommodative than they had been before the crisis.[16] The regulators approached this balancing act in different ways, decisions that shaped some of the key battles during the legislative and implementation stages. We show in the next sections that the unevenness in the international institutional context, and the availability (or not) of international soft law, was a critical factor in determining how, when, and even if regulators and other political entrepreneurs sought to balance these goals.

Banking: uneven soft law, coordinated capital rules, and the Fed's new cautious approach to systemically important foreign banks

In 2008, banking regulation was the most developed subsector of international financial soft law. As the political arena had expanded to the transnational level, so too had the orientation of US officials, notably in the Treasury and Federal Reserve Bank. They deemed it appropriate and necessary

[15] "Former Trading Regulator Scott O'Malia to Lead Derivatives Group," *New York Times*, July 23, 2014.

[16] The following are good examples: SEC, "Statement by the European Commission and the US Securities and Exchange Commission on Mutual Recognition in Securities Markets," February 1, 2008; SEC, "SEC Announces Next Steps for Implementation of Mutual Recognition Concept," March 24, 2008.

that US reforms would be intimately linked to Basel-centered processes. As we argued in Chapter 5, arena expansion had shifted the orientation of domestic actors toward the transnational process, shaping their goals and agendas. And in areas where the BCBS had experience—in capital reserves and home–host issues—these US actors used its credibility as a political tool to blunt opposition and justify the expansion of their autonomy. Yet the introduction of regimes in the United States and abroad to govern systemically important financial firms (based on a belief in the insufficiency of capital requirements) meant that new areas of transnational coordination through soft law were in 2009 and 2010 in their infancy. This unevenness, even within the same subsector, is reflected in what type of autonomy the Treasury and Fed wanted (and got) from Congress as well as the Fed's ultimate approach to international coordination and cross-border financial integration. In defending a more territorial principle, international soft law was the Fed's strongest weapon.

BASELIZATION OF REFORMED US CAPITAL REQUIREMENTS

The Treasury's and Fed's orientation toward the Basel arena spanned across administrations and political parties and was manifest at all stages of the US reform process. Both the Bush and Obama administrations were deeply enmeshed in this transnational political arena and, at least in the case of capital reserves (what one Fed official referred to as the pre-crisis "dominant prudential regulatory tool"[17]), had great faith that the international standard-setting process would eventually produce a third accord. This commitment to the international process shaped what authorities wanted from Congress—sufficient autonomy so that they could wait to create new home rules until Basel III negotiations were complete—and their goals for international cooperation.

The Bush administration's October 2008 "Progress Update on March Policy Statement on Financial Market Developments" by the President's Working Group on Financial Markets (composed of the Treasury, the Fed, SEC, and CFTC) reveals the extent to which US banking authorities were already anticipating Basel soft law to be the future basis of domestic regulatory reforms. In the section entitled "Enhancements to Prudential Regulatory Policies (19–23)," the President's Working Group relied heavily on international soft law with eleven of the seventeen initiatives mentioning the BCBS, its processes or its standards. The clear message was that, in the view of the authors (of which the FDIC was not one), US reforms would be made

[17] Daniel K. Tarullo, "Next Steps in Financial Regulatory Reform." Speech at George Washington University Center for Law, Economics, and Finance Conference on the Dodd-Frank Act, Washington, DC, November 12, 2010.

in conjunction with foreign jurisdictions: the BCBS is depicted as having the capacity to act swiftly and to create standards reliably enough to be a basis for US regulation.

Conveying a similar message, Geithner's Treasury released its legislative roadmap, *Financial Regulatory Reform: A New Foundation,*[18] in June 2009. It became the Obama administration's proposal for financial regulatory legislation and was authored by a team that included future and seconded Federal Reserve officials, including Daniel Tarullo. It recommended stiffer prudential requirements ("capital and liquidity requirements were simply too low" (19)) and supports "the Basel Committee's efforts to improve the Basel II Capital Accord" (28), pressing the Basel Committee, among other things, to "strengthen the definition of regulatory capital to improve the quality, quantity, and international consistency of capital." Fearing Congressional intervention, which would threaten international coordination, the Treasury encouraged BCBS to work at a rapid pace—urging it "to issue guidelines to harmonize the definition of capital by the end of 2009, and develop recommendations on minimum capital levels in 2010" (80). Ben Bernanke (2015: 454) makes a similar case in his memoir:

> Without international coordination tougher domestic regulation might result only in banking activity moving out of the United States to foreign financial centers. Moreover, even if foreign jurisdictions adopted comparably tough rules, in the absence of international coordination those rules might be inconsistent with US standards, which could fragment global capital markets and otherwise diminish the effectiveness of new rules. The potential solution to these problems lay in Basel, with the Bank for International Settlements. The BIS, besides being a gathering place for central bank governors, was also the host of an international forum called the Basel Committee on Banking Supervision.

The enmeshment of US regulators in the BCBS arena is also manifest during the legislative process. In a speech delivered in February 2010 (after the House, but before the Senate, had passed a bill), for instance, Daniel Tarullo, member of the Fed's Board of Governors, indicates the close affinities between the Basel Committee's thinking on prudential regulation and how he frames it in his own mind: "It is perhaps instructive to organize this [the US regulatory reform] agenda by reference to the 'three pillars' of financial regulation enunciated by the Basel Committee on Banking Supervision—minimum prudential requirements, supervisory oversight, and market discipline. Although the Basel Committee formulated the three-pillar approach in the context of the

[18] Department of the Treasury (2009); Brad Dennis, "Obama Turns Efforts to Financial Changes," *Washington Post*, September 14, 2009, A1.

Basel II arrangement for capital requirements, this frame of reference can also be applied to the broader set of reform measures."[19]

Invoking the Basel Committee and its soft law served Treasury and Fed efforts to preserve the latter's autonomy, which was frequently under attack during the Dodd-Frank legislative process. Many blamed the financial watchdogs, notably the Federal Reserve, for not preventing the crisis and wanted to see their independence curtailed. Even before publication of *A New Foundation*, the Treasury had to compromise on its original preference for having the Fed oversee the new regime for systemically important financial firms without what would be named the Financial Stability Oversight Council (Geithner 2014). Speeches like Tarullo's, which fostered an aura of legitimacy around existing soft law and the Basel arena, helped to ensure that Congress would leave the Fed with enough discretion and time to wait for the completion of Basel III before finalizing new capital requirements at home.

In the end, Congress gave banking regulators instructions to coordinate with foreign counterparts and broad powers to do so (DFA Title I, SEC 175; Title I, SEC 165, b(2); Geithner 2014: 645–7). Moreover, the text covering capital reserve and leverage requirements, apart from a minimum floor (the Collins Amendment, which had the support of the FDIC (Carpenter 2011)), stands out for its relative parsimony and for the discretion and time given to the Fed to negotiate international standards (DFA Title I, SEC 171).

Taking full advantage of the autonomy it had won, the Federal Reserve's rule-making was deeply intertwined with the Basel Committee's. In his November 2010 speech to a George Washington University audience, Tarullo's discussion on capital requirements lays out the remarkable melding of US and Basel processes.[20] After his description of five major improvements in BCBS soft law and how they relate to US changes, the imperfections in the Basel III agreement, the sources of successful cooperation, the need for strong BCBS monitoring, and the agenda of unfinished business, an unmistakable message emerges—that one cannot discuss US reforms without also understanding transnational developments (Turner 2012; Walker et al. 2012; Zaring 2015a).[21]

INCHOATE SOFT LAW FOR SIFIS AND A TERRITORIAL TURN

In contrast to capital reserve requirements with its long history of international soft law, the 2008 financial crisis for the first time elevated the issue

[19] Daniel K. Tarullo, "Financial Regulatory Reform." Speech at the US Monetary Policy Forum, New York, February 26, 2010.

[20] Daniel K. Tarullo, "Next Steps in Financial Regulatory Reform." Speech at George Washington University Center for Law, Economics, and Finance Conference on the Dodd-Frank Act, Washington, DC, November 12, 2010.

[21] Ibid.

of resolution regimes for SIFIs to the international level. The bankruptcies of AIG and Lehman Brothers and many banks in Europe such as ABN AMRO, Anglo Irish Bank, Northern Rock, and UBS, made it clear that the collapse of multinational financial conglomerates was a real threat for which governments had to be better prepared (Cohan 2009; Skeel 2010; Sorkin 2010). The realization turned attention to who should be responsible for the monitoring of such financial institutions (as their operations inherently fall under the auspices of multiple regulators) and who would cover the costs involved in providing orderly resolutions when they failed.

Resolution rules and other aspects of SIFI regulation represent a case of limited soft law with little in the way of existing best practices on how to manage the special circumstances surrounding these firms. Given this thin soft law environment, Federal Reserve Board officials, from an early stage in the legislative process, dampened expectations by publicly highlighting the futility of early coordination and the necessity of improving US prudential regulation unilaterally.

Even so, the SIFIs case is an exemplar of soft law's second-order effects disrupting regulatory politics—because it features Fed authorities invoking a long-existing body of international soft law (concerning relations between home and host regulators) to justify a territorial turn in the US treatment of foreign banks and to enhance the Federal Reserve's role domestically and globally. By dipping into the perceived legitimacy of this well-established soft law, the Fed diverged from the Treasury's original preference for coordinated US implementation, passed on the costs of regulatory adjustment to foreign banks, and diffused opposition from domestic industry and EU policy-makers—a sharp contrast to the OTC derivatives case discussed in the subsequent section.

Before the crisis, capital requirements had been the main regulatory tool for managing the risks related to bank insolvency. By revealing the tool's shortcomings, the crisis spawned the addition of complementary ones. In Fed Governor Tarullo's words, "The financial crisis showed that the concentrated, almost all-consuming regulatory focus on refining bank capital requirements in Basel II had come at the expense of attention to other risks in the financial system."[22] Yet international coordination in these new areas of prudential regulation had to be created from scratch and only got underway, in earnest, in the eighteen months following the DFA's enactment when US banking regulators were mandated to write new rules.

By calling on the BCBS to publish recommendations for the improved resolution of global financial firms, the US administration's June 2009 legislative

[22] Ibid.

proposal nodded to G20 commitments (Department of the Treasury 2009: 82). Nevertheless, international processes were moving slowly. At a summit in Pittsburgh in September of 2009, when the US House of Representatives was well on its way to passing a financial reform bill, the G20 still lacked concrete proposals and was only raising the too-big-to-fail (TBTF) issue and pointing to the need for coordination of SIFIs regulation (Goldstein and Véron 2011). Even a year later, four months after Dodd-Frank's passage and well into the implementation phase, the Financial Stability Board, the body delegated to oversee the international coordination effort, did not have a clear plan of action and instead made unspecified calls on its members to improve resolution regimes and monitoring of globally systemically important financial institutions (G-SIFIs) (Financial Stability Board 2010).

Soft law's underdeveloped state and the sluggish pace of coordination were influential factors behind the Federal Reserve's Congressional and implementation strategies to ensure more rigorous regulation of systemically important financial institutions. As early as the fall of 2009, during the legislative process but still months before Congress agreed on extending the FDIC's resolution authority to include systemically important financial firms (DFA, Title II), cautious Fed officials already lowered expectations for early international coordination. As Fed governor Tarullo (2009) explains:

> The task of harmonizing divergent legal regimes, and reconciling the principles underlying many of these regimes, would be challenge enough. But an effective international regime would also likely require agreement on how to share the losses and possible special assistance associated with a global firm's insolvency...we must acknowledge that satisfyingly clean and comprehensive solutions to the international difficulties occasioned by such insolvencies are not within sight.[23]

The concern was genuine. Not only did banking authorities lack preexisting soft law on which to build but they also confronted uncertain prospects that the slow-moving international process would succeed. Unlike in the United States, most other countries did not have a tradition of bank resolution. US officials doubted whether the Europeans—whose economies tended to rely more heavily on banks (as opposed to capital markets) for financing and had comparatively more concentrated banking industries—would ever put in place rigorous resolution regimes. For example, when asked in December 2011 where the major regulatory fault lines lie between the United States and the European Union, one Treasury official succinctly captured a general

[23] Daniel K. Tarullo, "Supervising and Resolving Large Financial Institutions." Speech at the Institute of International Bankers Convergence on Cross-Border Insolvency Issues, New York, November 10, 2009.

sentiment in Washington about bank resolution: "The US thinks banks should die; others don't."[24]

These uncertainties also contributed to the Federal Reserve's decision to have systemically important foreign financial firms operate in the United States under a variant of the national treatment principle. The final Dodd-Frank Act text includes fairly detailed provisions on how SIFIs should be regulated[25]—higher prudential standards, contingent capital and resolution plans—yet left the Fed with considerable discretion over implementation, including rules giving access to foreign banks.[26] The Fed used this discretion to adopt an approach to integration that moved the United States in a more territorial direction. Before the crisis, robust international coordination of stricter capital requirements might have given Fed officials enough confidence in foreign regulation to extend more liberal terms of access. The crisis had changed what they considered appropriate prudential regulation. In particular, the new integration principle was adopted to solve what its officials considered an untenable pre-crisis regime (Tafara and Peterson 2007; Turner 2012): the mixture of loose national rules concerning where banks had to keep capital, on the one hand, and cross-border differences in resolution processes, on the other, created risks to US financial stability. Tarullo explains:

> The location of capital and liquidity proved critical in the resolution of some firms that failed during the financial crisis. Capital and liquidity were in some cases trapped at the home entity, as in the case of the Icelandic banks and in our own country, Lehman Brothers. Actions by home-country authorities during this period showed that while a foreign bank regulatory regime designed to accommodate centralized management of capital and liquidity can promote efficiency during good times, it also increases the chances of ring-fencing by home and host jurisdictions at the moment of a crisis, as local operations come under severe strain and repayment of local creditors is called into question. Resolution regimes and powers remain nationally based, complicating the resolution of firms with large cross-border operations.[27]

The Fed's adopted approach makes foreign firms keep more capital and liquidity in US entities, rather than under a more permissive arrangement (preferred by industry associations and policy-makers in the European Union and elsewhere) based on either a firm-by-firm approach or mutual reliance on home-country regulation and supervision. In an effort to bolster US-located capital and liquidity positions, the final rule requires large foreign banking organizations

[24] Author interview with US Treasury official, December 20, 2011.

[25] Title I, SEC 165, 166, 606 and Title II, SEC 217 of Dodd-Frank.

[26] Daniel K. Tarullo, "Regulation of Foreign Banking Organizations." Yale Management Leader's Forum, New Haven, November 28, 2012.

[27] Ibid.

to create a US intermediate holding company to be treated in the same way as US bank holding companies and uses a threshold (of $50 billion or more non-branch assets) similar to the one used to determine systemically important banks in the United States.[28] In other words, foreign SIFIs had to cordon off more capital in the United States to be used in the case of a crisis.

The Fed's decision drew opposition from a wide spectrum of actors. A prominent theme of their objections was that the US rule undermined the G20 efforts to prevent regulatory fragmentation. Associations representing global banks, like the Institute of International Finance (see Chapter 5), saw the move as a blatant attack on the business practices of foreign banks. Timothy Adams, the IIF's President and CEO, argued:

> While progress is still being made toward globally harmonized resolution for large financial institutions, some major countries appear to assume that cross-border coordination will fail during a crisis, and thus have focused on securing supervisory information and resources within their jurisdictions. This has led to efforts to "ring fence" capital and liquidity within national boundaries—as reflected, for example, in the US Federal Reserve Board's proposal for enhanced supervision of Foreign Banking Operations (FBOs), among other national initiatives. These measures would raise costs and diminish global financial institutions' ability to manage capital and liquidity, reducing efficiency in global markets. By restricting the redeployment of capital and liquidity resources among affiliates of global groups, they could increase fragility of the global financial system, instead of making it more resilient.[29]

Officials representing major international financial centers echoed these arguments, focusing their opposition on the US rule's alleged contravention of the Basel Committee's aims. After citing that the European Union had lived up to its international commitments by adopting a more permissive approach to foreign banks, European Commissioner Michel Barnier accused the United States of creating a rule with aspects that "seem to be in substantial contradiction to global regulatory convergence and could have a negative impact on the implementation of Basel III, jeopardizing and/or delaying the process."[30] Likewise, Bank of Japan Executive Director, Hiroki Tanaka, raised concerns that the proposed rule would "hamper the effectiveness of the ongoing international collaborative efforts including the Basel III and initiatives to address Global Systemically Important Financial Institutions."[31]

[28] Federal Reserve Board, "Federal Reserve Board approves final rule strengthening supervision and regulation of large US bank holding companies and foreign banking organizations," February 18, 2014.

[29] Timothy D. Adams, President and CEO, Institute of International Finance, Letter to Tharman Shanmugaratnam, Chairman of International Monetary and Financial Committee at the IMF, and Marek Belka, Chairman of Development Committee at the World Bank, April 16, 2013.

[30] Michael Barnier, Letter to Ben Bernanke, BD/cq D(2013), April 18, 2013. Brussels.

[31] Hiroki Tanaka, Letter to Daniel K. Tarullo, April 30, 2013.

In response to such opposition, the Fed turned to a perhaps unlikely source—Basel Committee soft law. The Federal Reserve's regulatory point person at the time, Daniel Tarullo, defended the rule on numerous occasions and to various audiences. The reasons he gave were multifarious; however, the most effective was that, rather than undermining decades-old Basel Committee standards and processes, the Fed's rule was in fact a manifestation of them. Tarullo declared in a March 2014 speech:

> While the circumstances and risks may have changed, the issue of the appropriate roles of home and host countries is not a new one. Indeed, it was a key motivation for creation of the Basel Committee in 1975 following the failures of the Herstatt and Franklin National banks. Many of the Basel Committee's early activities were focused on the challenges created by gaps in the supervision of internationally active banks, as evidenced by the fact that Basel "Concordats" on supervision preceded Basel "Accords" and "Frameworks" on capital and other subjects.[32]

In particular, Tarullo held that the US rule, following the lead of the United Kingdom[33] and Switzerland, upholds the responsibilities of a financial center that hosts many foreign banks and does so in accordance with the stipulations and intentions of the BCBS's soft law concerning home–host supervisory relations. Tarullo continues:

> It is important to note that each Basel Committee declaration on the importance of home-country consolidated oversight [which is the responsibility of the home country] has also included a statement of the obligations and prerogatives of host states in which significant foreign bank operations are located... In accordance with this history, the current version of the "Core Principles for Effective Banking Supervision" sets out as one of its "essential criteria" for home-host relationships that "[t]he host supervisor's national laws or regulations require that the cross-border operations of foreign banks are subject to prudential, inspection and regulatory reporting requirements similar to those for domestic banks."[34]

After justifying the US rule by drawing on the BCBS's soft law that emanated from the 1975 Concordat, Tarullo goes on to extoll the committee's wisdom in identifying the host's role as a central part of ensuring financial stability:

[32] Daniel K. Tarullo, "Regulating Large Foreign Banking Organizations." Harvard Law School Symposium on Building the Financial System of the Twenty-first Century: An Agenda for Europe and the United States, Armonk, New York, March 27, 2014.

[33] Bank of England and European Commission officials counter that the UK's ring fencing (known as the Vickers rule because it is based on a report headed by Sir John Vickers) is directed at large UK-based banks and, unlike the Fed's FBO rule, does not discriminate against foreign banks. Author interview with Bank of England official, London, July 1, 2015.

[34] Daniel K. Tarullo, "Regulating Large Foreign Banking Organizations." Harvard Law School Symposium on Building the Financial System of the Twenty-first Century: An Agenda for Europe and the United States, Armonk, New York, March 27, 2014.

> In short, the work of the Basel Committee over the years has not been directed at restraining host-country authorities from supervising and regulating foreign banking operations in their country. On the contrary, the committee has repeatedly asserted the complementary responsibilities of both home and host countries to oversee large, internationally active banking groups, in the interests of both national and international financial stability. And the committee has frequently returned to this set of issues in responding to developments that pose a threat to the safety and soundness of the international financial system.[35]

The Fed's rhetorical strategies appear to have paid off. Despite making adjustments to its final rule in response to a number of these criticisms,[36] the Fed unmistakably moved the United States in a territorial direction. Yet the reaction has been surprisingly tempered and restrained. For example, in a reversal, the IIF, which had rebuked the Fed in 2013, appears won over by Tarullo's logic:

> One of the most challenging post-crisis issues was the resolution framework for globally systemically important banks. International standard-setters and domestic authorities have developed a co-operative regime on cross-border resolution through crisis coordination mechanisms of the authorities of home and host jurisdictions. Alongside the development of standards fair to all claimants that avoid inefficient and excessive ring-fencing, this has contributed to an environment which significantly improves the stability of international finance and the global economy. (Carr and Ekberg 2017: 5)

Tarullo's arguments, draped in the legitimacy of the BCBS's soft law, also apparently resonated with like-minded foreign counterparts—and help us understand why the transatlantic conflicts over the Fed's FBO rule did not escalate to the same degree as the conflicts over US approaches to jurisdictional issues related to OTC derivatives markets.

We do not suggest that all global conflicts have been eliminated in the banking sector. The United States and the European Union remain at odds over a Basel III revision concerning the use of banks' internal models to evaluate asset risk for establishing capital requirements.[37] Moreover, the European Union may still retaliate against the United States over the Fed's new rules for foreign banking organizations.[38] Yet for capital requirements and even the SIFI issue, the disagreements have mostly been managed through

[35] Ibid.

[36] The main examples are listed in the final paragraph of Federal Reserve Board, "Federal Reserve Board approves final rule strengthening supervision and regulation of large US bank holding companies and foreign banking organizations," February 18, 2014.

[37] Boris Groendahl and Silla Brush, "Global Bank Regulators Stick to Their Guns in Rebuff to EU," *Bloomberg*, November 30, 2016; Alexander Weber and Silla Brush, "Europe's Bank Lobby Finds New Lease on Life as Basel Deal Stalls," *Bloomberg*, March 13, 2017.

[38] Alex Barker, Jim Brunsden, and Martin Arnold, "EU to Retaliate Against US Bank Capital Rules," *Financial Times*, November 21, 2016.

Basel Committee processes. This pattern holds not only for the more formal procedures used to devise new standards for capital reserves requirements but also for the less formal discussions that contributed to revised norms concerning home–host responsibilities. There are examples of the European Union and United States managing difficult issues bilaterally, notably in the case of the FSB's development of higher ("additional loss absorbency") standards for G-SIBs.[39] Yet in banking, in contrast to derivatives, politicized bilateralism characterized by mutual threats of retaliatory action has been the exception.

Derivatives: a soft law void and the CFTC's extraterritorial gamble

The regulation of OTC derivatives differs in several ways from the banking cases. Early coordination efforts with foreign counterparts had little to build on, in contradistinction to the example of capital adequacy. Despite initial agreement on high principles, progress was slow, and US policy-makers and regulators began implementing Dodd-Frank derivatives rules before the FSB or IOSCO could produce sufficiently concrete international standards. And similar to the issue of resolving SIFIs, the CFTC, the regulator charged with implementing much of the derivatives provisions of the US law, developed rules (notably defining and governing the actions of non-US persons[40] and regulating swap execution facilities) that promised to transfer considerable adjustment costs onto internationally active firms. Unlike the Fed in the case of banking, the CFTC faced a remarkably contentious implementation process, in which it had to deal with unrelenting opposition (Pagliari 2018). This is all the more surprising as one might have expected the Fed's imposition of a less permissive, territorial principle for cross-border interoperability of foreign banks to be the more controversial and less manageable conflict (Greenberger 2011; Coffee 2014; Knaack 2015; Gravelle and Pagliari 2018; Posner 2018). Instead, the opposite occurred. The CFTC's insistence in key areas that transatlantic mutual recognition be granted on an extraterritorial basis sparked high-profile battles with industry groups and EU policy-makers (Johnson 2013; Coffee 2014; Knaack 2015), led to outcomes based on relative power as opposed to technocratic rationales (Posner 2018), and ultimately contributed to regulations with unintended loopholes and weaknesses (Gravelle and Pagliari 2018; Pagliari 2018).

This section shows that asymmetries across the subsectors of international soft law are central to explaining the contrast in outcomes. In some ways, the

[39] See the series of FSB reports and documents on Total Loss-Absorbing Capacity at <http://www.financialstabilityboard.org>.

[40] Technically, in the case of US persons, the CFTC issued a "proposed interpretive guidance." For a discussion, see Coffee (2014: 1277) and Gravelle and Pagliari (2018).

CFTC and the Fed were in similar positions as they both faced a high salience crisis of their sector. Yet the Fed had in its arsenal a political resource unavailable to Gary Gensler and the CFTC: soft law in the form of a decades-old deliberation over the responsibilities of home and host authorities in supervising foreign financial firms and their cross-border activities (Buxbaum 2016). Like Tarullo in the case of SIFI resolution rules, Gensler was determined to implement stringent and comprehensive regulation and lacked confidence in the commitment of other jurisdictions to act similarly. In a different context, he too might have pursued a strictly territorial integrationist approach. Yet unlike in the case of the Fed, the CFTC was not in a strong enough position to adopt such an approach in the face of expectations from foreign counterparts and industry associations. A main reason was that no established international standards existed to justify a territorial principle for cross-border interoperability in the derivatives markets. The CFTC thus sought what it hoped would be a close substitute: the exportation of US regulation through the back door, demanding foreign equivalence be based on similarity of rule rather than on outcome—an approach unworkable when the main interlocutor, the European Union, was equally powerful and seeking the same.

THE GENSLER FACTION AND THE PRIORITIZATION OF DOMESTIC STABILITY OVER GLOBAL COORDINATION

Derivatives are contracts between two or more parties who want to manage risks (i.e. to hedge) or exploit price differentials and volatility (i.e. to speculate) (Spagna 2018). The values of these financial products rely on underlying assets or variables that can be as tangible as the rights to the future delivery of a commodity (like corn or soybeans) or as intangible as the interest rate of a foreign central bank or corporate bond. "Over-the-counter" refers to transactions that do not take place on an organized exchange but rather between private parties. Dominated by a small number of dealers, mostly US-based banks and brokers (which is one of the reasons why regulators in the United States, who oversaw the largest OTC derivatives markets, had been reluctant to impose a regime of direct regulation), these contracts had been the sleepy cousin to other types of securities (Mügge 2009; Clapp and Helleiner 2012; Pagliari 2013; Helleiner et al. 2018; Spagna 2018).

By the first decade of the new millennium, however, OTC derivatives had become the world's largest financial markets (Spagna 2018). For much of the 1990s, the global outstanding value of OTC derivatives hovered around a few trillion dollars but by 2008 that number had grown exponentially to 35 trillion (a number that represents over half of global GDP; see Figure 6.2). And as has been memorialized in popular accounts of the financial crisis such as Michael Lewis's *The Big Short*, the rise of OTC products like credit default swaps and collateralized debt obligations is inextricably tied up with images of

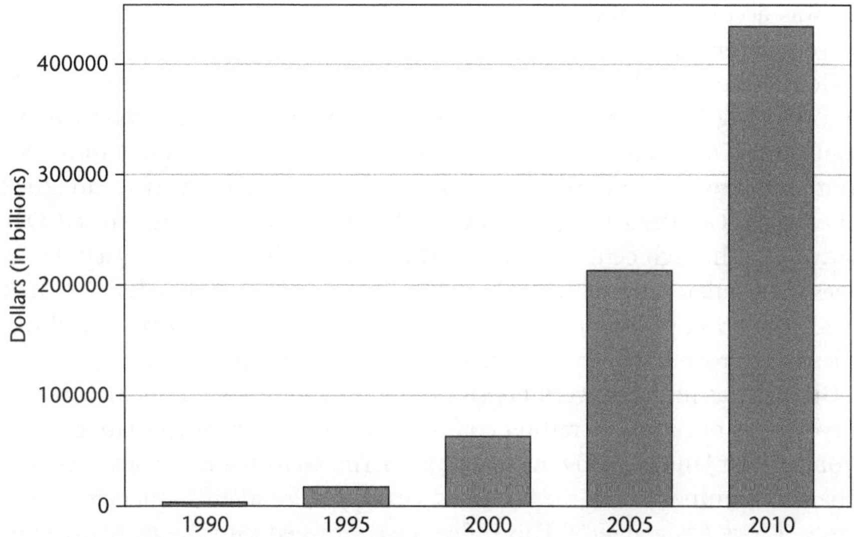

Figure 6.2. Outstanding interest rate and currency derivatives
Source: International Swaps and Derivatives Association (ISDA).

wild speculation and systemic instability (Cohan 2009; Lewis 2010; Sorkin 2010). After the collapse of Lehman Brothers, even defenders of the pre-crisis regulatory approach that relied on self-policing by industry conceded the need for greater public regulation (Pagliari 2013; Geithner 2014).

The OTC derivatives markets and dealers found themselves in the crosshairs of a regulatory faction that sought a thorough upgrading of US regulation. Fanned by the high salience of the issue, this faction gave priority to domestic stability over global coordination. Gary Gensler, whose CFTC team is credited with crafting the derivatives sections of the administration's plan as well as some of the key text of the DFA's Title VII,[41] was the central policy activist behind the US regulatory shake up of derivatives.[42] Gensler's past made him a surprising candidate for serious reformer. A Goldman Sachs financier-turned-Treasury official, Gensler had a hand in the 2000 Commodity Futures Modernization Act, which kept OTC derivatives markets free of direct and comprehensive regulation. His "Nixon to China" turnaround won him praise by the likes of Brooksley E. Born (the former CFTC chairwoman whom he had opposed during the 2000 reform), Barney Frank, and Elizabeth Warren.[43]

[41] Author interview with former CFTC official, telephone, April 18, 2017.

[42] Ibid.; Silla Brush and Robert Schmidt, "How the Bank Lobby Loosened US Reins on Derivatives," *Bloomberg*, September 4, 2013; Charles Levinson, "US Banks Moved Billions of Dollars in Trades Beyond Washington's Reach," *Reuters*, August 21, 2015.

[43] Bernie Sanders was not as forgiving: "Sanders opposed Gensler's nomination for months in early 2009, arguing that a Rubinite could never fit the bill. 'Gary Gensler, as part of the Treasury

He was accordingly reviled by much of Wall Street, especially the biggest players in the OTC markets.[44]

Gensler's proposals focused on breaking up what he saw as a dealers' cartel and bringing OTC derivatives markets and participants under robust public regulation (Department of the Treasury 2009). Taking a dramatic turn away from the pre-crisis model of self-governance by industry (Pagliari 2013: Chapter 4), Gensler's blueprint included the clearing of standardized OTC derivatives through central counterparties (CCPs), the trading of such derivatives on regulated exchanges or electronic trade execution systems, heightened regulation of major participants in OTC derivatives markets, and new rules to improve transparency (Department of the Treasury 2009: 46–9).

Gensler was in the powerful position not only of outlining the new regulatory regime but also of crafting core sections of the actual legislative text.[45] From at least January 2009, he (along with Tim Geithner and Mary Schapiro, Obama's nominee to run the SEC) was part of the President's inner circle, who wrote *A New Foundation*.[46] This influence continued into the legislative process. According to Bloomberg's in-depth 2013 investigation, "Dan Berkovitz, the CFTC general counsel at the time, and John Riley, the agency's head of legislative affairs, sent text and suggestions to Democratic staff members on the House Financial Services and Agriculture committees that ended up in the bill almost verbatim, e-mails show."[47] It was widely reported that "[t]he core financial industry won little in the drafts of Dodd-Frank, thanks in part to Gensler," whose team shaped the actual text.[48] After pushing his ideas behind the scenes and in public for eighteen months, "Most of what he and the administration had wanted, down to exact language in many cases, was now enshrined in law."[49]

In contrast to the example of capital adequacy for banks, the international financial architecture did not have on offer a clearly articulated strategy on how countries should address direct public regulation of OTC derivatives markets. Here the major transnational industry associations and regulatory

Department under Robert Rubin, pushed for the repeal of Glass-Steagall, the breakdown of those walls, which have led us precisely to where Citigroup is today, where AIG is today,' Sanders said in a March 2009 interview with Democracy Now. 'This is a hard-working guy. He is a decent guy. I don't have any animus against him personally. But I think President Obama has brought around him a lot of the Rubin mentality, which is not only deregulation, it's unfettered free trade." Jennifer Epstein, "Clinton's Progressive Beacon Is a Former Goldman Sachs Banker and Bob Rubin Protégé," *Bloomberg*, June 16, 2016.

[44] Ibid.; Graham Bowley, "Ex-Goldman Banker Urges Regulation," *New York Times*, March 11, 2010; Douwe Miedema, "Swaps Regulator Gensler: Banker Turned Wall Street Scourge," *Reuters*, January 3, 2014.

[45] Author interview with former CFTC official, telephone, April 18, 2017.

[46] Silla Brush and Robert Schmidt, "How the Bank Lobby Loosened US Reins on Derivatives," *Bloomberg*, September 4, 2013.

[47] Ibid. [48] Ibid. [49] Ibid.

groups had long pushed for self-regulation and light touch solutions. ISDA (founded in 1984 as the Swap Dealers Association), creator of the Master Agreement, is the best known but the field is also populated by other industry associations, such as the Emerging Markets Traders Association, Financial Industry Association, Derivatives Policy Group, Institute of International Finance, and the London Investment Banking Association as well as the G30, a private organization (Tsingou 2003; Pagliari 2013: Chapter 4; Spagna 2018). These private organizations provided technical and legal solutions to sustain the fast-expanding global derivatives markets (Porter 2003; McKeen-Edwards and Porter 2013). This field of private bodies represented the pre-crisis international face of US and UK domestic decisions not to impose direct regulation over derivatives markets. By assigning the industry to regulate itself, public officials had not developed best practices in prudential regulation (of capital, margins, CCPs, trading venues, transparency), nor felt pressure to harmonize home–host arrangements as access to foreign derivatives market participants went largely unhindered. The Committee on Payment and Settlement Systems[50] and IOSCO jointly published recommendations concerning CCPs but they did so in 2004, before there was a potential need to have them mutually recognized.[51]

This international institutional legacy meant that in September 2009 when the United States and other countries agreed at the G20 Summit in Pittsburgh to coordinate on a new derivatives regime of direct regulation (a regime mirroring the Obama administration's proposed legislation) no obvious transnational organization existed to support the task and certainly no organization with a reputation approaching the BCBS's (Pagliari 2013; Knaack 2015; Buxbaum 2016). In the fall of 2009, the SEC (which under the Dodd-Frank Act would continue to be a regulator of a much smaller portion of the derivatives sector), not the CFTC, represented the United States as its voting member at IOSCO (General Accounting Office 2004; Ryan 2013). Not only did the ISDA not have existing capacities for developing standards concerning the new cross-border issues surrounding direct regulation, but it had also long doubled as an industry lobby, which promoted self-regulation, rendering it unsuitable for the challenges of coordinating direct pubic regulation (Tsingou 2003). Thus, if there was going to be an institution to facilitate the heady G20 derivatives program, it would have had to commence from a rudimentary starting point. Even though the FSB was the G20's designee, as of 2016 it was not evolving into a Basel-like committee

[50] CPSS became CPMI in 2013. "About the CPMI," bis.org, last accessed July 26, 2017, <https://www.bis.org/cpmi/info.htm?m=3%7C16%7C29>.

[51] Author interview with two FSB officials, Basel, June 24, 2015; CPSS-IOSCO, "Recommendations for Central Counterparties." Basel & Madrid: BIS and IOSCO, 2004.

for derivatives. Instead, six distinct bodies[52] have produced or are in the process of writing twenty-five sets of standards, and these include only standards developed with public authorities and exclude the separate standard-setting processes of industry associations.[53]

The Treasury's June 2009 document reveals this disjointed and incipient international institutional landscape as well as the resulting domestic–international disjuncture. The G20 did not commit to a direct-regulation approach, as the United States had, until September of that year, and thus the best the Treasury could do (in *A New Foundation*'s Chapter V titled "Raise International Regulatory Standards and Improve International Cooperation") was to articulate reforms based on a pre-crisis reliance on industry solutions: "The G20 agreed to promote the standardization and central clearing of credit derivatives and called on industry to develop an action plan in that regard by autumn 2009" (Department of the Treasury 2009: 81). Chapter V also made it obvious that no transnational political arena existed equivalent to the one centered on the BCBS, nor was there a clear path in June 2009 to creating one around IOSCO, the FSB, or some new body.

Rather than being enmeshed in the processes of a transnational arena, Gensler and his team hardly knew their foreign counterparts and remained deeply suspicious of commitments to establish rigorous new regulation on par with what the team wanted for the United States. Unlike central bankers, derivatives regulators tended to be a more eclectic group. From different backgrounds, they were much less likely to have known each other before taking their positions.[54]

It is hard to exaggerate Gensler's concerns about foreign commitments. He was preoccupied by the European Union and London, in particular—and rightly so. At the time, 80–90 percent of OTC derivatives market activity took place in the United States and the European Union. So when Gensler spoke about the need to prevent evasion of US rules, he usually had in mind London's "light touch" tradition.[55] One of the first targets of Gensler's CFTC included the so-called "London loophole," the ability of New York traders to avoid US position limits and reporting requirements by executing transactions on a foreign exchange via terminals in the United States.[56] Indeed, Gensler's

[52] The OTC Derivatives Supervisors Group, IOSCO, CPMI (formerly CPSS), the FSB, the Committee on Global Financial Systems, and BCBS.

[53] According to the FSB, standard setting for derivatives markets has five work streams: Standardization (7), Reporting to Trade Repositories (6), Central Clearing (7), Exchange and Platform Trading (2), Capital and Margins Requirements (3). FSB, "OTC Derivatives Market Reforms Progress report on Implementation," Basel, 2014.

[54] Author interview with former CFTC official, telephone, April 18, 2017.

[55] Ibid.

[56] Gary Gensler, "Statement before the Senate Committee on Agriculture, Nutrition and Forestry," June 4, 2009; Jill E. Sommers, "The US Regulatory Landscape: The View from Washington." Speech to FIAFOA International Derivatives Expo, London, June 9, 2009.

team believed that US regulatory failures notwithstanding, those in the European Union had been worse.[57]

Gensler's concerns about foreign commitments and potential for regulatory arbitrage led to a number of extraterritorial provisions in the Dodd-Frank Act.[58] In October 2009, a Republican Congressman Spencer Bachus added an amendment to a discussion draft of the House's bill with the intent of keeping banks' foreign transactions outside the new US rules.[59] In testimony before the House Financial Services Committee, Gensler warned against the language[60] and, on Barney Frank's prompting, put his lawyers to work on the "extraterritorial provision."[61] Whether or not the Title VII language on the CFTC's jurisdiction was seen by others as a compromise (Coffee 2013; Gravelle and Pagliari 2018), the Gensler insertion, combined with its use as the main legal tool for the CFTC's expansive interpretation of US jurisdiction, demonstrates the Commissioner's determination to prevent what he feared would be foreign laxity.

In the same way that the international context (devoid of a transnational arena) influenced Gensler's lack of confidence in foreign regulation, it also served to undermine the ability of the industry groups who supported the Bachus amendment and might have done better in achieving their goals in Dodd-Frank if there had been credible international soft law in 2009 and 2010 from which to draw (Young 2013; Young and Park 2013; Pagliari and Young 2014). Unlike the case of banking, however, Gensler's detractors could not readily hide behind the campaigns of foreign counterparts, who also could not draw from agreed principles to help argue in favor of restraints on the extraterritorial reach of US rules.

Gensler was never under the delusion that he could prevent international coordination or that OTC derivatives markets would cease to be international.[62] In a perfect world of his own devising, he might have contemplated more

[57] Author interview with former CFTC official, telephone, April 18, 2017.

[58] The relevant DFA text can be found in Title VII, SEC 722, d: "The provisions of this Act relating to swaps that were enacted by the Wall Street Transparency and Accountability Act of 2010 (including any rule prescribed or regulation promulgated under that Act), shall not apply to activities outside the United States unless those activities—(1) have a direct and significant connection with activities in, or effect on, commerce of the United States; or (2) contravene such rules or regulations as the Commission may prescribe or promulgate as are necessary or appropriate to prevent the evasion of any provision of this Act that was enacted by the Wall Street Transparency and Accountability Act of 2010."

[59] Charles Levinson, "US Banks Moved Billions of Dollars in Trades Beyond Washington's Reach," *Reuters*, August 21, 2015; also see Coffee (2014) and Gravelle and Pagliari (2018).

[60] Gary Gensler, "Commodity Futures Trading Commission, Testimony before the House Committee on Financial Services," October 7, 2009.

[61] Silla Brush and Robert Schmidt, "How the Bank Lobby Loosened US Reins on Derivatives," *Bloomberg*, September 4, 2013; Charles Levinson, "US Banks Moved Billions of Dollars in Trades Beyond Washington's Reach," *Reuters*, August 21, 2015.

[62] Author interview with former CFTC official, telephone, April 18, 2017.

territorial terms for admitting foreign firms to participate in US markets. And he probably envied the Fed's ability to do so. Yet for derivatives, unlike for banking, there was no soft law from the pre-crisis era giving guidance on home–host issues and therefore no political cover that might have justified a territorial integration principle—even for the host regulator of the world's most important international financial center. Instead, because of the absence of such soft law and because of the constraints discussed above, Gensler adopted a strategy of giving priority to devising high quality US regulation and then figuring out how to get others to create regimes comparable enough to allow for deferment.

CONTENTIOUS IMPLEMENTATION AND DOMESTIC AND FOREIGN RESPONSES TO US EXTRATERRITORIALITY

The US law gives the CFTC wide discretion to forge an international strategy. The text extends its jurisdiction extraterritorially but also allows it to work with foreign counterparts and to commit to arrangements based on deference. For all practical purposes, however, Congress's final text, much influenced by Gensler himself, left the CFTC with few choices for how it would coordinate internationally and integrate US markets. The long list of rules to be devised had to be completed quickly and in conjunction with building up the CFTC's internal capacities. With the large gaps in the transnational arena and international soft law and with the European Union reforming at a slower pace, the CFTC could not practically coordinate internationally at the same time as implement at home. Despite having broad discretion, the CFTC found itself boxed into a strategy that promised to become highly controversial. Especially in 2010, 2011, and 2012, it was not in a strong position to create international soft law with foreign counterparts before writing its own rules, and with only a few exceptions, the coordination necessary for eventual deference arrangements came only after US rule-making.

The CFTC began implementing the 2010 US law at a rapid pace even though international coordination had just started. As the financial press and academic literature have observed, the CFTC did this in an effort to stymie industry efforts to gain during implementation what they could not achieve in the text.[63] Bloomberg News explained, "Staff members unaccustomed to working long hours, nights and weekends would occasionally sleep on the couches on the ninth floor, where the commissioners had their offices, the people said. With the industry arming for a major pushback, Gensler told them, speed and dedication were essential."[64]

[63] Coffee (2014); Silla Brush, "CFTC Chairman Wants New Derivatives Rules Implemented Quickly," *Bloomberg*, September 22, 2010.

[64] Silla Brush and Robert Schmidt, "How the Bank Lobby Loosened US Reins on Derivatives," *Bloomberg*, September 4, 2013.

Gensler's CFTC stretched the DFA to its limits in trying to prevent what it perceived as the erosion of US rules. Again, his team's efforts, the fierce reaction by the financial industry, and his increasing political isolation have been well documented (Coffee 2013; Johnson 2013; Gravelle and Pagliari 2018; Pagliari 2018). Bloomberg News continued, "At an October 2010 public meeting at the CFTC, Berkovitz, the general counsel, announced that the law gave the agency 'a wide reach and a broad reach' overseas. That could extend the rules to any branch or affiliate of a US bank, even if the branch was selling swaps to non-US customers. Bankers left the CFTC stunned, according to several participants."[65] Thus began the so-called US persons' controversy. In the United States by this time, the banks had recouped some of their lost sway on Capitol Hill (Pagliari 2018), and as Bloomberg News reported, "the lobby found sympathizers in both parties, including Representative Barney Frank... At a November 2011 hearing, he called the CFTC's proposal 'more intrusive and more complex than was necessary'."[66]

The CFTC's decision to implement first and develop a globally compatible cooperative framework afterwards also reverberated internationally, not only in "US persons" case but also in others such as the conflict over trading venues (Gravelle and Pagliari 2018; Knaack 2018).[67] By creating technically oriented detailed rules with only modest coordination, the United States inevitably came up with differences from the corresponding rules of the European Union, which was operating, albeit more slowly, within the same international institutional context. Regulators on both sides of the Atlantic faced pressure—for the same reasons—to establish mutual recognition arrangements on the basis of stringent equivalence requirements. Yet those differences fostered years of drawn-out contention that differed significantly with EU–US banking relations and with the stated goals of G20 commitments (Helleiner 2014a).

To preserve the international character of OTC derivatives markets, EU and US negotiators, without a Basel-like committee, felt compelled to work through the differences bilaterally, despite having mutually promoted multilateralism with the FSB's creation. Before the imposition of direct public regulation of OTC derivatives markets, cross-border interoperability was easy. Everyone agreed that some kind of regulatory equivalence would have to undergird mutual recognition. But on what grounds would comparability be determined? Given the underdeveloped transnational arena and little usable soft law, the European Union and the United States had to engage bilaterally—despite the increased chances that the terms would be set through tit-for-tat

[65] Ibid. [66] Ibid. [67] Parts of this section derive from Posner (2018).

bargaining rather than on the technical merits and the possibility that other jurisdictions would perceive bilateral agreements as less legitimate.[68]

In 2009, an OTC Derivatives Regulators' Forum (ODRF) had been set up to avoid just such an outcome. Yet as their own report explains, the group gained little traction: "Authorities participating in the ODRF have noted that several of the gaps and concerns the forum was initially formed to address are now more appropriately handled by these [FSB] standard setting bodies and domestic authorities."[69] Helleiner similarly concludes that "the unprecedented politicization of OTC derivatives in the wake of the crisis—particularly within the USA and Europe—has drawn many domestic groups into the policymaking process beyond those involved in the FSB's elite transgovernmental network" (Helleiner 2014a: 143). Over the next several months, the conflict escalated to the point that in the spring of 2013, the European Union along with seven finance ministers wrote a letter to the US Treasury warning about the CFTC position's potential for disrupting and fragmenting the derivatives market.[70]

The CFTC and the European Commission inaugurated the bilateral process, known as the Common Path, with great fanfare in July 2013.[71] In the official press release, there was even an optimistic suggestion that the CPSS and IOSCO's newly minted soft law (a revision of 2004 recommendations for regulating central counterparties) would be sufficient to ensure smooth resolution of outstanding issues.[72] But the new forum hardly seemed able to quell tensions, at least in a timely fashion. Indeed, one of the most visible spats that continued after the Common Path's launching centered on CCPs. CPSS and IOSCO's revised principles proved too imprecise for Brussels, which was reluctant to accept US CCPs regulation as equivalent because of a different margin requirement (Gravelle and Pagliari 2018; Posner 2018).[73] Central counterparties was not the only conflict that festered on. The CFTC's extraterritoriality resulting from its reading of Title VII provisions in Dodd-Frank and the subsequent expansive definition of "US persons" was also alive and well after.[74] In fact, the transatlantic negotiations reached their nadir

[68] Author interview with Bank of England official, London, July 1, 2015.

[69] Quoted in Buxbaum (2016).

[70] Financial Services Agency, "Ministerial-Level Joint Letter from the Financial Services Agency and nine Foreign Authorities on Cross-Border OTC Derivatives Reform to Jacob J. Lew, US Secretary of the Treasury," April 19, 2013.

[71] CFTC, "Cross Border Regulation of Swaps/Derivatives, Discussion between the Commodity Futures Trading Commission and the European Union—A Path Forward," July 11, 2013.

[72] Ibid.; CPSS–IOSCO, "Recommendations for Central Counterparties." Basel & Madrid: BIS and IOSCO 2004; and CPSS-IOSCO, "Principles for Financial Market Infrastructures." Basel & Madrid: BIS and IOSCO. April 2012.

[73] Philip Stafford, "Quick View: Clear Up Differences," *Financial Times*, June 16, 2014.

[74] Tom Braithwaite, Michael Mackenzie, Alex Barker, Philip Stafford, and Gina Chon, "US Rules 'Endanger' Derivatives Reforms," *Financial Times*, September 26, 2013; Gregg Wirth, "The Coming Clearing Turf Battle," *Traders Magazine*, October 30, 2014, Vol. 1(1); Anish Puaar, "US and Europe Lock Horns on Derivatives," *Financial News*, December 17, 2013.

in the summer of 2014 when the European Commission announced its intention to accept the regulation of clearinghouses in five countries but excluded the United States, and the CFTC suggested that to comply with US rules, European clearing of US-listed futures contracts should flow to the United States.[75] As this book goes to press, the two sides have painfully worked out many of the key disputes, including the ones surrounding US persons and CCPs.[76] And there may be a counter-example emerging that supports the chapter's arguments about BCBS: using soft law published in 2013 by BCBS and IOSCO, the United States and European Union (with Japan) have sought to coordinate first to devise margin requirements for non-centrally cleared derivatives (BCBS and IOSCO 2013; FSB 2016). Yet even though the EU and US authorities participate extensively in a fragmented field of transnational organizations (e.g. IOSCO and the OTC Derivatives Supervisors Group), bilateral negotiations have remained necessary and central in managing remaining conflicts.

The G20 financial regulatory agenda remains littered with outstanding issues. Nevertheless, the ones involving derivatives regulation have tended to last longer and be more contentious. The pattern is not just the observation of journalists or scholars (Coffee 2013; Knaack 2015; Gravelle and Pagliari 2018). In interviews during the summer of 2015, officials from IOSCO, BCBS, BIS, CPMI, the FSB, and US and European regulatory bodies always mentioned coordination of derivatives regulation as among the most challenging and contentious areas.

The fallout from the speedy and largely unilateral implementation of the Dodd-Frank derivatives rules has had consequences beyond the distribution of political authority between and within the United States and Europe. Finance watchers note disruptions for international markets. The uncertainty regarding derivatives regulation and the strict US and EU rules have caused considerable regulatory and market fragmentation and fueled debates about the de-globalization of finance (Gravelle and Pagliari 2018; Helleiner et al. 2018; Knaack 2018). The ISDA explained in 2015:

> Rather than being subject to multiple, potentially inconsistent requirements, derivatives users are increasingly choosing to trade with counterparties in their own jurisdictions. The result is a fragmentation of liquidity pools along geographic lines, which reduces choice, increases costs, and will make it more challenging for end users to enter into or unwind large transactions, particularly in stressed markets.[77]

[75] Timothy Massad, "Remarks of Chairman Timothy G. Massad before the FIA International Derivatives Conference." London, June 9, 2015.

[76] CFTC, "The United States Commodity Futures Trading Commission and the European Commission, Common Approach for Transatlantic CCPs," February 10, 2016.

[77] Briefing Notes, "The Dodd Frank Act: Five Years On," ISDA 2015.

One very real outcome of the slow pace of transatlantic rule setting has been an opening for other financial centers, particularly in Asia. Authorities there, according to Yu-wai Vic Li (2018), have used the prolonged transatlantic conflict to create autonomy from G20 pressures and to pursue the development of their own financial centers.

Other Arguments, Complementary and Alternative

US policy-making is notoriously messy, especially in the crowded field of financial regulation (Carpenter 2011; Konings 2011; Lavelle 2013). The post-crisis reform is no exception. A multitude of factors combined to produce its various trajectories, including the ones featured above: changes in international coordination, integration principles, and agency discretion that together comprise the interface between US banking and derivatives regulation and global finance. This section broadens the analysis to examine the importance and role of arguments other than ours featuring international soft law.

Did the particular individuals involved matter? Clearly, they did. CFTC Chairman Gensler as policy activist, rule implementer, and international negotiator launched a crusade that only a former financial insider could have carried off. He played a disproportionate role in the creation and implementation of Title VII and contributed to the confrontational tone of EU–US negotiations over derivatives regulation (Woolley and Ziegler 2012).[78] Still, we caution against giving too much weight to accounts based on Gensler or any other individuals. Prioritizing the role of one person misses how unevenness in the international soft law landscape defined what was and was not possible and thereby contributed to the differing orientations of policy activists (e.g. contrast Gensler with Tarullo) and created different opportunities and constraints for them.

Another possible argument attributes the observed outcomes to the inherent qualities of issue areas (Simmons 2001). By this logic, issue areas produce different cooperation challenges and need different types of institutional solutions. The regulatory problems confronting banking and derivatives authorities differed. Yet the politics and challenges may change dramatically over time even in the same issue area, and derivatives and SIFI regulation are cases in point. In both domains, crisis-induced ideational change sparked new political battles and innovative regulatory solutions at home and pressured officials to negotiate new terms of cross-border interoperability and create new transnational arenas. The derivatives example especially helps to highlight

[78] Ben Protess, "Regulator of Wall Street Loses Its Hard-Charging Chairman," *New York Times*, January 2, 2014.

the problems with the argument. In terms of what constitutes necessary international institutions, perceptions shifted before and after the crisis. Only with the post-crisis reframing did authorities begin to envision a need for internationally coordinated public regulation. Until then, officials believed existing private rules created by the ISDA and other industry associations sufficient. Given that an issue area is a "constant," other factors must account for change over time in regulatory solutions.

A related argument, attributing regulatory and institutional differences to variance in complexity across subsectors, merits separate consideration (Porter 2003, 2014; Morgan 2012; Carruthers 2013). By complexity in contemporary financial governance, scholars mean the growing number of transnational bodies, the expanded set of standards, and the more articulated architecture, characterized by increased differentiation and specialization and more defined linkages among the players and rules. They also refer to the greater complexity in the relationship between international, domestic, and regional rule-making (Porter 2014).

According to the argument, the observed differences in US reform trajectories are attributable to subsector variance in levels of complexity; the problems of derivatives regulators, by this logic, are simply harder to solve than those of banking authorities, and that is why Gary Gensler's CFTC, when compared to Tarullo's Fed, had fewer good options. We are sympathetic to the idea that increased complexity is central to understanding contemporary governance of finance, and scholars have long noted that international capital markets involve different and more complex technical issues than banking markets.[79]

Nevertheless, the argument offers a less robust explanation of the different US reform trajectories outlined in this chapter. While it is true that derivatives authorities, in adopting a whole new regulatory framework, confronted remarkably complex problems, it is no less true for banking authorities who had to struggle with novel approaches to regulating systemically important financial institutions. And did the challenges surrounding capital reserve requirements appear any less complex to the innovating banking authorities of the 1980s? The governance issues surrounding the internationalization of derivatives markets might very well be more complex. But they are not insurmountable.

What matters in the post-crisis Dodd-Frank reforms is the presence of well-developed international soft law in some areas but not others. Rather than natural differences in levels of complexity, this unevenness had more to do with the pattern of US and UK domestic regulatory approaches, which ultimately determined whether and when American and foreign authorities began

[79] For example, Porter (2003: 536–7).

grappling with the coordination and home–host problems. Because Washington and London accepted industry-policed OTC derivatives markets, less demand existed for (and therefore prompted deliberation about) home–host relations, in contrast to the banking world where authorities began working on these issues in 1975.

Are the trajectories of US financial reform and the subsequent international interactions better understood as reflections of differing arrays of interests, ultimately traceable to subsector and cross-national variance in industrial organization? As other scholars have shown, material interests mattered (Fioretos 2010; Hardie and Howarth 2013; Pagliari and Young 2014), and no explanation would be complete without reference to them. However, one should be cautious about taking the argument too far. The interest-based argument starts with factions and policy entrepreneurs who entered the reform period with fairly well-formed preferences. Yet the core policy activists in the United States and elsewhere did not always have fixed preferences (suggesting the need to examine preference-formation processes). Even when they did, the more interesting question centers on why some actors were more successful than others in seeing their preferences realized (Sell 2003; Shaffer 2012; Kirshner 2015). Working in an atmosphere of high levels of public salience and uncertainty, policy-makers satisficed in pasting together reform programs. Whether the end product resulted in continuity of market-friendly regulation is a topic of contentious debate (Helleiner 2014b). What is certain from our vantage is that positions concerning many of the provisions in the Dodd-Frank Act and the detailed implementation rules were frequently indeterminate and fluid, that some policy activists proved more successful than others in achieving their goals, and that soft law and the international institutional context influenced both preference formation patterns and the availability of political resources. This chapter thus shows that material interests hardly explain everything we want to know. The international institutional context—as an influence on preferences and a source of political resources—affected core decisions behind the changed US interface with international financial markets and governance.

Conclusion

This chapter supports the book's theoretical framework by challenging prevalent assumptions about the relationship between US regulation and the international financial architecture (Simmons 2001). Portrayals of the United States as only or primarily a source and setter of global rules miss the extensive interpenetration of the two. By establishing how the evolution of international soft law shaped the US politics of financial reform and its global interface, we demonstrate the explanatory limits of the one-way image. Rather than American exceptionalism, this chapter suggests that US financial regulation-making has a complex relationship with international institutions and processes similar to that of the European Union and other rising financial regulatory powers discussed in Chapter 4.

The detailed case studies comparing post-crisis reform trajectories of banking and derivatives bring out the effects of different international institutional contexts on international coordination, integration principles, and regulatory discretion and showcase the roles of arena expansion and legitimacy claims. In the case of capital adequacy requirements and regulations for systemically important financial institutions, key US policy entrepreneurs were already oriented toward the transnational arena, so much so that their legislative, implementation, and cooperation strategies were embedded within it. Asymmetries of international banking soft law account for much of the Fed's observed actions. To preserve discretion to devise US capital requirements concurrently with international coordination processes, it borrowed the legitimacy of the Basel Committee's highly developed international standards. To combat opposition, the Fed used the Basel Concordat principles on home–host relations to contain a backlash from industry associations and foreign counterparts as it moved toward a territorial market-access principle.

In derivatives regulation, reformers operated without a similar soft law infrastructure. Their policies were less oriented toward the transnational setting, and they had fewer relationships with foreign counterparts. The CFTC lacked a set of voluntary prescriptions that it could invoke to justify agendas, undermine opposition, and dampen conflict when it erupted over the US adoption of extraterritorial rules. The comparison with banking illustrates how variance in the soft law environment explains whether regulatory battles were contained within technocratic channels or followed a more politicized form of contestation that has had far-reaching, unintended ramifications for international finance.

These US cases—arguably the hardest from the standpoint of theory and observation—complete the book's chapters providing evidence in support of our argument about international soft law's second-order effects and the key role of legitimacy claims and arena expansion. In the conclusion, we consider the future of international soft law in finance, how these arguments might apply in other political arenas outside of finance, and lessons for international relations.

7

Conclusion

On January 31, 2017, Patrick McHenry (R-NC), the vice-chairman of the US House of Representatives Financial Services Committee, wrote a letter to Janet Yellen, Chair of the Federal Reserve. In no uncertain terms, he levels an attack against international soft law for lacking sufficient democratic accountability, giving too much autonomy to unelected bureaucrats and harming US banks and companies. "The Federal Reserve," he argues, "continues negotiating international standards for financial institutions among global bureaucrats in foreign lands without transparency, accountability, or authority to do so. This is unacceptable." He continues, "The international standards were then turned into domestic regulation that forced American firms of various sizes to substantially raise their capital requirements, leading to slower economic growth here in America . . . the Federal Reserve must cease all attempts to negotiate binding standards burdening American business."[1]

McHenry's diatribe against international soft law reflects the Trump-era campaign to revisit Obama-era financial regulatory battles, and the Basel III accord lists among the prime targets. However, the anecdote also reveals this book's central argument: international soft law not only represents solutions to the problems posed by globalization but is also a disruptive force woven into the political fabric of Washington, Brussels, and Beijing, as well as transnational regulatory arenas. Like other social and economic institutions, soft law has the potential to generate distributive consequences for markets and politics. Going beyond scholarship concerned with the short-term effects (e.g. whether it is adopted or not), the book turns attention to soft law's second-order implications and to how it destabilizes existing regulatory contests by becoming a resource to policy activists (our "legitimacy claims" mechanism) and restructuring and reorienting political actors and organizations (our "arena expansion" mechanism).

[1] Patrick McHenry, "Letter to Janet Yellen," January 31, 2017. On file with the author.

In terms of legitimacy claims, those seeking to upset the political status quo draw on the perceived legitimacy (or illegitimacy) of soft law to bolster their position and undermine support for alternatives (or assertions that none exist). Here, policy activists frequently borrow from soft law's reputation of being impartial and technically sound. As McHenry's example illustrates, however, they also advance their agendas by framing soft law as illegitimate and unaccountable. Their target is not only the particular soft law rule but also the authority of a competing faction (in McHenry's view the Fed and those seeking coordinated rules). In the case of arena expansion, soft law's generation and implementation shifts the locus of contestation away from Brussels and Washington to transnational regulatory arenas, unsettling existing pathways to political engagement, restructuring political organizations and interest group landscapes, and generating incentives for the relevant parties to reorient their focus, agendas, and strategies. Yet not all actors are equally suited to this new ecosystem. Through these two mechanisms, soft law's temporal disruptive effects influence the winners and losers of regulatory politics.

Over the course of the book, we use these theoretical tools to better understand the politics of finance. The empirical chapters apply this lens to answer policy-relevant questions about pre-crisis EU regulatory harmonization and transatlantic alignment, the rise of transnational industry associations, and the peculiar pattern by which post-crisis US reforms interface with foreign jurisdictions and global markets. These chapters invoke a wide array of evidence including elite interviews, archival material, press coverage, and primary sources to assess what happens to political battles and actors in the presence and absence of soft law and at different levels of its development. Methodologically, we compare across and within cases from multiple financial regulatory subsectors and various national, supranational, and transnational political arenas, at different moments in time. We also evaluate our arguments against competing and complementary ones. The results show that regulatory policy activists in Europe and the United States leverage the presence or absence of international soft law to win internal contests over a wide selection of issues from capital requirements to accounting standards to derivatives regulation; and that soft law's gravitational pull alters the interest group landscape and particular associations like the Institute of International Finance, which in reorienting to the transnational level sidelined competitors. The evidence also reveals how these second-order effects reshuffled the distribution of power elevating some financial regulatory actors (like the US Federal Reserve and the European Commission) but subordinating others (like the Federal Deposit Insurance Commission and national associations representing small to medium-sized banks in continental countries such as Germany or Italy). International soft law disrupts financial regulatory contests in national, supranational, and transnational political arenas, blurring traditional divisions between domestic and international levels while transforming both, and creating winners and losers in its wake.

Rethinking International Financial Regulatory Soft Law

This book identifies and clarifies how politics permeates many, if not most, aspects of international financial soft law; it also maps out the complex relationships between soft law and powerful financial actors, both public and private. In doing so, it aims to recast debates on the politics, power, and law of financial regulation.

Contestation, not just coordination

First and foremost, we challenge scholars and policy-makers who depict international soft law primarily as a solution for resolving coordination problems. By contrast, we stress how soft law reflects and provokes discord among competing political factions. We are not the first to suggest that a given body of financial regulatory soft law provides more than objective best practices or reflects bargains resulting from overlapping and competing national interests. Scholars have observed, for instance, that soft law may also mirror intellectual and governance monocultures (McNamara 2009; Drezner and McNamara 2013), which seem quite vibrant in periods of stability but also predispose economies to quick and rapid collapse. The alignment between the two transatlantic economic heavyweights described in Chapter 4 was based on regulatory principles very different from post-war national European ones that might have prevented the levels of risk-taking that led to the 2008 financial crisis.[2] Moreover, without embracing McHenry's perspective in its entirety, we agree that Fed officials' preferences for early and extensive coordination with foreign counterparts stem in part from their enmeshment in Basel Committee processes (Baker 2013; Farrell and Quiggin 2017). Critics on the Left as well as the Right see Basel III as an incremental reform that does not go far enough to rid the international banking system of unwanted risk-taking.[3]

Unlike these ideational arguments, we demonstrate regular and important ways that soft law generates political contestation, not just consensus. For

[2] Mark Blyth and Len Seabrooke, "Benefits of Unlevel Playing Fields," *Financial Times*, February 16, 2010, 12.

[3] Mike Konczal, "Sherrod Brown and David Vitter Have a New Bipartisan Bill to End Too Big to Fail. Here's What It Does," *Washington Post*, April 9, 2013.

example, as discussed in Chapter 6, US Federal Reserve officials had multiple motivations for promoting the quality of the Basel Committee's capital adequacy and home–host relations soft law. And preserving its own bureaucratic discretion over bank regulatory matters ranked high among them. This was not simply a story of regulators cooperating to ward off future crisis and political oversight (Singer 2007). Regulatory factions deploy soft law to achieve a number of political ends such as inter-agency or factional competition, which may result in economic consequences very different from those imagined by its creators (Moschella and Tsingou 2014; Kalyanpur and Newman 2017). Even where soft law does not resolve market problems, it often addresses political ones.

To give a further example (from Chapter 3) of soft law's political expedience, domestic bureaucratic turf wars created perverse and unintended effects of international banking standards. In the 1980s, the Fed hoped to replace risk assessment by individual bank examiners with a more scientific model, better suited to its organizational capacities (i.e. limited staff and resources compared to competing bank regulators) and mission (i.e. the guardian of the monetary system). Fed officials saw in Basel Committee soft law a strategy to outflank domestic political opposition. Ultimately, however, the Fed-championed model skewed decision-making as banks amassed allegedly low-risk securitized products such as mortgage-backed and asset-backed securities at a seemingly unbound pace (Wood 2005; Hemel 2011; Thiemann 2014). In this way, international soft law, driven in part by political motives, contributed to the 2008 banking crisis and its wildly uneven impact.

Such illustrations—and the more systematic evidence of our empirical chapters—do not militate against soft law's potential for harmonizing or coordinating approaches across borders. But they widen the aperture by showing that soft law regularly alters the prospects of competing factions in addition to generating market stability or otherwise serving the "public interest." This observation might give pause to policy-makers considering soft law's potential as a governance tool, or at least make them mindful that regulatory factions shape its substance and deploy it in ways that transform domestic policy.

A related theme running orthogonally through these examples is that financial regulatory battles continue over long stretches of time. Ongoing and dynamic processes, they feature disgruntled parties attempting to use changing economic, technological, and political conditions to recast regulatory bargains. Throughout these temporal trajectories of contestation, soft law may appear and reappear in various guises. This observation suggests the insufficiency of research that treats soft law as a discrete and stable outcome and limits analysis to an evaluation of its implementation or non-implementation at single points in time. The compliance debate in political science and international law (discussed in Chapter 2) gives a false sense of stability and social orderliness—as if markets would be safe if actors simply followed the rules. Equally important, political actors, anticipating the benefits and costs of soft law's multiple roles, use it for different purposes at different times. As McHenry's quotation suggests, for factions who lose in round one, they fight another day. The point is that soft law's content, deployment, and evolution are politically charged. We thus argue against research that uses the false distinction between agenda setting and compliance and in favor of approaches that integrate the two into a more fluid and ongoing research program. One way forward is to think more systematically about how rule implementation feeds back into rule development processes (Sandholtz 2007; Mahoney and Thelen 2009).

Finally, we consider a main thread of McHenry's letter: the relationship between arena expansion and legitimacy. Distrust of expertise has been part of a widespread backlash to expanding international economic interdependence. The increased scrutiny of expertise in the aftermath of the financial crisis has tarnished the sheen of science and technical knowledge and diminished its potential as a basis of authority (Fischer 1991; Eriksson et al. 2010; Mügge 2011b; Sending 2015; Nichols 2017). Anti-expertise disdain reached fever pitch in Donald Trump's rhetoric, which his administration and the Republican Congress are using to carry out a campaign against regulation in general, and financial regulation in particular, with the demise of international soft law as a primary aim. A House of Representatives bill, known as the Financial Choice Act of June 8, 2017, would roll back many of the central provisions of the Dodd-Frank Act, including several pertaining to international soft law.[4] The new bill would, for example, require that prior to their negotiation global standards be vetted through the administrative procedures used in domestic regulation, including notice and comment systems.[5] While the Fed requested comments when implementing Basel II and Basel III, pre-negotiation consultation is the exception rather than the rule. If the Choice Act were to pass, international soft law would face many more of the traditional veto points and players typical of domestic rule-making and treaty-based international governance (Newman and Bach 2014).

While the fate of the bill is highly uncertain, the inclusion of this provision captures an interesting relationship between the two key mechanisms identified in the book. As arena expansion progresses, excluded and disadvantaged stakeholders have incentives to protect themselves from transnational processes (Farrell and Newman 2014) and to use their political

[4] <https://www.congress.gov/bill/114th-congress/house-bill/5983>.

[5] See section 371 of the draft legislation.

resources—including perceptions of soft law's legitimacy—to do so. From this angle, these factions leverage claims of soft law's illegitimacy to limit its further development. The example of the US bill thus illustrates the response of a regulatory faction seeking to promote light touch regulation without international coordination. What might this political current portend for international soft law and the politics of finance? It is worth considering briefly the potential impact for soft law's second-order effects.

We believe that legitimacy claims of either positive or negative valence will continue to play a central role in the fight over financial regulation. The McHenry example demonstrates the persistence of soft law's second-order effects, by way of the "(il)legitimacy claims" mechanisms. Here, we anticipate battles between those who support international collaboration and those who oppose it, as well as between those who seek light touch regulation and those who support more consumer protection. While scrambling the existing constellation of factions, the Trump administration's position and similar future ones will likely amplify the importance of claims about soft law's legitimacy in the evolution of financial regulatory contests.

Despite campaigns to curtail reliance on international standards and diminish the relevance of transnational regulatory arenas, it is difficult to unwind existing arrangements—including regulatory discretion to cooperate with foreign counterparts—without resistance. A broad swath of industry, policymakers, and regulators has vested interests in international soft law. In a remarkable development, the IIF, in response to the Republican bid to renationalize financial regulation, defends international soft law:

> The role of international regulatory processes and standard setters is currently in focus, with some advocating a greater (and often, almost exclusive) emphasis on national regulation . . . This presents a genuine threat to the effectiveness of the global regulatory framework and the functioning of markets. Internationally consistency could be undermined, or even unravel, which would come at a cost to economies around the world. (Carr and Ekberg 2017: 1)

The IIF continues:

> The United States should continue to support and remain actively engaged with global standard setting bodies like the Basel Committee, the Financial Stability Board, IOSCO and the IAIS. Large, globally-active financial institutions should operate under a common consistent rulebook as capital moves around the world. A more fragmented, regionally-focused approach to regulation traps capital, inhibits cross-border capital flows and makes the global financial system more brittle and potentially unstable.[6]

[6] Tim Adams, "It's Time for a Review of Regulations, But Which Ones?," *IIF CEO Corner*, April 27, 2017.

As part of its strategy to blunt the claims of illegitimacy, the IIF and others in the pro-soft law faction are promoting ways to increase its credibility, notably by enhancing transparency on the part of standard-setting bodies (Carr and Ekberg 2017).

From this book's perspective, the debate over the Financial Choice Act reads as a testament to the arena expansion argument. Factions excluded from transnational processes fight to renationalize policy-making as a means to improve their ability to get what they want, while those enmeshed in and benefiting from the transnational arena defend it. Given the inchoate nature of the legislation and its unknown political ramifications, we can only speculate how the contest will evolve. We do know that competing political factions will continue to struggle over the boundaries and effects of transnational policy-making in finance.

False dichotomies, analytic silos, and contextualized power

This book takes power, in its many guises, seriously, which is why the empirical chapters focus on the behavior of the most important rule-making polities—the United States and the European Union—and the most influential industry associations. Explaining how international financial soft law contextualizes powerful financial actors complicates debates that paint it as either in opposition to or an extension of their interests. We highlight two points.

The first is that much of the literature on the global politics of finance separates the "state-centered" perspectives from "network" perspectives or domestic-oriented approaches from international ones.[7] Similarly, scholars of international law focus on whether soft law is a complement to or substitute for more traditional forms of state-led, intergovernmental rules, an emphasis that draws research back to questions of coordination rather than distribution (Shaffer and Pollack 2009; Brummer 2011). Too often the results yield false dichotomies and generate predictions that soft law, alternatively, reflects state or industry interests, or demonstrates the relevance and efficacy of new networked forms of governance. The Financial Stability Board, for example, is cast on the one hand as an example of states reasserting control over global financial regulation (Helleiner 2010; Reisenbichler 2015) and on the other as the quintessential example of complex governance at work (Campbell-Verduyn and Porter 2014). Our historical institutionalist and temporal arguments, by contrast, cut across these perspectives, incorporating contentious and cooperative interactions of the full range of participants in

[7] On the merits of synthesizing analytical approaches, see Grossman and Leblond (2011); Helleiner and Pagliari (2011); Helleiner (2014b).

the politics of regulation: state executive officials, independent agencies, and other members of domestic regulatory factions, along with transnational industry associations and standard-setting bodies. Thus we see organizations like the FSB as transnational sites of contestation that expand rather than replace the political arena for at least some traditional domestic and international participants but also spawn new ones (Halliday and Shaffer 2015).

The second point is that power in financial regulatory arenas does not operate in an institutional vacuum. The international institutional context matters. In complex ways that cross national, regional, and international boundaries (Grossman and Leblond 2011; Helleiner et al. 2018), soft law penetrates the politics of post-crisis financial regulatory reform in the United States, just as it infiltrates the politics of pre-crisis EU harmonization. Likewise, soft law reconstituted the IIF, turning it into the most influential financial industry association and, in doing so, reordered the interest group landscape. Approaches that emphasize a particular actor constellation from great powers to firms would do well to take soft law's second-order effects into account or risk introducing biases into their explanations.

Ultimately, policy-makers and therefore scholars want to know whether international financial soft law works: that is, whether a soft law centric international financial architecture creates rules and processes that meet social values and public policy aims. The answer lies outside the book's purview. However, our findings about soft law's distributional and temporal effects do place us in a position to comment on the related questions of for whom soft law works and to what end. As we have been arguing, financial regulation reflects ongoing political struggles among competing factions. Regulatory debates may start with issues of market stability or efficiency, but to understand policy consequences it is necessary to decipher the particular interests and organizational dynamics of the actors involved.

If one of the public policy goals for international soft law is to prevent the dominance of a narrow set of interests or the ideas of a technocratic monoculture, policy-makers must ensure a wide range of stakeholders have access to the political arena (Kingsbury et al. 2005). Yet not all voices are equally capable of engaging in such participatory schemes, particularly at the transnational level (Barr and Miller 2006). In the existing transnational arenas for financial regulation, it is hard to be optimistic. In addition to the challenges inherent in engaging directly at the transnational level, the political organization of non-firm societal interests in the area of finance has been perennially weak (Hacker and Pierson 2010; Pagliari and Young 2016). Even with the post-crisis amplification of these voices, no equivalent exists in finance to the transnational mobilization one finds over environmental, property rights, labor, or Internet issues, to name a few (Sell 2003, 2013; Cashore et al. 2004; Seidman 2007; Bartley 2011). If one believes, as we do, that the current architecture holds promise for encouraging rigorous regulation and facilitating a cross-border finance with socially acceptable risk-taking, then there is reason to reject both McHenry's draconian renationalization proposal that seeks lax rules and even more sensible renationalization schemes that strive for more stringent regulation. Opening up the process, however, will not be enough to shield public goals from specialized interests. Instead, governments and regulators should engage in an active effort to expand representation and the groups that are included in such policy discussions. Policy-makers might take their cues from the European Union, where the European Commission and the European Parliament, in the name of fostering more balanced political arenas, spurred the formation of new lobby organizations representing marginalized voices (Posner 2005, 2009b).[8]

Voluntary Disruptions in Labor and Environmental Markets?

The book's empirical focus has been on the relationship between international soft law and the governance of finance. In this section, we outline parallel processes at work in the areas of labor and environmental regulation in order to probe the plausibility of the theoretical claims obtaining in additional sectors. A brief review of the secondary literature suggests signs of soft law's disruptive potential across issue areas and actor constellations.

As in finance, extensive international soft law exists in the regulatory areas of labor and the environment. Transnational public and private organizations have issued a host of best practices, certification schemes, and voluntary guidance for public–private partnerships. As with finance, much of the existing academic research focuses on first-order effects—the generation of soft law and compliance with it (Cashore et al. 2004; Potoski and Prakash 2005; Green 2013; Locke 2013).

Scholars across fields—from sociologists and political scientists, to legal scholars and environmental scientists—call for greater attention to second-order consequences (Bartley 2011; Shaffer 2012). In the area of labor market reform, for example, the European Union relies on soft law as it has little binding legal authority in the policy field. Over the last decade, it has developed a set of best practices known as the European Employment Strategy (EES), which lays out a set of voluntary prescriptions. Much like our findings

[8] Examples include the creation of the European Venture Capital Association in 1983 (EVCA later kept its acronym but became the European Private Equity and Venture Capital Association, and then in 2015 changed its name to Invest Europe in 2015; <https://www.investeurope.eu/about-us/who-we-are/>), the Financial Services User Group in 2010 (<https://ec.europa.eu/info/node/8611/#latest>), and Finance Watch in 2011 (<http://www.finance-watch.org/about-us/why-finance-watch>).

featuring the legitimacy claims mechanism, research shows that reformists use the European Union's best practices to narrow agendas in member states. In part, policy entrepreneurs deploy these advisory practices to shape the framing of problems, limit agenda cycling, and refute arguments that no clear policy solutions exist (López-Santana 2006). Yet the European Union's soft law also acts as a source of legitimacy for opposing factions seeking labor market flexibility in domestic markets (Stiller and van Gerven 2012). Over time, the EES has altered the way that regulatory factions understand the policy agenda and their calculations about potential reform strategies.

Other studies indicate that international soft law not only affects the agendas and strategies of regulatory factions but may also transform domestic institutions as they gravitate toward transnational arenas. Amengaul and Chirot (2016) examine the Indonesian case of the Better Work's program to enhance garment industry compliance with the ILO's international soft law. A collaboration between the International Labour Organization and the International Financial Corporation, the Better Work program assists local NGOs and the apparel industry improve and monitor working conditions.[9] The study demonstrates that even when Better Work failed to improve compliance and factory labor conditions (for instance, with the introduction of long-term contracts for apparel workers), it was still able to harness the perceived legitimacy of ILO standards to help vitalize domestic institutions committed to collective bargaining. This second-order effect contributed to wage improvements and to the overall strength of unions (Amengual and Chirot 2016). Competing local and central government regulatory factions used the international standards as a tool in their efforts to reorganize authority between the two levels of government.

Seidman (2007) makes similar points in *Beyond the Boycott*, which examines the impact of fair-trade standards on domestic NGOs in Guatemala. Reminiscent of the IIF's reconstitution detailed in Chapter 5, Seidman demonstrates how international fair-trade soft law catalyzes the creation of an NGO, the Commission for the Verification of Codes of Conduct (COVERCO). Inspecting and reporting breaches of international soft law, COVERCO monitors global supply chains with subcontractors in Guatemala. In addition, COVERCO supports the rule of law and transparency in Guatemalan politics. "Its engagement with international audiences," writes Seidman, "stems not from a desire to bypass local institutions in favor of global ones, but from a broader effort to construct a more democratic and responsive state at home" (Seidman 2007: 104). Much like this book's finance examples, COVERCO shows how policy

[9] <http://betterwork.org/>.

activists use international soft law as a resource that then transforms the power dynamics of domestic politics.

Finally, additional evidence of the arena expansion theme comes from research on fair-trade coffee. As the salience of transnational standard-setting bodies has increased, industry has shifted its attention from national to transnational certification systems, a move with distributive effects similar to those revealed in Chapter 5's IIF–Basel Committee example. Jaffee (2012) explores this phenomenon in standards generated by Fairtrade International, noting that the creation of international soft law prompted large multinationals like Starbucks and Nestlé to organize transnationally and engage directly with the codes-creation process (Jaffee 2012). The companies shape the codes, in contrast to many local NGOs, which did not recognize the shift in governance arena and have less access to the standards development process. Over time, international soft law eclipsed local certification systems and thus, paradoxically, helped promote the interests of transnational firms.

Scholarship on environmental regulation offers further evidence of soft law's second-order effects. Research demonstrates that regulatory factions use international environmental soft law to mobilize and transform state institutions. Auld et al. (2008) show this in forestry certification processes, and Andonova (2014) uncovers similar evidence in public–private partnerships aimed at preserving the Brazilian rainforest. In both instances, private and public actors leverage the legitimacy of international soft law to promote policy reforms designed to strengthen state institutions and thereby protect the environment (Auld et al. 2008; Andonova 2014). As the political arena shifts to the transnational level, environmental standards and certification systems also produce uneven political effects as not all players have equal access to these new regulatory bodies. International certification systems developed by the Marine Stewardship Council to maintain fisheries, for example, have had wide-ranging distributional consequences in South Africa (Ponte 2008). Ponte demonstrates how arena expansion to the transnational level offers differential access to groups, resulting in significant second-order consequences. In particular, these fishing standards benefit white over black fishers, furthering inequality and undermining the latter's political mobilization efforts (Ponte 2008). Seidman makes a similar point in fair trade, as certification standards often put pressure on small and medium-sized firms that have difficulty complying with monitoring regimes imposed by such soft law (Seidman 2007). This example is part of a larger theme that spans finance, labor, and the environment, in which transnational policy-making disrupts the representation of interests (Cashore et al. 2004; Barr and Miller 2006).

The purpose of these illustrations is not to suggest that international soft law in finance, labor, or the environment uniformly has these effects. Our argument depends on an underlying level of competition among competing regulatory factions, which use international soft law to alter the balance among them. In those areas characterized by limited competition—because of weak domestic institutions or weak organization and mobilization of certain segments of the population (Bartley 2011)—we do not expect soft law to have such far-ranging consequences. Future research will map these boundary conditions and consider how they do or do not apply across different policy domains.

Voluntary Disruptions and Global Politics

In addition to shedding light on a phenomenon that may have relevance in sectors beyond finance, this book invites scholars of international relations, comparative politics, international law, and sociology to look again at the relationship between soft law and global politics. Over the course of the chapters, we built an argument that reconsiders the interaction of actors, institutions, and power in international political economy.

First, our argument draws attention to the importance of collective actors and individuals below the level of the state. Research on global finance and regulation that uses the analogy of systems clashing (i.e. great powers going head to head to set the terms of global competition) sacrifices too much for the sake of theoretical parsimony (Drezner 2007). Our theory and evidence establish that there is often no "United States" or "European Union" position. Instead, global politics is marked by competing regulatory factions within and across jurisdictions that hope to defend or transform the domestic and international rules affecting them. They engage domestic and regional as well as transnational channels of politics (Farrell and Newman 2014). In some regulatory contests over international rules, the main fights are not between jurisdictions but among groups that span them. As we demonstrate for the United States and the European Union, regulators, other public officials, and private actors often ally with counterparts in other countries and use soft law to do battle at home as well as abroad.

We do not discount the importance of nationally (and regionally, in the European Union) bounded markets and regulations. To the contrary, large internationalized markets can be a source of power (Newman 2008b; Posner 2009b; Newman and Posner 2011). Part of bureaucratic infighting involves factions and activists vying for regulatory control over national markets, precisely because market size offers a powerful weapon for fighting internal and external battles. National markets, however, are not the captives of a single unitary actor called the "state." They are political resources that serve the whims of certain regulatory agencies or factions as opposed to others. We encourage a theoretical shift away from emphasizing "states" as the primary unit of analysis to incorporating the diverse struggles transpiring between and among political actors below the level of the chief executive. We do not envision a chaotic proliferation of endless actor-types. Instead, we see ample room for research to focus on the coherent patterns of regulatory factions appearing within and across jurisdictions.

As a result, we reject sharp distinctions between levels of politics. Scholars of international relations and comparative politics bracket the international from the domestic either through arguments about exogenous shocks or second-image reversed dynamics. While allowing for global–domestic interactions, these approaches miss the fundamental interpenetration of the two (Callaghan 2010; Oatley 2011; Weinberg 2016). As we show through our empirical studies, domestic political disputes structure transnational efforts that feed back into domestic institutional changes and, in turn, transform global interactions. We thus see little value in maintaining such sharp disciplinary subfield divides given these dynamic and endogenous interconnections. We call on scholars active in both international relations and comparative politics to incorporate the transnational dynamics, which influence both.

Second, scholars do not have to be structural realists to be interested in issues of power. The artificial divide among IR rationalists and institutionalists, pitting those interested in power and those interested in institutions, is too stark and occupies too much intellectual space. The former, falling under realism's wide umbrella, tend to emphasize state-centric accounts and the distributive consequences of cooperation (Krasner 1991). With respect to global regulation and finance, these scholars focus on the role of relative power, defined largely by market size, in shaping the ability of states to externalize adjustment costs and set global rules (Helleiner 1996; Simmons 2001; Drezner 2007). Rational institutionalists, by contrast, emphasize how institutions tame power (i.e. by making commitments believable or by providing information) and enhance welfare (Koremenos et al. 2001).

While rejecting the traditional structural realist stance that institutions are epiphenomenal to great power interests, behavior, and relations, our book is not a frontal attack on rationalist accounts of power and institutions. Instead, it adds to a growing chorus of voices contending that institutions generate, contextualize, and disrupt power (Knight 1992; Moe 2005; Newman 2008b; Posner 2009a, 2009b; Farrell and Newman 2014; Newman and Posner 2016a, 2016b; Voeten Forthcoming). *Voluntary Disruptions* attests to the independent and measurable effects of institutions on powerful actors and relations among them. In Chapters 4 and 6, for example, we show that institutions largely explain why the rise of bipolarity in finance sometimes generates relatively harmonious interactions but other times conflictual ones. Institutions, here, provide resources for activists—an understanding of institutions that harks back to an earlier literature on interdependence that asked how the complexity of global governance might offer new political opportunities to multifarious actors including regulators, firms, and non-governmental organizations (Keohane and Nye 1977; Risse-Kappen 1995). A second generation of research in this vein depicts global governance in terms of problem solving rather than politics (Slaughter 2004; Sabel and Zeitlin 2010). Here too, we challenge those rationalist institutional accounts that emphasize the ability of institutions to promote—through information or commitment mechanisms—the social welfare. We hope this book reinvigorates the more political aspects of contestation and redistribution (Knight 1992; Moe 2005; Voeten Forthcoming).

In Chapter 5, like many accounts of domestic institutions, we observe that international institutions affect who has access to and influence over decision-making and structure the interests and organization of political actors. Many of the things we claim that institutions do—structure, orient, and constitute—are consistent with an amalgam of ideas put forth by constructivists, critical IR scholars, historical institutionalists, sociological and rationalist institutionalists (Fligstein 1996; Blyth 2002; McNamara 2002; Sell 2003) and we unapologetically encourage others to borrow and synthesize as well.

Lastly, our approach to international institutions benefits from insights drawn from domestic-level research on the importance of time and temporality. A tenet of historical institutionalism, originally developed in the fields of comparative politics and American political development, is that institutions have temporal effects capable of altering political dynamics (Thelen 2003; Pierson 2004; Mahoney and Thelen 2009). This book belongs to the recent trend in IR scholarship that borrows from the historical institutionalist toolkit (Farrell and Newman 2010; Posner 2010a; Fioretos 2011). It is an explicit attempt to integrate concepts like policy feedback (an endogenous process of change in which governance decisions over time shape actor preferences, resources, and capabilities) into the study of international politics. The takeaway, we think, is that soft law is similar to other domestic and international institutions, and thus the politics surrounding it can rarely be captured in an atemporal analytical snapshot.

The politics of institutions is an ongoing struggle, and international soft law is as much a powerful disruptive force as an attempt to resolve market frictions or failures. In making these points, *Voluntary Disruptions* calls on scholars and policy-makers to take seriously the ramifications of international soft law as it ripples through global politics.

Bibliography

Abbott, Kenneth W., and Duncan Snidal. 2000. "Hard and Soft Law in International Governance." *International Organization* 54 (3): 421–56.

Abbott, Kenneth W., and Duncan Snidal. 2002. "Values and Interests: International Legalization in the Fight against Corruption." *Journal of Legal Studies* 31 (s1): 141–77.

Abbott, Kenneth W., Jessica F. Green, and Robert O. Keohane. 2016. "Organizational Ecology and Institutional Change in Global Governance." *International Organization* 70 (2): 247–77.

Abdelal, Rawi. 2007. *Capital Rules: The Construction of Global Finance*. Cambridge, MA: Harvard University Press.

Alexander, Kern, Rahul Dhumale, and John Eatwell. 2006. *Global Governance of Financial Systems: The International Regulation of Systemic Risk*. Oxford: Oxford University Press.

Alter, Karen. 1998. "Who Are the 'Masters of the Treaty'? European Governments and the European Court of Justice." *International Organization* 52 (1): 121–47.

Amengual, Matthew, and Laura Chirot. 2016. "Reinforcing the State: Transnational and State Labor Regulation in Indonesia." *ILR Review* 69 (5): 1056–80.

Amyx, Jennifer Ann. 2004. *Japan's Financial Crisis: Institutional Rigidity and Reluctant Change*. Princeton, NJ: Princeton University Press.

Andonova, Liliana B. 2014. "Boomerangs to Partnerships? Explaining State Participation in Transnational Partnerships for Sustainability." *Comparative Political Studies* 47 (3): 481–515.

Andonova, Liliana B., Michele M. Betsill, and Harriet Bulkeley. 2009. "Transnational Climate Governance." *Global Environmental Politics* 9 (2): 52–73.

Andonova, Liliana B., and Ioana A. Tuta. 2014. "Transnational Networks and Paths to EU Environmental Compliance: Evidence from New Member States." *JCMS: Journal of Common Market Studies* 52 (4): 775–93.

Andrews, David M. 1994. "Capital Mobility and State Autonomy: Toward a Structural Theory of International Monetary Relations." *International Studies Quarterly* 38 (2): 193–218.

Auld, Graeme, Lars H. Gulbrandsen, and Constance L. McDermott. 2008. "Certification Schemes and the Impacts on Forests and Forestry." *Annual Review of Environment and Resources* 33 (1): 187–211.

Ayadi, Rym. 2007. "Solvency II: A Revolution for Regulating European Insurance and Re-Insurance Companies." *Journal of Insurance Regulation* 26 (1): 11–35.

Bach, David. 2010. "Varieties of Cooperation: The Domestic Institutional Roots of Global Governance." *Review of International Studies* 36 (3): 561–89.

Bach, David, and Abraham Newman. 2007. "The European Regulatory State and Global Public Policy: Micro-Institutions and Macro-Influence." *Journal of European Public Policy* 16 (4): 827–46.

Bach, David, and Abraham Newman. 2010. "Transgovernmental Networks and Domestic Policy Convergence: Evidence from Insider Trading Regulation." *International Organization* 64 (3): 505–28.

Baily, Martin Neil, Aaron Klein, and Justin Schardin. 2017. "The Impact of the Dodd-Frank Act on Financial Stability and Economic Growth." *RSF* 3 (1): 20–47.

Bair, Sheila. 2013. *Bull by the Horns: Fighting to Save Main Street from Wall Street and Wall Street from Itself.* New York: Simon & Schuster.

Baker, Andrew. 2006. *The Group of Seven: Finance Ministries, Central Banks, and Global Financial Governance.* London: Routledge.

Baker, Andrew. 2010. "Restraining Regulatory Capture? Anglo-America, Crisis Politics and Trajectories of Change in Global Financial Governance." *International Affairs* 86 (3): 647–63.

Baker, Andrew. 2013. "The New Political Economy of the Macroprudential Ideational Shift." *New Political Economy* 18 (1): 112–39.

Barnett, Michael, and Martha Finnemore. 2004. *Rules for the World: International Organizations in Global Politics*. Ithaca, NY: Cornell University Press.

Barr, Michael S., and Geoffrey P. Miller. 2006. "Global Administrative Law: The View from Basel." *European Journal of International Law* 17 (1): 15–46.

Bartley, Tim. 2011. "Transnational Governance as the Layering of Rules: Intersections of Public and Private Standards." *Theoretical Inquiries in Law* 12 (2): 517–42.

Baumgartner, Frank R., Jeffrey M. Berry, and Marie Hojnacki. 2009. *Lobbying and Policy Change: Who Wins, Who Loses, and Why*. Chicago, IL: University of Chicago Press.

BCBS and IOSCO. 2013. "Margin Requirements for Non-Centrally Cleared Derivatives." September. <http://www.bis.org/publ/bcbs261.pdf>.

Berger, Suzanne, ed. 1983. *Organizing Interests in Western Europe.* Cambridge: Cambridge University Press.

Berger, Suzanne, and Ronald P. Dore. 1996. *National Diversity and Global Capitalism.* Ithaca, NY: Cornell University Press.

Bernanke, Ben S. 2015. *The Courage to Act: A Memoir of a Crisis and Its Aftermath.* New York: W. W. Norton.

Bernstein, Steven, and Benjamin Cashore. 2007. "Can Non-State Global Governance Be Legitimate? An Analytical Framework." *Regulation & Governance* 1 (4): 347–71.

Block, Fred, and Frances Fox Piven. 2010. "Déjà Vu, All Over Again: A Comment on Jacob Hacker and Paul Pierson, 'Winner-Take-All Politics.'" *Politics & Society* 38 (2): 205–11.

Blustein, Paul. 2003. *The Chastening: Inside the Crisis That Rocked the Global Financial System and Humbled the IMF.* New York: Public Affairs.

Blyth, Mark. 2002. *Great Transformations: Economic Ideas and Institutional Change in the Twentieth Century.* Cambridge: Cambridge University Press.

Botzem, Sebastian. 2008. "Transnational Expert-Driven Standardisation: Accountancy Governance from a Professional Point of View." In *Transnational Private Governance and its Limits*, ed. Jean-Christophe Graz and Andreas Nölke, 44–57. London: Routledge.

Botzem, Sebastian. 2012. *The Politics of Accounting Regulation: Organizing Transnational Standard Setting in Financial Reporting*. London: Edward Elgar.

Boyle, Alan E. 1999. "Some Reflections on the Relationship of Treaties and Soft Law." *International & Comparative Law Quarterly* 48 (4): 901–13.

Bradford, Anu. 2012. "The Brussels Effect." *Northwestern University Law Review* 107 (1): 1–68.

Braumüller, Peter. 2007. "Cross-Border Exchange of Information and Cooperation Between Insurance Supervisors." *The Geneva Papers on Risk and Insurance—Issues and Practice* 32 (3): 301–18.

Brooks, Sarah M., Raphael Cunha, and Layna Mosley. 2015. "Categories, Creditworthiness, and Contagion: How Investors' Shortcuts Affect Sovereign Debt Markets." *International Studies Quarterly* 59 (3): 587–601.

Brown, Elizabeth F. 2009. "The Development of International Norms for Insurance Regulation Symposium: Ruling the World—Generating International Legal Norms." *Brooklyn Journal of International Law* 34: 953–98.

Brummer, Chris. 2011. *Soft Law and the Global Financial System: Rule Making in the 21st Century*. Cambridge: Cambridge University Press.

Buerkle, Tom. 2002. "European Disunion." *Institutional Investor*, July 1. <http://www.institutionalinvestor.com/Article/1027364/european-disunion.html>.

Burley, Anne-Marie. 1993. "Regulating the World: Multilateralism, International Law, and the Projection of the New Deal Regulatory State." In *Multilateralism Matters*, ed. John Ruggie, 125–56. New York: Columbia University Press.

Burley, Anne-Marie, and Walter Mattli. 1993. "Europe before the Court: A Political Theory of Legal Integration." *International Organization* 47 (1): 41–76.

Büthe, Tim. 2002. "Taking Temporality Seriously: Modeling History and the Use of Narratives as Evidence." *American Political Science Review* 96 (3): 481–93.

Büthe, Tim, and Walter Mattli. 2011. *The New Global Rulers: The Privatization of Regulation in the World Economy*. Princeton, NJ: Princeton University Press.

Büthe, Tim, and Helen V. Milner. 2008. "The Politics of Foreign Direct Investment into Developing Countries: Increasing FDI through International Trade Agreements?" *American Journal of Political Science* 52 (4): 741–62.

Buxbaum, Hannah. 2016. "Transnational Legal Ordering and Regulatory Conflict: Lessons from the Regulation of Cross-Border Derivatives." *UC Irvine Journal of International, Transnational, and Comparative Law* 1: 91–116.

Callaghan, Helen. 2010. "Beyond Methodological Nationalism: How Multilevel Governance Affects the Clash of Capitalisms." *Journal of European Public Policy* 17 (4): 564–80.

Callaghan, Helen, and Martin Hopner. 2005. "European Integration and the Clash of Capitalisms: Political Cleavages over Takeover Liberalization." *Comparative European Politics* 3 (3): 307–32.

Calomiris, Charles W., and Stephen H. Haber. 2014. *Fragile by Design: The Political Origins of Banking Crises and Scarce Credit*. Princeton, NJ: Princeton University Press.

Camfferman, Kees, and Stephen A. Zeff. 2007. *Financial Reporting and Global Capital Markets: A History of the International Accounting Standards Committee, 1973–2000*. Oxford: Oxford University Press.

Campbell, Andrea. 2003. *How Policies Make Citizens: Senior Political Activism and the American Welfare State*. Princeton, NJ: Princeton University Press.

Campbell, John L. 2004. *Institutional Change and Globalization*. Princeton, NJ: Princeton University Press.

Campbell-Verduyn, Malcolm, and Tony Porter. 2014. "Experimentalism in European Union and Global Financial Governance: Interactions, Contrasts, and Implications." *Journal of European Public Policy* 21 (3): 408–29.

Cardoso, Daniel, Philani Mthembu, Marc Venhaus, and Miguelángel Verde Garrido, eds. 2014. *The Transatlantic Colossus: Global Contributions to Broaden the Debate on the EU–US Free Trade Agreement*. Berlin: Internet & Gesellschaft Collaboratory.

Carnegie, Allison. 2014. "States Held Hostage: Political Hold-Up Problems and the Effects of International Institutions." *American Political Science Review* 108 (1): 54–70.

Carpenter, Charli. 2011. "Vetting the Advocacy Agenda: Network Centrality and the Paradox of Weapons Norms." *International Organization* 65 (1): 69–102.

Carpenter, Daniel. 2001. *Forging of Bureaucratic Autonomy: Reputations, Networks, and Policy Innovation in Executive Agencies*. Princeton, NJ: Princeton University Press.

Carpenter, Daniel. 2010. "Institutional Strangulation: Bureaucratic Politics and Financial Reform in the Obama Administration." *Perspectives on Politics* 8 (3): 825–46.

Carpenter, Daniel. 2011. "The Contest of Lobbies and Disciplines: Financial Politics and Regulatory Reform." In *Reaching for a New Deal: Ambitious Governance, Economic Meltdown, and Polarized Politics in Obama's First Two Years*, ed. Theda Skocpol and Lawrence R. Jacobs, 139–88. New York: Russell Sage Foundation.

Carpenter, Daniel, and David A. Moss, eds. 2013. *Preventing Regulatory Capture: Special Interest Influence and How to Limit It*. Cambridge: Cambridge University Press.

Carr, Brad, and Matthew Ekberg. 2017. "International Regulatory Standards: Vital for Economic Growth." Institute of International Finance, March 15. <https://www.iif.com/publication/regulatory-report/international-regulatory-standards-vital-economic-growth>.

Carruthers, Bruce. 2013. "Diverging Derivatives: Law, Governance and Modern Financial Markets." *Journal of Comparative Economics* 41 (2): 386–400.

Cashore, Benjamin. 2002. "Legitimacy and the Privatization of Environmental Governance: How Non-State Market-Driven (NSMD) Governance Systems Gain Rule-Making Authority." *Governance* 15 (4): 503–29.

Cashore, Benjamin William, Graeme Auld, and Deanna Newsom. 2004. *Governing Through Markets: Forest Certification and the Emergence of Non-State Authority*. New Haven, CT: Yale University Press.

Cerny, Philip G. 2010. *Rethinking World Politics: A Theory of Transnational Neopluralism*. Oxford: Oxford University Press.

Chey, Hyoung-kyu. 2014. *International Harmonization of Financial Regulation? The Politics of Global Diffusion of the Basel Capital Accord*. London: Routledge.

Chinkin, Christine M. 1989. "The Challenge of Soft Law: Development and Change in International Law." *International & Comparative Law Quarterly* 38 (4): 850–66.

Claessens, Stijn, Erik Feijen, and Luc Laeven. 2008. "Political Connections and Preferential Access to Finance: The Role of Campaign Contributions." *Journal of Financial Economics* 88 (3): 554–80.

Clapp, Jennifer, and Eric Helleiner. 2012. "Troubled Futures? The Global Food Crisis and the Politics of Agricultural Derivatives Regulation." *Review of International Political Economy* 19 (2): 181–207.

Coates, Katherine. 2001. "Regulation: Passport to Change." *Reinsurance Magazine*, August 16.

Coffee, John C. Jr. 2011. "Political Economy of Dodd-Frank: Why Financial Reform Tends to Be Frustrated and Systemic Risk Perpetuated Symposium: Financial Regulatory Reform in the Wake of the Dodd-Frank Act." *Cornell Law Review* 97: 1019–82.

Coffee, John C. Jr. 2014. "Extraterritorial Financial Regulation: Why E.T. Can't Come Home." Symposium on Extraterritoriality: Essay. *Cornell Law Review* 99: 1259–302.

Cohan, William D. 2009. *House of Cards: A Tale of Hubris and Wretched Excess on Wall Street*. New York: Knopf Doubleday.

Cohen, Joshua, and Charles F. Sabel. 2005. "Global Democracy?" *NYU Journal of International Law & Politics* 37: 763–97.

Coleman, William D. 1996. *Financial Services, Globalization, and Domestic Policy Change*. New York: St. Martin's Press.

Coleman, William D., and Geoffrey R. D. Underhill. 1995. "Globalization, Regionalism and the Regulation of Securities Markets." *Journal of European Public Policy* 2 (3): 488–513.

Conti, Joseph A. 2010. "Producing Legitimacy at the World Trade Organization: The Role of Expertise and Legal Capacity." *Socio-Economic Review* 8 (1): 131–55.

Cooke, Peter. 1990. "International Convergence of Capital Adequacy Measurement and Standards." In *The Future of Financial Systems and Services*, ed. Edward Gardener, 310–35. New York: St Martin's Press.

Corrigan, E. Gerald, J. Virgil Mattingly, and William Taylor. 1992. "The Federal Reserve's Views on BCCI." *The International Lawyer* 26 (4): 963–86.

Culpepper, Pepper D. 2010. *Quiet Politics and Business Power: Corporate Control in Europe and Japan*. Cambridge: Cambridge University Press.

Culpepper, Pepper D. 2015. "Structural Power and Political Science in the Post-Crisis Era." *Business and Politics* 17 (3): 391–409.

Cummins, J. David, and Mary Weiss. 2000. "The Global Market for Reinsurance." In *Papers on Financial Services*, ed. Robert E. Litan and Anthony M. Santomero, 159–222. Washington, DC: Brookings Institution Press.

Cutler, Claire. 2010. "The Legitimacy of Private Transnational Governance: Experts and the Transnational Market for Force." *Socio-Economic Review* 8 (1): 157–85.

Cutler, Claire, Virginia Haufler, and Tony Porter. 1999. *Private Authority and International Affairs*. Albany, NY: SUNY.

Dale, Richard. 1984. *The Regulation of International Banking*. Cambridge: Woodhead-Faulkner.

David, Paul A. 1985. "Clio and the Economics of QWERTY." *American Economic Review* 75 (2): 332–7.

Davies, Howard, and David Green. 2008. *Global Financial Regulation: The Essential Guide*. Cambridge: Polity Press.

Davis, Christina L. 2004. "International Institutions and Issue Linkage: Building Support for Agricultural Trade Liberalization." *American Political Science Review* 98 (1): 153–69.

Deeg, Richard. 1999. *Financial Capitalism Unveiled: Banks and the German Political Economy*. Ann Arbor, MI: University of Michigan Press.

Deeg, Richard. 2010. "Institutional Change in Financial Systems." In *The Oxford Handbook of Comparative Institutional Analysis*, ed. Glenn Morgan, John Campbell, Colin Crouch, Peer Hull Kristensen, Ove Kai Pedersen, and Richard Whitley, 309–34. Oxford: Oxford University Press.

Deeg, Richard, and Susanne Lütz. 2000. "Internationalization and Financial Federalism." *Comparative Political Studies* 33 (3): 374–405.

Della Porta, Donatella, and Sidney G. Tarrow, eds. 2005. *Transnational Protest and Global Activism*. Lanham, MD: Rowman & Littlefield.

Demirgüç-Kunt, Asli, Baybars Karacaovali, and Luc Laeven. 2005. "Deposit Insurance Around the World: A Comprehensive Database." SSRN Scholarly Paper ID 756851. World Bank Policy Research Working Paper No. 3628. Washington, DC: World Bank. <https://papers.ssrn.com/abstract=756851>.

Department of the Treasury. 2009. "Financial Regulatory Reform: A New Foundation." Washington, DC. <https://www.treasury.gov/initiatives/Documents/FinalReport_web.pdf>.

Derthick, Martha, and Paul J. Quirk. 1985. *The Politics of Deregulation*. Washington, DC: Brookings Institution Press.

Deutsch, Klaus. 2014. "Transatlantic Consistency? Financial Regulation, the G20 and the TTIP." Deutsche Bank Research. July 9. <https://www.dbresearch.com/PROD/DBR_INTERNET_EN-PROD/PROD0000000000336924/Transatlantic+consistency%3F+Financial+regulation,+the+G20+and+the+TTIP.pdf>.

DiMaggio, Paul, and Walter W. Powell. 1983. "The Iron Cage Revisited: Collective Rationality and Institutional Isomorphism in Organizational Fields." *American Sociological Review* 48 (2): 147–60.

Djelic, Marie-Laure, and Sigrid Quack. 2010. *Transnational Communities: Shaping Global Economic Governance*. Cambridge: Cambridge University Press.

Dorf, Michael, and Charles Sabel. 1998. "A Constitution of Democratic Experimentalism." *Columbia Law Review* 98 (2): 267–473.

Drezner, Daniel. 2007. *All Politics Is Global: Explaining International Regulatory Regimes*. Princeton, NJ: Princeton University Press.

Drezner, Daniel. 2014. *The System Worked: How the World Stopped Another Great Depression*. Oxford: Oxford University Press.

Drezner, Daniel, and Kathleen R. McNamara. 2013. "International Political Economy, Global Financial Orders and the 2008 Financial Crisis." *Perspectives on Politics* 11 (1): 155–66.

Egan, Michelle. 2001. *Constructing a European Market: Standards, Regulation, and Governance*. Oxford: Oxford University Press.

Eichengreen, Barry. 1999. *Toward a New International Financial Architecture*. Washington, DC: Peterson Institute for International Economics.

Eriksson, Johan, Mikael Karlsson, and Marta Reuter. 2010. "Technocracy, Politicization, and Noninvolvement: Politics of Expertise in the European Regulation of Chemicals." *Review of Policy Research* 27 (2): 167–85.

European Commission. 1983. "Financial Integration." *Official Journal* COM 83/207, April 20.

European Commission. 1985. "Completing the Internal Market: White Paper from the Commission to the European Council." *Official Journal* COM 85/310 final, June 14.

European Commission. 1995. "Accounting Harmonisation: A New Strategy vis-à-vis International Harmonisation." <http://ec.europa.eu/internal_market/accounting/docs/com-95-508/com-95-508_en.pdf>.

European Commission. 1998. "Financial Services: Building a Framework for Action." *Official Journal* IP/98/941, October 28.

European Commission. 1999. "Financial Services: Implementing the Framework for Financial Markets: Action Plan." *Official Journal* COM 232, May 11.

Evans, Peter, Harold Jacobson, and Robert Putnam, eds. 1993. *Double-Edged Diplomacy: International Bargaining and Domestic Politics*. Berkeley, CA: University of California Press.

Fairfield, Tasha. 2015. *Private Wealth and Public Revenue in Latin America: Business Power and Tax Politics*. New York: Cambridge University Press.

Falkner, Gerda, Oliver Treib, Miriam Hartlapp, and Simone Leiber. 2005. *Complying with Europe: EU Harmonisation and Soft Law in the Member States*. Cambridge: Cambridge University Press.

Falleti, Tulia G., and Julia F. Lynch. 2009. "Context and Causal Mechanisms in Political Analysis." *Comparative Political Studies* 42 (9): 1143–66.

Farrell, Henry, and Abraham Newman. 2010. "Making Global Markets: Historical Institutionalism in International Political Economy." *Review of International Political Economy* 17 (4): 609–38.

Farrell, Henry, and Abraham Newman. 2014. "Domestic Institutions beyond the Nation-State: Charting the New Interdependence Approach." *World Politics* 66 (02): 331–63.

Farrell, Henry, and Abraham Newman. 2015. "The New Politics of Interdependence: Cross-National Layering in Trans-Atlantic Regulatory Disputes." *Comparative Political Studies* 48 (4): 497–526.

Farrell, Henry, and Abraham Newman. 2016. "The New Interdependence Approach: Theoretical Development and Empirical Demonstration." *Review of International Political Economy* 23 (5): 713–36.

Farrell, Henry, and John Quiggin. 2017. "Consensus, Dissensus, and Economic Ideas: Economic Crisis and the Rise and Fall of Keynesianism." *International Studies Quarterly* 61 (2): 269–83.

Ferran, Eilis, and Kern Alexander. 2010. "Can Soft Law Bodies Be Effective? Soft Systemic Risk Oversight Bodies and the Special Case of the European Systemic Risk Board." SSRN Scholarly Paper ID 1676140. Social Science Research Network. <http://papers.ssrn.com/abstract=1676140>.

Financial Stability Board. 2010. "Reducing the Moral Hazard Posed by Systemically Important Financial Institutions." October 20.

Financial Stability Board. 2016. "OTC Derivatives Market Reforms: Eleventh Progress Report on Implementation." August 26. Basel: FSB. <http://www.fsb.org/wp-content/uploads/OTC-Derivatives-Market-Reforms-Eleventh-Progress-Report.pdf>.

Finnemore, Martha. 1996. *National Interests in International Society*. Ithaca, NY: Cornell University Press.

Finnemore, Martha, and Stephen J. Toope. 2001. "Alternatives to 'Legalization': Richer Views of Law and Politics." *International Organization* 55 (3): 743–58.

Fioretos, Orfeo. 2001. "The Domestic Sources of Multilateral Preferences." In *Varieties of Capitalism*, ed. Peter Hall and David Soskice, 213–45. Oxford: Oxford University Press.

Fioretos, Orfeo. 2009. "The Regulation of Transnational Corporate Identity in Europe." *Comparative Political Studies* 42 (9): 1167–92.

Fioretos, Orfeo. 2010. "Capitalist Diversity and the International Regulation of Hedge Funds." *Review of International Political Economy* 17 (4): 696–723.

Fioretos, Orfeo. 2011. "Historical Institutionalism in International Relations." *International Organization* 65 (2): 367–99.

Fischer, Frank. 1991. "American Think Tanks: Policy Elites and the Politicization of Expertise." *Governance* 4 (3): 332–53.

Flanagan, Sean M. 2001. "The Rise of a Trade Association: Group Interactions within the International Swaps and Derivatives Association." *Harvard Negotiation Law Review* 6: 211–63.

Fligstein, Neil. 1996. "Markets as Politics: A Political-Cultural Approach to Market Institutions." *American Sociological Review* 61: 656–73.

Fligstein, Neil. 2001. "Social Skill and Theory of Fields." *Sociological Theory* 19 (2): 105–25.

Fligstein, Neil. 2009. *Euroclash: The EU, European Identity, and the Future of Europe*. Oxford: Oxford University Press.

Fligstein, Neil, and Iona Mara-Drita. 1996. "How to Make a Market: Reflections on the European Union's Single Market Program." *American Journal of Sociology* 102 (1): 1–33.

Foot, Rosemary, and Andrew Walter. 2010. *China, the United States, and Global Order*. Cambridge: Cambridge University Press.

Fourcade, Marion. 2009. *Economists and Societies: Discipline and Profession in the United States, Britain, and France, 1890s to 1990s*. Princeton, NJ: Princeton University Press.

Fox, Justin, and Matthew C. Stephenson. 2015. "The Constraining, Liberating, and Informational Effects of Nonbinding Law." *Journal of Law, Economics, and Organization* 31 (2): 320–46.

Gadinis, Stavros. 2013. "The Financial Stability Board: The New Politics of International Financial Regulation." *Texas International Law Journal* 48: 157.

Galbraith, Jean, and David Zaring. 2013. "Soft Law as Foreign Relations Law." *Cornell Law Review* 99: 735–94.

Garrett, Geoffrey, and Barry Weingast. 1993. "Ideas, Interests, and Institutions: Constructing the European Community's Internal Market." In *Ideas and Foreign Policy: Beliefs, Institutions, and Political Change*, ed. Judith Goldstein and Robert Keohane, 173–206. Ithaca, NY: Cornell University Press.

Geithner, Timothy F. 2014. *Stress Test: Reflections on Financial Crises*. New York: Broadway Books.

George, Andrew, and Andrew Bennett. 2005. *Case Studies and Theory Development in the Social Sciences*. Cambridge, MA: MIT Press.

Gereffi, Gary, John Humphrey, and Timothy Sturgeon. 2005. "The Governance of Global Value Chains." *Review of International Political Economy* 12 (1): 78–104.

Gill, Stephen R., and David Law. 1989. "Global Hegemony and the Structural Power of Capital." *International Studies Quarterly* 33 (4): 475–99.

Gilpin, R. 1987. *The Political Economy of International Relations*. Princeton, NJ: Princeton University Press.

Glaum, Martin. 2000. "Bridging the GAAP: The Changing Attitude of German Managers towards Anglo-American Accounting and Accounting Harmonization." *Journal of International Financial Management & Accounting* 11 (1): 23–47.

Goldbach, Roman. 2015a. "Asymmetric Influence in Global Banking Regulation." *Review of International Political Economy* 22 (6): 1087–127.

Goldbach, Roman. 2015b. *Global Governance and Regulatory Failure: The Political Economy of Banking*. London: Palgrave Macmillan.

Goldsmith, Jack, and Eric A. Posner. 2006. *The Limits of International Law*. New York: Oxford University Press.

Goldstein, Judith. 1996. "International Law and Domestic Institutions: Reconciling North American 'Unfair' Trade Laws." *International Organization* 50 (4): 541–64.

Goldstein, Morris, and Nicolas Véron. 2011. "Too Big to Fail: The Transatlantic Debate." SSRN Scholarly Paper ID 1746982. Washington, DC: Peterson Institute for International Economic Working Paper. <https://papers.ssrn.com/abstract=1746982>.

Goodhart, Charles. 2011. *The Basel Committee on Banking Supervision: A History of the Early Years 1974–1997*. Cambridge: Cambridge University Press.

Government Accountability Office. 2004. "Financial Regulation: Industry Changes Prompt Need to Reconsider US Regulatory Structure." Washington, DC.

Government Accountability Office. 2016. "Financial Regulation: Complex and Fragmented Structure Could Be Streamlined to Improve Effectiveness." Washington, DC.

Gravelle, Matthew, and Stefano Pagliari. 2018. "Global Markets, National Toolkits: Extraterritorial Derivatives Rulemaking in Response to the Global Financial Crisis." In *Governing the World's Biggest Market: The Politics of Derivatives Regulation after the 2008 Crisis*, ed. Eric Helleiner, Stefano Pagliari, and Irene Spagna, 82–106. Oxford: Oxford University Press.

Gray, Julia. 2009. "International Organization as a Seal of Approval: European Union Accession and Investor Risk." *American Journal of Political Science* 53 (4): 931–49.

Green, Jessica F. 2013. *Rethinking Private Authority: Agents and Entrepreneurs in Global Environmental Governance*. Princeton, NJ: Princeton University Press.

Greenberger, Michael. 2012. "The Extraterritorial Provisions of the Dodd-Frank Act Protects US Taxpayers from Worldwide Bailouts." *UMKC Law Review* 80: 965–88.

Grossman, Emiliano. 2004. "Bringing Politics Back In: Rethinking the Role of Economic Interest Groups in European Integration." *Journal of European Public Policy* 11 (4): 637–54.

Grossman, Emiliano, and Patrick Leblond. 2011. "European Financial Integration: Finally the Great Leap Forward?" *JCMS: Journal of Common Market Studies* 49 (2): 413–35.

Grossman, Emiliano, and Cornelia Woll. 2013. "Saving the Banks: The Political Economy of Bailouts." *Comparative Political Studies* 47 (4): 574–600.

Gruson, Michael. 2004. "Supervision of Financial Conglomerates in the European Union." *Journal of International Banking Law and Regulation* 19: 363–81.

Guzman, Andrew T., and Timothy L. Meyer. 2010. "International Soft Law." *Journal of Legal Analysis* 2 (1): 171–225.

Haas, Peter. 1992. "Introduction: Epistemic Communities and International Policy Coordination." *International Organization* 46 (1): 1–35.

Hacker, Jacob S., and Paul Pierson. 2002. "Business Power and Social Policy: Employers and the Formation of the American Welfare State." *Politics & Society* 30 (2): 277–325.

Hacker, Jacob S., and Paul Pierson. 2010. *Winner-Take-All Politics: How Washington Made the Rich Richer—and Turned its Back on the Middle Class*. New York: Simon & Schuster.

Hafner-Burton, Emilie M., and Kiyoteru Tsutsui. 2007. "Justice Lost! The Failure of International Human Rights Law to Matter Where Needed Most." *Journal of Peace Research* 44 (4): 407–25.

Haldane, Andrew G., and Robert M. May. 2011. "Systemic Risk in Banking Ecosystems." *Nature* 469 (7330): 351–5.

Hale, Thomas. 2015. "The Rule of Law in the Global Economy: Explaining Intergovernmental Backing for Private Commercial Tribunals." *European Journal of International Relations* 21 (3): 483–512.

Hall, Peter. 1986. *Governing the Economy*. Oxford: Oxford University Press.

Hall, Peter, and David Soskice, eds. 2001. *Varieties of Capitalism*. Oxford: Oxford University Press.

Halliday, Terence C., and Bruce Carruthers. 2009. *Bankrupt: Global Lawmaking and Systemic Financial Crisis*. Stanford, CA: Stanford University Press.

Halliday, Terence C., and Gregory Shaffer. 2015. *Transnational Legal Orders*. New York: Cambridge University Press.

Halliday, Terence C., Susan Block-Lieb, and Bruce G. Carruthers. 2010. "Rhetorical Legitimation: Global Scripts as Strategic Devices of International Organizations." *Socio-Economic Review* 8 (1): 77–112.

Hamilton, Daniel Sheldon, and Joseph P. Quinlan, eds. 2005. *Deep Integration: How Transatlantic Markets Are Leading Globalization*. Brussels: CEPS.

Hamilton, Daniel Sheldon, and Joseph P. Quinlan 2008. *The Transatlantic Economy 2008: Annual Survey of Jobs, Trade and Investment between the United States and Europe*. Washington, DC: Center for Transatlantic Relations, Johns Hopkins University.

Hardie, Iain, and David Howarth. 2013. *Market-Based Banking and the International Financial Crisis*. Oxford: Oxford University Press.

Hardie, Iain, David Howarth, Sylvia Maxfield, and Amy Verdun. 2013. "Banks and the False Dichotomy in the Comparative Political Economy of Finance." *World Politics* 65 (4): 691–728.

Hawkins, Darren, David Lake, Daniel Nielson, and Michael Tierney, eds. 2006. *Delegation and Agency in International Organizations*. Cambridge: Cambridge University Press.

Hay, Colin. 2000. "Contemporary Capitalism, Globalization, Regionalization and the Persistence of National Variation." *Review of International Studies* 26 (4): 509–31.

Helfer, Laurence, Karen Alter, and M. Florencia Guerzovich. 2009. "Islands of Effective International Adjudication: Constructing an Intellectual Property Rule of Law in the Andean Community." *American Journal of International Law* 103 (1): 1–46.

Helleiner, Eric. 1996. *States and the Reemergence of Global Finance*. Ithaca, NY: Cornell University Press.

Helleiner, Eric. 2010. "What Role for the New Financial Stability Board? The Politics of International Standards after the Crisis." *Global Policy* 1 (3): 282–90.

Helleiner, Eric. 2014a. "Towards Cooperative Decentralization: The Post-Crisis Governance of Global OTC Derivatives." In *Transnational Financial Regulation After the Crisis*, ed. Tony Porter, 132–53. London: Routledge.

Helleiner, Eric. 2014b. *The Status Quo Crisis: Global Financial Governance After the 2008 Meltdown*. Oxford: Oxford University Press.

Helleiner, Eric. 2015. "Regulating the Regulators: The Emergence and Limits of the Transnational Financial Legal Order." In *Transnational Legal Orders*, ed. Terrence Halliday and Gregory Shaffer, 231–57. Cambridge: Cambridge University Press.

Helleiner, Eric. 2016. "Incremental Origins of Bretton Woods." In *The Oxford Handbook of Historical Institutionalism*, ed. Orfeo Fioretos, Tulia Falleti, and Adam Sheingate, 627–41. Oxford: Oxford University Press.

Helleiner, Eric, and Stefano Pagliari. 2011. "The End of an Era in International Financial Regulation? A Postcrisis Research Agenda." *International Organization* 65 (1): 169–200.

Helleiner, Eric, Stefano Pagliari, and Irene Spagna. 2018. "Governing the World's Biggest Market: The Politics of Derivatives Regulation After the 2008 Crisis." In *Governing the World's Biggest Market: The Politics of Derivatives Regulation After the 2008 Crisis*, ed. Eric Helleiner, Stefano Pagliari, and Irene Spagna, 1–26. Oxford: Oxford University Press.

Helmke, Gretchen, and Steven Levitsky. 2004. "Informal Institutions and Comparative Politics: A Research Agenda." *Perspectives on Politics* 2 (4): 725–40.

Hemel, Daniel. 2011. "Regulatory Consolidation and Cross-Border Coordination: Challenging the Conventional Wisdom." *Yale Journal on Regulation* 28: 213–52.

Henderson, Jeffrey, Peter Dicken, Martin Hess, Neil Coe, and Henry Wai-Chung Yeung. 2002. "Global Production Networks and the Analysis of Economic Development." *Review of International Political Economy* 9 (3): 436–64.

Hillgenberg, Harmut. 1999. "A Fresh Look at Soft Law." *European Journal of International Law* 10 (3): 499–515.

Ho, Daniel E. 2002. "Compliance and International Soft Law: Why Do Countries Implement the Basle Accord?" *Journal of International Economic Law* 5 (3): 647–88.

Hopkins, Raymond F. 1976. "The International Role of 'Domestic' Bureaucracy." *International Organization* 30 (3): 405–32.

Hopwood, Anthony G. 1994. "Some Reflections on 'The Harmonization of Accounting within the EU.'" *European Accounting Review* 3 (2): 241–54.

Hulle, K. Van. 1993. "Harmonization of Accounting Standards in the EC." *European Accounting Review* 2 (2): 387–96.

Hurd, Ian. 1999. "Legitimacy and Authority in International Politics." *International Organization* 53 (2): 379–408.

Hurrell, Andrew, and Sandeep Sengupta. 2012. "Emerging Powers, North–South Relations and Global Climate Politics." *International Affairs* 88 (3): 463–84.

IIF. 2007. "Institute of International Finance: The First 25 Years." Washington, DC. <https://www.scribd.com/document/355801717/IIF-The-First-25-Years-1982-2007>.

Ikenberry, G. John. 2001. *After Victory: Institutions, Strategic Restraint, and the Rebuilding of Order After Major Wars*. Princeton, NJ: Princeton University Press.

International Monetary Fund. 2001. "Quarterly Report on the Assessments of Standards and Codes." Washington, DC, June 29. <https://www.imf.org/external/pubs/ft/stand/q/2001/eng/062901.htm>.

International Monetary Fund and World Bank. 2002a. "Experience with the Assessments of the IOSCO Objectives and Principles of Securities Regulation under the Financial Sector Assessment Program." Washington, DC, April 18. <https://www.imf.org/external/np/mae/IOSCO/2002/eng/041802.htm>.

International Monetary Fund and World Bank. 2002b. "The Standards and Codes Initiative: Is it Effective? and How Can it be Improved?" Washington, DC, June 1. <https://www.imf.org/external/np/pp/eng/2005/070105a.pdf>.

Jabko, Nicolas. 2006. *Playing the Market: A Political Strategy for Uniting Europe*. Ithaca, NY: Cornell University Press.

Jaffee, Daniel. 2012. "Weak Coffee: Certification and Co-optation in the Fair Trade Movement." *Social Problems* 59 (1): 94–116.

Joachim, Jutta. 2003. "Framing Issues and Seizing Opportunities: The UN, NGOs, and Women's Rights." *International Studies Quarterly* 47 (2): 247–74.

Johnson, Christian. 2013. "Regulatory Arbitrage, Extraterritorial Jurisdiction, and Dodd-Frank: The Implications of US Global OTC Derivative Regulation." *Nevada Law Journal* 14: 542–619.

Jupille, Joseph Henri, Walter Mattli, and Duncan Snidal. 2013. *Institutional Choice and Global Commerce*. Cambridge: Cambridge University Press.

Kahler, Miles. 2016. "Complex Governance and the New Interdependence Approach (NIA)." *Review of International Political Economy* 23 (5): 825–39.

Kaldor, Mary. 2013. *Global Civil Society: An Answer to War*. New York: John Wiley.

Kalinowski, Thomas. 2013. "Regulating International Finance and the Diversity of Capitalism." *Socio-Economic Review* 11 (3): 471–96.

Kalyanpur, Nikhil, and Abraham Newman. 2017. "Form over Function in Finance: International Institutional Design by Bricolage." *Review of International Political Economy* 24 (3): 363–92.

Kapstein, Ethan B. 1989. "Resolving the Regulator's Dilemma: International Coordination of Banking Regulations." *International Organization* 43 (2): 323–47.

Kapstein, Ethan B. 1992. "Between Power and Purpose: Central Bankers and the Politics of Regulatory Convergence." *International Organization* 46 (1): 265–87.

Kapstein, Ethan B. 1994. *Governing the Global Economy: International Finance and the State*. Cambridge, MA: Harvard University Press.

Karlsson-Vinkhuyzen, Sylvia I., and Antto Vihma. 2009. "Comparing the Legitimacy and Effectiveness of Global Hard and Soft Law: An Analytical Framework." *Regulation & Governance* 3 (4): 400–20.

Kastner, Lisa. 2017. "Tracing Policy Influence of Diffuse Interests: The Post-Crisis Consumer Finance Protection Politics in the US." *Journal of Civil Society* 13 (2): 130–48.

Kaya, Devrimi, Robert J. Kirsch, and Klaus Henselmann. 2016. "The Role of Non-Governmental Organizations (NGOs) as Intermediaries of the European Union Decision to Adopt International Accounting Standards: 1973–2002." *Accounting Historians Journal* 43 (2): 59–127.

Keck, Margaret, and Kathryn Sikkink. 1998. *Activists Beyond Borders: Advocacy Networks in International Politics*. Ithaca, NY: Cornell University Press.

Kempthorne, David. 2013. "Governing International Securities Markets: IOSCO and the Politics of International Securities Market Standards." Dissertation, Waterloo University. <https://uwspace.uwaterloo.ca/handle/10012/7661>.

Kempthorne, David. 2015. "The FSB and the Politics of Cross-Sector Financial Standards: Inter-Agency Regulatory Conflict Beyond the State." Manuscript.

Keohane, Robert, and Joseph Nye. 1977. *Power and Interdependence: World Politics in Transition*. Boston, MA: Little, Brown.

Kern, Steffen. 2008. "EU–US Financial Market Integration–A Work in Progress." Deutsche Bank Research, June 4. <http://www.dbresearch.in/PROD/DBR_INTERNET_DE-PROD/PROD0000000000225963/EU-US+financial+market+integration+-+a+work+in+progress.pdf>.

Kerner, Andrew, and Jeffrey Kucik. 2010. "The International and Domestic Determinants of Insider Trading Laws." *International Studies Quarterly* 54 (3): 657–82.

Khademian, Anne. 1992. "The SEC and Capital Market Regulation: The Politics of Expertise." University of Pittsburgh.

Khademian, Anne. 1996. *Checking on Banks: Autonomy and Accountability in Three Federal Agencies*. London: Jessica Kingsley.

Kingsbury, Benedict, Nico Krisch, and Richard B. Stewart. 2005. "The Emergence of Global Administrative Law." *Law and Contemporary Problems* 68 (3/4): 15–61.

Kirshner, Jonathan. 2015. "The Economic Sins of Modern IR Theory and the Classical Realist Alternative." *World Politics* 67 (1): 155–83.

Kirton, John J., Marina Larionova, and Paolo Savona. 2010. *Making Global Economic Governance Effective: Hard and Soft Law Institutions in a Crowded World*. London: Ashgate.

Klabbers, Jan. 1998. "The Undesirability of Soft Law." *Nordic Journal of International Law* 67: 381–91.

Kleibl, Johannes. 2015. "Coercion and the Global Spread of Securities Regulation." *International Interactions* 41 (1): 1–25.

Knaack, Peter. 2015. "Innovation and Deadlock in Global Financial Governance: Transatlantic Coordination Failure in OTC Derivatives Regulation." *Review of International Political Economy* 22 (6): 1217–48.

Knaack, Peter. 2018. "A Web without a Center: Fragmentation in the OTC Derivatives Trade Reporting System." In *Governing the World's Biggest Market: The Politics of Derivatives Regulation after the 2008 Crisis*, ed. Eric Helleiner, Stefano Pagliari, and Irene Spagna, 226–256. Oxford: Oxford University Press.

Knight, Jack. 1992. *Institutions and Social Conflict*. Cambridge: Cambridge University Press.

Konings, Martijn. 2011. *The Development of American Finance*. Cambridge: Cambridge University Press.

Koremenos, Barbara, Charles Lipson, and Duncan Snidal. 2001. "The Rational Design of International Institutions." *International Organization* 55 (4): 761–99.

Krasner, Stephen. 1976. "State Power and the Structure of International Trade." *World Politics* 28 (2): 317–47.

Krasner, Stephen. 1991. "Global Communications and National Power: Life on the Pareto Frontier." *World Politics* 43 (3): 336–66.

Kudrna, Zdenek, and Patrick Müller. 2017. "Harmonizing Internationally to Harmonize Internally: Accounting for a Global Exit from the EU's Decision Trap." *JCMS: Journal of Common Market Studies* 55 (4): 815–31.

Kurzer, Paulette. 1993. *Business and Banking: Political Change and Economic Integration in Western Europe*. Ithaca, NY: Cornell University Press.

Lake, David A. 2009. "Open Economy Politics: A Critical Review." *Review of International Organizations* 4 (3): 219–44.

Lall, Ranjit. 2012. "From Failure to Failure: The Politics of International Banking Regulation." *Review of International Political Economy* 19 (4): 609–38.

Lall, Ranjit. 2014. "Timing as a Source of Regulatory Influence: A Technical Elite Network Analysis of Global Finance." *Regulation & Governance* 9 (2): 125–43.

Lamfalussy, Alexandre. 2001. "Final Report of the Committee of Wise Men on the Regulation of European Securities Markets." European Union, February 15. <http://ec.europa.eu/internal_market/securities/docs/lamfalussy/wisemen/final-report-wise-men_en.pdf>.

Laurence, Henry. 2001. *Money Rules: The New Politics of Finance in Britain and Japan*. Ithaca, NY: Cornell University Press.

Lavelle, Kathryn. 2013. *Money and Banks in the American Political System*. New York: Cambridge University Press.

Lavelle, Kathryn. 2014. "Implementing the Volcker Rule in National and International Politics." In *Transnational Financial Regulation After the Crisis*, ed. Tony Porter, 115–31. New York: Routledge.

Leland, Hayne E. 1992. "Insider Trading: Should It Be Prohibited?" *Journal of Political Economy* 100 (4): 859–87.

Levitt, Arthur. 2001. "The World According to GAAP." *Financial Times*, May 2, p. 21.

Levy, Jonah D. 1999. *Tocqueville's Revenge: State, Society, and Economy in Contemporary France*. Cambridge, MA: Harvard University Press.

Lewis, Michael. 2010. *The Big Short: Inside the Doomsday Machine*. New York: W. W. Norton.

Li, Quan, and Adam Resnick. 2003. "Reversal of Fortunes: Democratic Institutions and Foreign Direct Investment Inflows to Developing Countries." *International Organization* 57 (1): 175–211.

Li, Yu-wai Vic. 2018. "Power Plays from the Fringe: East Asian Responses to Derivatives Regulatory Reform." In *Governing the World's Biggest Market: The Politics of Derivatives Regulation after the 2008 Crisis*, ed. Eric Helleiner, Stefano Pagliari, and Irene Spagna, 107–136. Oxford: Oxford University Press.

Lindblom, Charles Edward. 1977. *Politics and Markets: The World's Political Economic Systems*. New York: Basic Books.

Lo, Andrew W. 2012. "Reading About the Financial Crisis: A Twenty-One-Book Review." *Journal of Economic Literature* 50 (1): 151–78.

Locke, Richard M. 2013. *The Promise and Limits of Private Power: Promoting Labor Standards in a Global Economy*. New York: Cambridge University Press.

López-Santana, Mariely. 2006. "The Domestic Implications of European Soft Law: Framing and Transmitting Change in Employment Policy." *Journal of European Public Policy* 13 (4): 481–99.

Lütz, Susanne. 1998. "The Revival of the Nation-State? Stock Exchange Regulation in an Era of Globalized Financial Markets." *Journal of European Public Policy* 5 (1): 153–68.

McCaffrey, David P. 2016. "The Transformation of the Over-the-Counter Derivatives Market, 1984–2016." SSRN Scholarly Paper ID 2642216. Rochester, NY: Social Science Research Network. <https://papers.ssrn.com/abstract=2642216>.

McKeen-Edwards, Heather, and Tony Porter. 2013. *Transnational Financial Associations and the Governance of Global Finance: Assembling Wealth and Power*. London: Routledge.

Mackenzie, Donald. 2006. *An Engine, Not a Camera: How Financial Models Shape Markets*. Cambridge, MA: MIT Press.

McNamara, Kathleen. 1998. *The Currency of Ideas*. Ithaca, NY: Cornell University Press.

McNamara, Kathleen. 2002. "Rational Fictions: Central Bank Independence and the Social Logic of Delegation." *West European Politics* 25 (1): 47–76.

McNamara, Kathleen. 2009. "Of Intellectual Monocultures and the Study of IPE." *Review of International Political Economy* 16 (1): 72–84.

McNamara, Kathleen. 2015. *The Politics of Everyday Europe: Constructing Authority in the European Union*. Oxford: Oxford University Press.

Mahoney, James. 2000. "Strategies of Causal Inference in Small-N Analysis." *Sociological Methods & Research* 28 (4): 387–424.

Mahoney, James. 2003. "Strategies of Causal Assessment in Comparative Historical Analysis." In *Comparative Historical Analysis in the Social Sciences*, ed. James Mahoney and Dietrich Rueschemeyer, 131–76. Cambridge: Cambridge University Press.

Mahoney, James, and Kathleen Thelen. 2009. *Explaining Institutional Change: Ambiguity, Agency, and Power*. Cambridge: Cambridge University Press.

Mahoney, Paul G. 1990. "Securities Regulation by Enforcement: An International Perspective." *Yale Journal on Regulation* 7: 305–20.

Majone, Giandomenico. 1984. "Science and Trans-Science in Standard Setting." *Science, Technology, & Human Values* 9 (1): 15–22.

Marcacci, Antonio. 2014. "IOSCO and the Spreading of a US-Like Regulatory Philosophy around the World." *European Business Law Review* 25 (6): 759–809.

March, James G., and Johan P. Olsen. 1983. "The New Institutionalism: Organizational Factors in Political Life." *American Political Science Review* 78 (3): 734–49.

Martin, Lisa L. 1993. *Coercive Cooperation: Explaining Multilateral Economic Sanctions*. Princeton, NJ: Princeton University Press.

Martinez-Diaz, Leonardo. 2005. "Strategic Experts and Improvising Regulators: Explaining the IASC's Rise to Global Influence, 1973–2001." *Business and Politics* 7 (3): 1–26.

Matthews, Barbara C. 1992. "The Second Banking Directive: Conflicts, Choices, and Long-Term Goals." *Duke Journal of Comparative & International Law* 2: 89–128.

Matthews, Barbara C. 2009. "Emerging Public International Banking Law: Lessons from the Law of the Sea Experience Symposium: International Law and the Economic Crisis." *Chicago Journal of International Law* 10: 539–80.

Mattli, Walter, and Tim Büthe. 2003. "Setting International Standards: Technological Rationality or Primacy of Power?" *World Politics* 56 (1): 1–42.

Mattli, Walter, and Ngaire Woods. 2009. *The Politics of Global Regulation*. Princeton, NJ: Princeton University Press.

Mian, Atif, and Amir Sufi. 2014. *House of Debt: How They (and You) Caused the Great Recession, and How We Can Prevent It from Happening Again*. Chicago, IL: University of Chicago Press.

Milner, Helen. 1997. *Interests, Institutions, and Information*. Princeton, NJ: Princeton University Press.

Moe, Terry M. 2005. "Power and Political Institutions." *Perspectives on Politics* 3 (2): 215–33.

Moran, Michael. 1991. *The Politics of the Financial Services Revolution: The USA, UK, and Japan*. London: Springer.

Moran, Michael. 1994. "The State and the Financial Services Revolution: A Comparative Analysis." *European Politics* 17 (3): 158–77.

Morgan, Glenn. 2010. "Legitimacy in Financial Markets: Credit Default Swaps in the Current Crisis." *Socio-Economic Review* 8 (1): 17–45.

Morgan, Glenn. 2012. "Reforming OTC Markets: The Politics and Economics of Technical Fixes." *European Business Organization Law Review* 13 (3): 391–412.

Moschella, Manuela. 2013. "Designing the Financial Stability Board: A Theoretical Investigation of Mandate, Discretion, and Membership." *Journal of International Relations and Development* 16 (3): 380–405.

Moschella, Manuela, and Eleni Tsingou, eds. 2014. *Great Expectations, Slow Transformations: Incremental Change in Post-Crisis Regulation*. Colchester: ECPR Press.

Mosley, Layna. 2010. "Regulating Globally, Implementing Locally: The Financial Codes and Standards Effort." *Review of International Political Economy* 17 (4): 724–61.

Mosley, Layna, and David Singer. 2009. "The Global Financial Crisis: Lessons and Opportunities for International Political Economy." *International Interactions* 35 (4): 420–9.

Mourlon-Druol, Emmanuel. 2016. "Banking Union in Historical Perspective: The Initiative of the European Commission in the 1960s–1970s." *JCMS: Journal of Common Market Studies* 54 (4): 913–27.

Mügge, Daniel. 2009. "Tales of Tails and Dogs: Derivatives and Financialization in Contemporary Capitalism." *Review of International Political Economy* 16 (3): 514–26.

Mügge, Daniel. 2010. *Widen the Market, Narrow the Competition: Banker Interests and the Making of a European Capital Market*. Colchester: ECPR Press.

Mügge, Daniel. 2011a. "From Pragmatism to Dogmatism: European Union Governance, Policy Paradigms and Financial Meltdown." *New Political Economy* 16 (2): 185–206.

Mügge, Daniel. 2011b. "Limits of Legitimacy and the Primacy of Politics in Financial Governance." *Review of International Political Economy* 18 (1): 52–74.

Mutersbaugh, Tad. 2005. "Fighting Standards with Standards: Harmonization, Rents, and Social Accountability in Certified Agrofood Networks." *Environment and Planning A* 37 (11): 2033–51.

Naughton, Barry. 2007. *The Chinese Economy: Transitions and Growth*. Cambridge, MA: MIT Press.

Nelson, Stephen. 2014. "Playing Favorites: How Shared Beliefs Shape the IMF's Lending Decisions." *International Organization* 68 (2): 297–328.

Newman, Abraham. 2008a. "Building Transnational Civil Liberties: Transgovernmental Entrepreneurs and the European Data Privacy Directive." *International Organization* 62 (1): 103–30.

Newman, Abraham. 2008b. *Protectors of Privacy: Regulating Personal Data in the Global Economy*. Ithaca, NY: Cornell University Press.

Newman, Abraham. 2010. "International Organization Control Under Conditions of Dual Delegation: A Transgovernmental Politics Approach." In *Who Governs the Globe?*, ed. Deborah Avant, Martha Finnemore, and Susan Sell, 131–52. Cambridge: Cambridge University Press.

Newman, Abraham, and David Bach. 2014. "The European Union as Hardening Agent: Soft Law and the Diffusion of Global Financial Regulation." *Journal of European Public Policy* 21 (3): 430–52.

Newman, Abraham, and Elliot Posner. 2011. "International Interdependence and Regulatory Power: Authority, Mobility, and Markets." *European Journal of International Relations* 17 (4): 589–610.

Newman, Abraham, and Elliot Posner. 2016a. "Transnational Feedback, Soft Law, and Preferences in Global Financial Regulation." *Review of International Political Economy* 23 (1): 123–52.

Newman, Abraham, and Elliot Posner. 2016b. "Structuring Transnational Interests: The Second-Order Effects of Soft Law in the Politics of Global Finance." *Review of International Political Economy* 23 (5): 768–98.

Nichols, Tom. 2017. *The Death of Expertise*. Oxford: Oxford University Press.

Noble, Gregory W., and John Ravenhill. 2000. *The Asian Financial Crisis and the Architecture of Global Finance*. Cambridge: Cambridge University Press.

Nölke, Andreas, and James Perry. 2008. "The Power of Transnational Private Governance: Financialization and the IASB." *Business and Politics* 9 (3): 1–25.

Norton, Joseph Jude. 1988. "Capital Adequacy Standards: A Legitimate Regulatory Concern for Prudential Supervision of Banking Activities Symposium: Scholarship in Banking Law." *Ohio State Law Journal* 49: 1299–364.

Oatley, Thomas. 2011. "The Reductionist Gamble: Open Economy Politics in the Global Economy." *International Organization* 65 (2): 311–41.

Oatley, Thomas, and Robert Nabors. 1998. "Redistributive Cooperation: Market Failure, Wealth Transfers, and the Basle Accord." *International Organization* 52 (1): 35–54.

Orban, Agnes. 2016. "Mobilizing Moral Boundaries: The Politics of Derivatives Reform in the US." *New Political Economy* 21 (6): 555–73.

Overdevest, Christine. 2010. "Comparing Forest Certification Schemes: The Case of Ratcheting Standards in the Forest Sector." *Socio-Economic Review* 8 (1): 47–76.

Padel, Susanne, Helena Röcklinsberg, and Otto Schmid. 2009. "The Implementation of Organic Principles and Values in the European Regulation for Organic Food." *Food Policy* 34 (3): 245–51.

Pagliari, Stefano. 2012a. "Who Governs Finance? The Shifting Public–Private Divide in the Regulation of Derivatives, Rating Agencies and Hedge Funds." *European Law Journal* 18 (1): 44–61.

Pagliari, Stefano, ed. 2012b. *Making Good Financial Regulation: Towards a Policy Response to Regulatory Capture.* London: Grosvenor House Publishing.

Pagliari, Stefano. 2013. "Public Salience and International Financial Regulation: Explaining the International Regulation of OTC Derivatives, Rating Agencies, and Hedge Funds." Dissertation, University of Waterloo. <https://uwspace.uwaterloo.ca/handle/10012/7344>.

Pagliari, Stefano. 2018. "The Second Half: Interest Group Conflicts and Coalitions in the Implementation of the Dodd-Frank Act Derivatives Rules." In *Governing the World's Biggest Market: The Politics of Derivatives Regulation after the 2008 Crisis*, ed. Eric Helleiner, Stefano Pagliari, and Irene Spagna, 137–167. Oxford: Oxford University Press.

Pagliari, Stefano, and Kevin L. Young. 2014. "Leveraged Interests: Financial Industry Power and the Role of Private Sector Coalitions." *Review of International Political Economy* 21 (3): 575–610.

Pagliari, Stefano, and Kevin L. Young. 2016. "The Interest Ecology of Financial Regulation: Interest Group Plurality in the Design of Financial Regulatory Policies." *Socio-Economic Review* 14 (2): 309–37.

Papadopoulos, Yannis. 2007. "Problems of Democratic Accountability in Network and Multilevel Governance." *European Law Journal* 13 (4): 469–86.

Patashnik, Eric M., and Julian E. Zelizer. 2013. "The Struggle to Remake Politics: Liberal Reform and the Limits of Policy Feedback in the Contemporary American State." *Perspectives on Politics* 11 (4): 1071–87.

Patel, Keyur. 2013. "Batting for the City: Do the Trade Associations Get It Right?" Center for the Study of Financial Innovation, June. <https://static1.squarespace.com/static/54d620fce4b049bf4cd5be9b/t/551e5ad6e4b0827b2174e5c8/1428052694695/Batting+for+the+City%2C+by+Keyur+Patel_WEB.pdf>.

Pauly, Louis W. 2009. "The Old and the New Politics of International Financial Stability." *JCMS: Journal of Common Market Studies* 47 (5): 955–75.

Pauwelyn, Joost, Ramses Wessel, and Jan Wouters. 2012. *Informal International Lawmaking.* Oxford: Oxford University Press.

Pearson, Margaret M. 2005. "The Business of Governing Business in China: Institutions and Norms of the Emerging Regulatory State." *World Politics* 57 (2): 296–322.

Pelc, Krzysztof J. 2009. "Seeking Escape: The Use of Escape Clauses in International Trade Agreements." *International Studies Quarterly* 53 (2): 349–68.

Pempel, T. J. 1999. "Structural Gaiatsu: International Finance and Political Change in Japan." *Comparative Political Studies* 32 (8): 907–32.

Pempel, T. J. 2006. "The Political Economy of International Accounting Standards." *Review of International Political Economy* 13 (4): 559–86.

Perry, James, and Andreas Nölke. 2005. "International Accounting Standard Setting: A Network Approach." *Business and Politics* 7 (3): 1–32.

Perry, James, and Andreas Nölke. 2006. "The Political Economy of International Accounting Standards." *Review of International Political Economy* 13 (4): 559–86.

Pierson, Paul. 1993. "When Effect Becomes Cause: Policy Feedback and Political Change." *World Politics* 45 (4): 595–628.

Pierson, Paul. 1996. "The Path to European Integration." *Comparative Political Studies* 29 (2): 123–63.

Pierson, Paul. 2004. *Politics in Time: History, Institutions, and Social Analysis*. Princeton, NJ: Princeton University Press.

Polanyi, Karl. 1944. *The Great Transformation*. Boston, MA: Beacon Press.

Pollack, Mark. 2003. *The Engines of Integration? Delegation, Agency, and Agenda Setting in the European Union*. New York: Oxford University Press.

Pollack, Mark, and Gregory C. Shaffer. 2009. *When Cooperation Fails: The International Law and Politics of Genetically Modified Foods*. New York: Oxford University Press.

Ponte, Stefano. 2008. "Greener than Thou: The Political Economy of Fish Ecolabeling and Its Local Manifestations in South Africa." *World Development* 36 (1): 159–75.

Porter, Tony. 1993. *States, Markets and Regimes in Global Finance*. New York: St. Martin's Press.

Porter, Tony. 2001. "The Democratic Deficit in the Institutional Arrangements for Regulating Global Finance." *Global Governance* 7: 427–39.

Porter, Tony. 2003. "Technical Collaboration and Political Conflict in the Emerging Regime for International Financial Regulation." *Review of International Political Economy* 10 (3): 520–51.

Porter, Tony. 2005a. *Globalization and Finance*. Cambridge: Polity Press.

Porter, Tony. 2005b. "Private Authority, Technical Authority, and the Globalization of Accounting Standards." *Business and Politics* 7 (3): 1–30.

Porter, Tony, ed. 2014. *Transnational Financial Regulation After the Crisis*. London: Routledge.

Posner, Elliot. 2005. "Sources of Institutional Change: The Supranational Origins of Europe's New Stock Markets." *World Politics* 58 (1): 1–40.

Posner, Elliot. 2007. "Financial Transformation in the European Union." In *Making History: European Integration and Institutional Change at Fifty*, ed. Kathleen McNamara and Sophie Meunier, 139–58. Oxford: Oxford University Press.

Posner, Elliot. 2009a. "Making Rules for Global Finance: Transatlantic Regulatory Cooperation at the Turn of the Millennium." *International Organization* 63 (4): 665–99.

Posner, Elliot. 2009b. *The Origins of Europe's New Stock Markets*. Cambridge, MA: Harvard University Press.

Posner, Elliot. 2010a. "Sequence as Explanation: The International Politics of Accounting Standards." *Review of International Political Economy* 17 (4): 639–64.

Posner, Elliot. 2010b. "The Lamfalussy Process: Polyarchic Origins of Networked Financial Rulemaking in the EU." In *EU Governance: Towards a New Architecture?*, ed. Charles F. Sabel and Jonathan Zeitlin, 43–60. Oxford: Oxford University Press.

Posner, Elliot. 2015. "International Financial Regulatory Cooperation: An Experimentalist Turn?" In *Extending Experimentalist Governance? The European Union and Transnational Regulation*, ed. Jonathan Zeitlin, 196–225. Oxford: Oxford University Press.

Posner, Elliot. 2018. "Financial Regulatory Cooperation: Coordination of Derivatives Markets." In *Governing the World's Biggest Market: The Politics of Derivatives Regulation after the 2008 Crisis*, ed. Eric Helleiner, Stefano Pagliari, and Irene Spagna, 54–81. Oxford: Oxford University Press.

Posner, Elliot, and Nicolas Véron. 2010. "The EU and Financial Regulation: Power without Purpose?" *Journal of European Public Policy* 17 (3): 400–15.

Posner, Elliot, and Nicolas Véron. 2016. "The End of EU Financial Regulatory Internationalism?" Presented at the 28th Annual Meeting of the Society for the Advancement of Socio-Economics, June 24–26, Berkeley, CA.

Potoski, Matthew, and Aseem Prakash. 2005. "Green Clubs and Voluntary Governance: ISO 14001 and Firms' Regulatory Compliance." *American Journal of Political Science* 49 (2): 235–48.

Poulsen, Lauge, and Emma Aisbett. 2013. "When the Claim Hits: Bilateral Investment Treaties and Bounded Rational Learning." *World Politics* 65 (2): 273–313.

Putnam, Robert D. 1988. "Diplomacy and Domestic Politics: The Logic of Two-Level Games." *International Organization* 42 (3): 427–60.

Quack, Sigrid. 2009. "Law, Expertise and Legitimacy in Transnational Economic Governance: An Introduction." *Socio-Economic Review* 8 (1): 3–16.

Quack, Sigrid. 2010. "Law, Expertise and Legitimacy in Transnational Economic Governance: An Introduction." *Socio-Economic Review* 8 (1): 3–16.

Quaglia, Lucia. 2010. *Governing Financial Services in the European Union: Banking, Securities and Post-Trading*. London: Routledge.

Quaglia, Lucia. 2013. "The European Union, the USA and International Standard Setting by Regulatory Fora in Finance." *New Political Economy* 19 (3): 427–44.

Quaglia, Lucia. 2014. *The European Union and Global Financial Regulation*. Oxford: Oxford University Press.

Raustiala, Kal. 2002. "The Architecture of International Cooperation: Transgovernmental Networks and the Future of International Law." *Virginia Journal of International Law* 43 (1): 1–92.

Reinicke, Wolfgang H. 1995. *Banking, Politics and Global Finance*. London: Edward Elgar.

Reisenbichler, Alexander. 2015. "The Domestic Sources and Power Dynamics of Regulatory Networks: Evidence from the Financial Stability Forum." *Review of International Political Economy* 22 (5): 996–1024.

Richards, John. 1999. "Toward a Positive Theory of International Institutions: Regulating International Aviation Markets." *International Organization* 53 (1): 1–37.

Risse, Thomas, and Mareike Kleine. 2007. "Assessing the Legitimacy of the EU's Treaty Revision Methods." *JCMS: Journal of Common Market Studies* 45 (1): 69–80.

Risse-Kappen, Thomas. 1994. "Ideas Do Not Float Freely: Transnational Coalitions, Domestic Structures, and the End of the Cold War." *International Organization* 48 (2): 185–214.

Risse-Kappen, Thomas. 1995. *Bringing Transnational Actors Back In*. Cambridge: Cambridge University Press.

Rogoff, Kenneth. 1999. "Institutions for Reducing Global Financial Instability." *Journal of Economic Perspectives* 13: 21–42.

Romano, Roberta. 2004. "The Sarbanes-Oxley Act and the Making of Quack Corporate Governance." SSRN Scholarly Paper ID 596101. Rochester, NY: Social Science Research Network. <https://papers.ssrn.com/abstract=596101>.

Rosenau, James N. 1990. *Turbulence in World Politics: A Theory of Change and Continuity*. Princeton, NJ: Princeton University Press.

Rosenbluth, Frances. 1989. *Financial Politics in Contemporary Japan*. Ithaca, NY: Cornell University Press.

Rosenbluth, Frances, and Michael F. Thies. 2001. "The Electoral Foundations of Japan's Banking Regulation." *Policy Studies Journal* 29 (1): 23–37.

Ruggie, John. 1982. "International Regimes, Transactions, and Change: Embedded Liberalism in the Postwar Economic Order." *International Organization* 36 (2): 379–415.

Ryan, Peter. 2013. "Charting a Course to Autonomy: Bureaucratic Politics and the Transformation of Wall Street." Dissertation, University of California, Berkeley, CA.

Sabel, Charles, and Jonathan Zeitlin. 2010. *Experimentalist Governance in the European Union: Towards a New Architecture*. Oxford: Oxford University Press.

Sandholtz, Wayne. 2007. *Prohibiting Plunder: How Norms Change*. Oxford: Oxford University Press.

Sandholtz, Wayne, and John Zysman. 1989. "1992: Recasting the European Bargain." *World Politics* 42 (1): 95–128.

Schäfer, Armin. 2006. "A New Form of Governance? Comparing the Open Method of Co-ordination to Multilateral Surveillance by the IMF and the OECD." *Journal of European Public Policy* 13 (1): 70–88.

Scharpf, Fritz. 1999. *Governing in Europe: Effective and Democratic*. Oxford: Oxford University Press.

Schmidt, Vivien A. 2013. "Democracy and Legitimacy in the European Union Revisited: Input, Output and 'Throughput.'" *Political Studies* 61 (1): 2–22.

Schwartz, Herman M. 2009. *Subprime Nation: American Power, Global Capital, and the Housing Bubble*. Ithaca, NY: Cornell University Press.

Scott, Joanne. 2014. "The New EU Extraterritoriality." *Common Market Law Review* 51 (5): 1343–80.

Seabrooke, Leonard, and Eleni Tsingou. 2009. "Power Elites and Everyday Politics in International Financial Reform." *International Political Sociology* 3 (4): 457–61.

Seidman, Gay W. 2007. *Beyond the Boycott: Labor Rights, Human Rights, and Transnational Activism*. New York: Russell Sage Foundation.

Seidman, William. 1986. "Bank Supervision in the United States." In *Financial Deregulation*, ed. Richard Dale, 64–80. Cambridge: Woodhead-Faulkner.

Seligman, Joel. 2003. *The Transformation of Wall Street: A History of the Securities and Exchange Commission and Modern Corporate Finance*. New York: Aspen Publishers.

Sell, Susan K. 2003. *Private Power, Public Law: The Globalization of Intellectual Property Rights*. New York: Cambridge University Press.

Sell, Susan K. 2010. "The Rise and Rule of a Trade-Based Strategy: Historical Institutionalism and the International Regulation of Intellectual Property." *Review of International Political Economy* 17 (4): 762–90.

Sell, Susan K. 2013. "Revenge of the 'Nerds': Collective Action against Intellectual Property Maximalism in the Global Information Age." *International Studies Review* 15 (1): 67–85.

Sending, Ole Jacob. 2015. *The Politics of Expertise*. Ann Arbor, MI: University of Michigan Press.

Shaffer, Gregory C. 2012. *Transnational Legal Ordering and State Change*. Cambridge: Cambridge University Press.

Shaffer, Gregory C., and Mark A. Pollack. 2009. "Hard vs. Soft Law: Alternatives, Complements, and Antagonists in International Governance." *Minnesota Law Review* 94: 706–99.

Sheingate, Adam D. 2003. "Political Entrepreneurship, Institutional Change, and American Political Development." *Studies in American Political Development* 17 (2): 185–203.

Shelton, Dinah. 2003. *Commitment and Compliance: The Role of Non-Binding Norms in the International Legal System*. Oxford: Oxford University Press.

Shickler, Eric. 2001. *Disjointed Pluralism: Institutional Innovation and the Development of the US Congress*. Princeton, NJ: Princeton University Press.

Shih, Victor. 2008. *Factions and Finance in China*. Cambridge: Cambridge University Press.

Shirley, Jonathan. 2004. "International Law and the Ramifications of the Sarbanes-Oxley Act of 2002." *Boston College International and Comparative Law Review* 27: 501–28.

Sikkink, Kathryn. 2005. "Patterns of Dynamic Multilevel Governance and the Insider–Outsider Coalition." In *Transnational Protest and Global Activism*, ed. Donatella Della Porta and Sidney Tarrow, 151–74. Lanham, MD: Rowman & Littlefield.

Simmons, Beth. 2000. "International Law and State Behavior: Commitment and Compliance in International Monetary Affairs." *American Political Science Review* 94 (4): 819–35.

Simmons, Beth. 2001. "The International Politics of Harmonization: The Case of Capital Market Regulation." *International Organization* 55 (3): 589–620.

Simmons, Beth. 2004. "The International Politics of Harmonization." In *Dynamics of Regulatory Change: How Globalization Affects National Regulatory Policies*, ed. David Vogel and Robert Kagan, 42–83. Berkeley, CA: University of California Press.

Sinclair, Timothy. 2005. *The New Masters of Capital: American Bond Rating Agencies and the Politics of Creditworthiness*. Ithaca, NY: Cornell University Press.

Singer, David Andrew. 2007. *Regulating Capital: Setting Standards for the International Financial System*. Ithaca, NY: Cornell University Press.

Skeel, David. 2010. *The New Financial Deal: Understanding the Dodd-Frank Act and Its (Unintended) Consequences*. New York: John Wiley.

Slaughter, Anne-Marie. 2004. *A New World Order*. Princeton, NJ: Princeton University Press.

Sobel, Andrew Carl. 1994. *Domestic Choices, International Markets: Dismantling National Barriers and Liberalizing Securities Markets*. Ann Arbor, MI: University of Michigan Press.

Soederberg, Susanne. 2004. *The Politics of the New International Financial Architecture: Reimposing Neoliberal Domination in the Global South*. London: Zed Books.

Solomon, Steven. 1995. *The Confidence Game: How Unelected Central Bankers Are Governing the Changed Global Economy*. New York: Simon & Schuster.

Sommer, A. A. Jr. 1996. "IOSCO: Its Mission and Achievement Symposium—Internationalization of Securities." *Northwestern Journal of International Law & Business* 17: 15–29.

Sorkin, Andrew Ross. 2010. *Too Big to Fail: The Inside Story of How Wall Street and Washington Fought to Save the Financial System—and Themselves*. New York: Penguin Press.

Spagna, Irene. 2018. "Becoming the World's Biggest Market: OTC Derivatives before the Global Financial Crisis of 2008." In *Governing the World's Biggest Market: The Politics of Derivatives Regulation after the 2008 Crisis*, ed. Eric Helleiner, Stefano Pagliari, and Irene Spagna, 27–53. Oxford: Oxford University Press.

Steffek, Jens. 2010. "Public Accountability and the Public Sphere of International Governance." *Ethics & International Affairs* 24 (1): 45–68.

Stigler, George. 1971. "The Theory of Economic Regulation." *Bell Journal of Economics and Management Science* 1: 3–21.

Stiller, Sabina, and Minna van Gerven. 2012. "The European Employment Strategy and National Core Executives: Impacts on Activation Reforms in the Netherlands and Germany." *Journal of European Social Policy* 22 (2): 118–32.

Stone Sweet, Alec, Wayne Sandholtz, and Neil Fligstein, eds. 2001. *The Institutionalization of Europe*. Oxford: Oxford University Press.

Story, Jonathan, and Ingo Walter. 1997. *Political Economy of Financial Integration in Europe: The Battle of the Systems*. Manchester: Manchester University Press.

Sunstein, Cass R. 1998. *Legal Reasoning and Political Conflict*. New York: Oxford University Press.

Tafara, Ethiopis. 2004. "Global Markets, National Regulation, and Cooperation: Statement before the House Financial Services Committee." Washington, DC, US House of Representatives Committee on Financial Services.

Tafara, Ethiopis, and Robert J. Peterson. 2007. "A Blueprint for Cross-Border Access to U.S. Investors: A New International Framework." *Harvard International Law Journal* 48: 31–68.

Tamura, Kentaro. 2003. "A Regulator's Dilemma and Two-Level Games: Japan in the Politics of International Banking Regulation." *Social Science Japan Journal* 6 (2): 221–40.

Tamura, Kentaro. 2005. "Challenges to Japanese Compliance with the Basel Capital Accord: Domestic Politics and International Banking Standards." *Japanese Economy* 33 (1): 23.

Tarrow, Sidney. 2001. "Transnational Politics: Contention and Institutions in International Politics." *Annual Review of Political Science* 4 (1): 1–20.

Tarullo, Daniel K. 2008. *Banking on Basel: The Future of International Financial Regulation*. Washington, DC: Peterson Institute for International Economics.

Tarullo, Daniel K. 2014. "Regulating Large Foreign Banking Organizations." Presented at the Symposium on Building the Financial System of the Twenty-First Century: An Agenda for Europe and the United States, Harvard Law School.

Thelen, Kathleen. 2003. "How Institutions Evolve: Insights from Comparative Historical Analysis." In *Comparative Historical Analysis in the Social Sciences*, ed. James Mahoney and Dietrich Rueschemeyer, 208–40. Cambridge: Cambridge University Press.

Thelen, Kathleen. 2004. *How Institutions Evolve: The Political Economy of Skills in Germany, Britain, the United States, and Japan*. Cambridge: Cambridge University Press.

Thelen, Kathleen, and Sven Steinmo. 1992. "Historical Institutionalism in Comparative Politics." In *Structuring Politics: Historical Institutionalism in Comparative Analysis*, ed. Kathleen Thelen and Sven Steinmo, 1–32. Cambridge: Cambridge University Press.

Thiemann, Matthias. 2014. "In the Shadow of Basel: How Competitive Politics Bred the Crisis." *Review of International Political Economy* 21 (6): 1203–39.

Trubek, David M., and Louise G. Trubek. 2005. "Hard and Soft Law in the Construction of Social Europe: The Role of the Open Method of Co-ordination." *European Law Journal* 11 (3): 343–64.

Tsingou, Eleni. 2003. "Transnational Policy Communities and Financial Governance: The Role of Private Actors in Derivatives Regulation." Working Paper. January. <http://www2.warwick.ac.uk/fac/soc/csgr/research/workingpapers/2003/wp11103.pdf>.

Tsingou, Eleni. 2008. "Transnational Private Governance and the Basel Process: Banking Regulation and Supervision, Private Interests and Basel II." In *Transnational Private Governance and its Limits*, ed. Jean-Christophe Graz and Andreas Nölke, 58–68. London: Routledge.

Tsingou, Eleni. 2015. "Club Governance and the Making of Global Financial Rules." *Review of International Political Economy* 22 (2): 225–56.

Turner, Nicholas W. 2012. "Dodd-Frank and International Regulatory Convergence: The Case for Mutual Recognition." *New York Law School Law Review* 57: 391–422.

Underhill, Geoffrey R. D. 1995. "Keeping Governments Out of Politics: Transnational Securities Markets, Regulatory Cooperation, and Political Legitimacy." *Review of International Studies* 21 (3): 251–78.

Underhill, Geoffrey R. D., Jasper Blom, and Daniel Mügge. 2010. *Global Financial Integration Thirty Years On: From Reform to Crisis*. Cambridge: Cambridge University Press.

Underhill, Geoffrey R. D., and Xiaoke Zhang. 2008. "Setting the Rules: Private Power, Political Underpinnings, and Legitimacy in Global Monetary and Financial Governance." *International Affairs* 84 (3): 535–54.

Vabulas, Felicity, and Duncan Snidal. 2013. "Organization without Delegation: Informal Intergovernmental Organizations (IIGOs) and the Spectrum of Intergovernmental Arrangements." *Review of International Organizations* 8 (2): 193–220.

Verdier, Pierre-Hugues. 2009. "Transnational Regulatory Networks and Their Limits." *Yale Journal of International Law* 34 (1): 113–72.

Véron, Nicolas. 2007. "The Global Accounting Experiment." *Bruegel Blueprint Series* 2.

Victor, David G. 2006. "Toward Effective International Cooperation on Climate Change: Numbers, Interests and Institutions." *Global Environmental Politics* 6 (3): 90–103.

Voeten, Erik. Forthcoming. *A Distributive Theory of International Institutions*. Washington, DC.

Vogel, David. 1983. "The Power of Business in America: A Re-Appraisal." *British Journal of Political Science* 13 (1): 19–43.

Vogel, David. 1989. *Fluctuating Fortunes: The Political Power of Business in America*. New York: Basic Books.

Vogel, David. 2012. *The Politics of Precaution: Regulating Health, Safety, and Environmental Risks in Europe and the United States*. Princeton, NJ: Princeton University Press.

Vogel, Steven. 1996. *Freer Markets, More Rules: Regulatory Reform in Advanced Industrial Countries*. Ithaca, NY: Cornell University Press.

Vogelgesang, Ralph, and Matthias Kubicek. 2007. "Towards a Global Approach to Reinsurance Regulation." *The Geneva Papers on Risk and Insurance—Issues and Practice* 32 (3): 413–25.

Volcker, Paul. 1985. "Statement of Paul A. Volcker, Chairman of the Board of Governors of the Federal Reserve System before the Committee on Banking, Housing, and Urban Affairs, United States Senate." Washington, DC: US Government Printing Office.

Walker, Jerome, Rosali Pretorius, Michael Zolandz, and Gary Goldberg. 2012. "Reconciling the Dodd-Frank and Basel Committee Capital Requirements." *Banking Law Journal* 129 (7): 627–63.

Walter, Andrew. 2006. "From Developmental to Regulatory State: Japan's New Financial Regulatory System." *Pacific Review* 19 (4): 405–28.

Walter, Andrew. 2008. *Governing Finance*. Ithaca, NY: Cornell University Press.

Walter, Andrew. 2010. "Chinese Attitudes towards Global Financial Regulatory Cooperation: Revisionist or Status Quo?" In *Global Finance in Crisis: The Politics of International Regulatory Change*, ed. Eric Helleiner, Stefano Pagliari, and Hubert Zimmermann, 121–36. London: Routledge.

Weinberg, Joe. 2016. "European Union Member States in Cross-National Analyses: The Dangers of Neglecting Supranational Policymaking." *International Studies Quarterly* 60 (1): 98–106.

Whytock, Christopher A. 2005. "A Rational Design Theory of Transgovernmentalism: The Case of E.U.–U.S. Merger Review Cooperation." *Boston University International Law Journal* 23: 1–54.

Wicks, Nigel. 2005. "Comments." In *The Future of Transatlantic Economic Relations: Continuity Amid Discord*, ed. David Andrews, Mark Pollack, Gregory Shaffer, and Helen Wallace, 269–73. Florence: Robert Schuman Centre for Advanced Studies.

Wilf, Meredith. 2016. "Credibility and Distributional Effects of International Banking Regulations: Evidence from US Bank Stock Returns." *International Organization* 70 (4): 763–96.

Woll, Cornelia. 2008. *Firm Interests: How Governments Shape Business Lobbying on Global Trade*. Ithaca, NY: Cornell University Press.

Woll, Cornelia. 2014. *The Power of Inaction: Bank Bailouts in Comparison*. Ithaca, NY: Cornell University Press.

Wood, Duncan Robert. 2005. *Governing Global Banking: The Basel Committee and the Politics of Financial Globalisation*. London: Ashgate.

Woolley, John T., and J. Nicholas Ziegler. 2012. "The Two-Tiered Politics of Financial Regulation in the United States." In *Crisis and Control: Institutional Change in Financial Market Regulation*, ed. Renate Mayntz, 29–66. Frankfurt: Campus Verlag.

Xi, Chao. 2014. "Basel III in China?" In *Reconceptualising Global Finance and its Regulation*, ed. Ross P. Buckley, Emilios Avgouleas, and Douglas W. Arner, 91–105. Cambridge: Cambridge University Press.

Young, Kevin L. 2012. "Transnational Regulatory Capture? An Empirical Examination of the Transnational Lobbying of the Basel Committee on Banking Supervision." *Review of International Political Economy* 19 (4): 663–88.

Young, Kevin L. 2013. "Financial Industry Groups' Adaptation to the Post-Crisis Regulatory Environment: Changing Approaches to the Policy Cycle." *Regulation & Governance* 7 (4): 460–80.

Young, Kevin L., and Sung Ho Park. 2013. "Regulatory Opportunism: Cross-National Patterns in National Banking Regulatory Responses Following the Global Financial Crisis." *Public Administration* 91 (3): 561–81.

Zaring, David. 1998. "International Law by Other Means: The Twilight Existence of International Financial Regulatory Organizations." *Texas International Law Journal* 33: 281–330.

Zaring, David. 2004. "Informal Procedure, Hard and Soft, in International Administration." *Chicago Journal of International Law* 5 (2): 547–603.

Zaring, David. 2011. "Finding Legal Principle in Global Financial Regulation." *Virginia Journal of International Law* 52 (3): 683–722.

Zaring, David. 2015a. "Financial Reform's Internationalism." *Emory Law Journal* 65: 1255–311.

Zaring, David. 2015b. "Legal Obligation in International Law and International Finance." *Cornell International Law Journal* 48 (1): 175–217.

Zavvos, George S. 1988. "Towards a European Banking Act." *Common Market Law Review* 25: 263–89.

Zeitlin, Jonathan, ed. 2015. *Extending Experimentalist Governance? The European Union and Transnational Regulation*. Oxford: Oxford University Press.

Zito, Anthony. 2001. "Epistemic Communities, Collective Entrepreneurship and European Integration." *Journal of European Public Policy* 8 (4): 585–603.

Zysman, John. 1983. *Governments, Markets, and Growth: Financial Systems and the Politics of Industrial Change*. Ithaca, NY: Cornell University Press.

Zysman, John. 1994. "How Institutions Create Historically Rooted Trajectories of Growth." *Industrial and Corporate Change* 3 (1): 243–83.

Index